Islam in America

Islam in America

Exploring the Issues

Craig Considine

Religion in Politics and Society Today

ABC-CLIO®

An Imprint of ABC-CLIO, LLC
Santa Barbara, California • Denver, Colorado

Library of Congress Cataloging-in-Publication Data

Names: Considine, Craig, author.
Title: Islam in America : exploring the issues / Craig Considine.
Description: Santa Barbara : ABC-CLIO, 2019. | Series: Religion in politics and society today | Includes bibliographical references and index.
Identifiers: LCCN 2019023092 (print) | LCCN 2019023093 (ebook) | ISBN 9781440866302 (cloth) | ISBN 9781440866319 (ebook)
Subjects: LCSH: Islam—United States.—Dictionaries.
Classification: LCC BP67.U6 C658 2019 (print) | LCC BP67.U6 (ebook) | DDC 297.0973/03—dc23
LC record available at https://lccn.loc.gov/2019023092
LC ebook record available at https://lccn.loc.gov/2019023093

ISBN: 978-1-4408-6630-2 (print)
    978-1-4408-6631-9 (ebook)

23 22 21 20 19   1 2 3 4 5

This book is also available as an eBook.

ABC-CLIO
An Imprint of ABC-CLIO, LLC

ABC-CLIO, LLC
147 Castilian Drive
Santa Barbara, California 93117
www.abc-clio.com

This book is printed on acid-free paper ∞

Manufactured in the United States of America

To you, the reader, for showing interest in my fourth book. I hope that it brings you knowledge, lifts your spirit, and encourages you to stand for humanity when you see it attacked.

Contents

Alphabetical List of Entries, ix

Topical List of Entries, xi

Series Foreword, xiii

Preface, xv

Acknowledgments, xvii

Overview, xix

Chronology, xxix

A to Z, 1

Annotated Bibliography, 195

Index, 207

Alphabetical List of Entries

Abrahamic Tradition
African American Muslims
Ahadith
Ahmadiyya
Apostasy
Arab American Muslims
Asian American Muslims
Civil Rights
Clash of Civilizations
Converts
Countering Violent Extremism
  (CVE)
Dhimmi
European American Muslims
Foreign Policies
Freedom of Religion
Freedom of Speech
Hate Crimes
Hijab
Integration
Islamophobia
Jesus and Mary
Jihad
Jizya
Latin American Muslims
LGBTQ

Media Coverage and the
  Entertainment Industry
Mosques and Organizations
The Muslim Brotherhood
Muslim Travel Ban and
  Immigration Policies
Pluralism
Polygamy
The Prophet Muhammad
Qur'an
Racialization
Refugees
Sharia
Shi'ism
Slavery
Social Justice Activism
Sufism
Sunnism
Taqiyya
Turkish American Muslims
Ummah
U.S. Founding Fathers
Wahhabism
Women's Rights
Zakat

Topical List of Entries

Community and Service
Civil Rights
Mosques and Organizations
Pluralism
Ummah
Zakat

Islamophobia
Hate Crimes
Hijab
Jihad
Islamophobia
Media Coverage and the
    Entertainment Industry
Polygamy
Refugees
Taqiyya

National Identity
Freedom of Religion
Freedom of Speech
Integration
Slavery
Social Justice Activism
U.S. Founding Fathers
Women's Rights

Politics
Clash of Civilizations
Countering Violent Extremism
    (CVE)
Foreign Policies
Freedom of Speech
The Muslim Brotherhood
Muslim Travel Ban and
    Immigration Policies
Sharia
Wahhabism

Race and Ethnicity
African American Muslims
Arab American Muslims
Asian American Muslims
European American Muslims
Latin American Muslims
Turkish American Muslims
Racialization

**Theology and Interfaith
Relations**
Abrahamic Tradition
Ahadith
Dhimmi

Jesus and Mary

Jizya

The Prophet Muhammad

Qur'an

Unity and Difference

Ahmadiyya

Apostasy

Converts

LGBTQ

Shi'ism

Sufism

Sunnism

Series Foreword

Religion is a pervasive and powerful force in modern society, and its influence on political structures and social institutions is inescapable, whether in the United States or around the world. Wars have been fought in the name of faith; national boundaries have been shaped as a result; and social policies, legislation, and daily life have all been shaped by religious beliefs. Written with the reference needs of high school students and undergraduates in mind, the books in this series examine the role of religion in contemporary politics and society. While the focus of the series is on the United States, it also explores social and political issues of global significance.

Each book in the series is devoted to a particular issue, such as anti-Semitism, atheism and agnosticism, and women in Islam. An overview essay surveys the development of the religious dimensions of the subject and discusses how religion informs contemporary discourse related to that issue. A chronology then highlights the chief events related to the topic. This is followed by a section of alphabetically arranged reference entries providing objective information about people, legislation, ideas, movements, events, places, and other specific subjects. Each entry cites works for further reading and in many cases provides cross-references. At the end of each volume is an annotated bibliography of the most important print and electronic resources suitable for student research.

Authoritative and objective, the books in this series give readers a concise introduction to the dynamic interplay of religion and politics in modern society and provide a starting point for further research on social issues.

Preface

Islam in America: Exploring the Issues is a follow-up to *Muslims in America: Examining the Facts,* which was published by ABC-CLIO in July 2018. While *Examining the Facts* focused on the lived experiences and views of U.S. Muslims through the lens of primary documents, statistics, and evidence-based resources, *Exploring the Issues* dives further into Islamic theology, Islamic history, the history of U.S. Muslims, and specific religious and ethnic communities living in the United States. Both of these books are reference works that are written in accessible prose to account for a range of people including academics, religious leaders, politicians, activists, and everyday U.S. citizens.

Islam in America: Exploring the Issues is inspired by my love of our common humanity and my hope that bridge building between diverse groups of people is a remedy to cure our country and world of its ills. As an Irish/Italian Catholic and U.S. citizen from Boston, Massachusetts, I am inspired by the journey of my immigrant ancestors, who struggled to make their way in the United States, by my Catholic faith, which calls on me to love my neighbor as I love myself, and by my affiliation with U.S. identity, which I see as rooted in civic national principles like religious pluralism, racial equality, constitutional rights, and democratic governance.

Islam in America: Exploring the Issues is structured around 48 entries, ranging from Islamic concepts like *jihad, sharia,* and *taqiyya,* to the Prophet Muhammad's life, and to historic profiles of ethno-religious Muslim communities like African American Muslims, Arab American Muslims, Asian American Muslims, as well as Turkish American Muslims. Each entry provides an overview of various terms or issues pertaining to the Islamic faith and subsequently places these topics in the context of U.S. Muslims themselves. In one example, the life of the Prophet Muhammad is summarized and then analyzed through the lens of contemporary depictions of him in U.S. society. In a second case, the matter of women's rights according to

Islamic traditions is addressed and then examined through the lens of the lived experiences and views of U.S. Muslim women themselves.

The last decade of my life has been an extraordinary journey into our common humanity, especially as it pertains to the dialogue of civilizations and the fostering of stronger bonds between Muslims and Christians. By God's grace, my path has taken me into hundreds of mosques around the world and into the neighborhoods, homes, schools, and businesses of Muslims as well as people of all walks of life. This personal and on-the-ground approach toward bridge building has allowed me to learn from Muslims themselves instead of simply learning through the theories, peer-reviewed journal articles, or books offered by scholars. *Islam in America: Exploring the Issues* is my fourth book and represents, perhaps more so than any other book, the most comprehensive piece of scholarship that I have published to date.

Dr. Craig Considine
Houston, TX
May 1, 2019

Acknowledgments

This book has been made possible through the scholarship, journalism, and activism of a range of people who are living (or have lived) around the world. I am grateful to all of those who have provided invaluable resources and critical insight into some of the most pressing issues facing our common humanity today. I would also like to extend my gratitude to those people who follow me on social media. Your words of encouragement keep me going in times when critics question my character, conduct, and intentions.

Overview

There is a tendency to treat both the Islamic faith and Muslims as mono-liths. Representations in this skewed manner are typically driven, whether consciously or subconsciously, by people who believe in an influential theory called the "clash of civilizations." The clash of civilizations posits that Western civilization (and the United States itself) is positioned in an epic struggle against Islamic civilization (or the "Muslim world"), which is viewed by proponents of the theory as a totalitarian ideology that op-poses basic "American values" like gender equality, freedom of religion, freedom of speech, racial equality, religious tolerance, and separation of Church and State. Critics who espouse this theory may believe in, or say, one of the following statements: "Islam does not give equal rights to women, gays, and religious as well as racial minority populations"; "Islam is not a religion—it is a political doctrine"; "Muslims are working to in-stall the *sharia* over the U.S. Constitution"; "Muslims are commanded by the Prophet Muhammad to engage in 'holy war' against non-believers"; "Muhammad was a terrorist, a pedophile, and a tyrant"; and "ISIS repre-sents the true Islamic teachings found in the Qur'an." These categoriza-tions erroneously depict the Islamic faith and Muslims as inherently "anti-American." Further, these categorizations do a serious disservice to the rich diversity of the U.S. Muslim population, and the dynamic internal discussions pertaining to their Islamic traditions that occur within Muslim communities in the United States.

The Qur'an, the holy book for Muslims, may be a single book, but it is by no means interpreted in only one way by U.S. Muslims, or by Muslims around the world. Muslims and people of various faiths alike frequently cherry-pick verses of the Qur'an to justify their self-serving actions and prophecies, but rarely is the Qur'an digested in a manner that captures the heart and essence of the teachings of Muhammad, the prophet of Islam. Muhammad's sayings and teachings, known across the world as *ahadith* (singular *hadith*), are also used and abused by Muslims and people of various faiths to justify social, cultural, economic, or political objectives. Absent in many of the current discussions of both the Qur'an and *ahadith* is the essence of the Islamic message as taught by Muhammad. This book looks at the essence of Muhammad's teachings and shares that essence in the context of U.S. Muslims as well as "American values." In doing so, this book explains why Islamic texts—mainly the Qur'an and *ahadith*—are compatible with the finest traditions of the United States as a society, culture, and government.

Anti-Muslim activists frequently turn to the Prophet Muhammad as the source of pure evil and anti-American behavior by Muslims living in the United States. Protesters and critics have berated Muhammad as the founder of a religion that is violent, misogynistic, intolerant of other religious traditions, and ultimately backward, especially in comparison to "Western civilization." Anti-Muhammad commentators claim that he lowered Jews, Christians, and other religious minority populations to the status of *dhimmi,* in which these populations were treated as second-class citizens under the *sharia.* Another Arabic term—*jizya,* or a tax levied on Jews, Christians, and other religious minority populations—is frequently deployed by Islamophobes in their criticism of Muhammad, suggesting that he made Christians, Jews, and other religious minority populations pay the tax for the simple reason that they would not embrace Islam. In light of these characterizations, Muslims and their allies have stepped up to defend the honor of Muhammad. These groups typically turn to historical treaties and the *ahadith* as a way to highlight how his teachings are in harmony with the values outlined in the U.S. Constitution. The Constitution of Medina, a treaty that the Prophet of Islam entered into with a range of groups including Jews and pagans, created a new kind of civic nation in which all people were treated equally before the law. Muhammad's "Farewell Sermon," delivered on Mount Arafat in 632 CE, made the revolutionary claim of racial equality among Arabs and non-Arabs as well as whites and non-whites. The Covenants of the Prophet Muhammad with the Christians of his time also laid the groundwork for a pluralistic society in which Christians' and Muslims' livelihoods and well-being were dependent upon one another.

Representing the Islamic tradition as fundamentally intolerant of other religions and religious people contradicts several key passages of the Qur'an. Jews and Christians are classified as "People of the Book," or *Ahl al-Kitab,* a term of honor and esteem, in Islamic scripture. The Qur'an recognizes and praises all prophets in the Old Testament and New Testament. Jesus is acknowledged as the "Messiah" in the Qur'an, while Mary, his mother, has an entire *surah,* or chapter of the Qur'an, named after her. Mary, in fact, is mentioned in the Qur'an more than she is in the New Testament. According to the Qur'an, God chose Mary above all women in history. Relations between Jews, Christians, and Muslims in the United States are, nevertheless, increasingly under pressure due to domestic political tension and conflicts around the world, especially in the Middle East. Yet people who identify with these three faith traditions point to Abraham, the prophet who is said to be the first person to believe in God, as a unifying link across the monotheistic spectrum.

Another equally important element of the Qur'an is its stance on freedom of religion. The Qur'an (2:256) states in unequivocal terms: "There shall be no compulsion in religion: true guidance has become distinct from error." Other passages in the Qur'an clearly stand for freedom of religion, and U.S. Muslims themselves actively participate in the process of religious pluralism and frequently stand by their neighbors, most of whom are Christians, during times of strife. There are countless examples in recent years showing that U.S. Muslims have taken political action, or raised funds, to protect religious and racial minority populations living on U.S. soil. Social activism is, therefore, an increasingly important act and value among U.S. Muslims, especially among the younger generations, many of whom are currently involved in causes for equality and equity in U.S. society. These causes range from, but are by no means limited to, anti-racism, anti–police brutality, LGBTQ+ rights, Deferred Action for Childhood Arrival (DACA) rights, and immigrant rights (especially on the U.S.-Mexico border). Several U.S. Muslims serve as leading voices of the social justice and anti-racist movements across the country. For example, Linda Sarsour, the co-founder of the Women's March in Washington, DC, proudly stands by the Black Lives Matter movement and the DACA population.

The entirety of the *ummah,* or global Muslim nation, is represented in the United States. In fact, no other country in the world has a more diverse Islamic representation of ethnicities, races, and theological beliefs than U.S. Muslims, who may be native-born U.S. citizens, immigrants, gay or straight people, doctors, lawyers, academics, cab drivers, musicians, actors, or athletes. U.S. Muslims may be fervent followers of the Islamic faith, or they may be more flexible in their everyday religious practices. Muslim women in the United States may wear the headscarf, or they may not. The U.S. Muslim population is made up of people who trace their ancestral origins to Africa, Central Asia, East Asia, Europe, the Middle East, South Asia, and Southeast Asia, among other regions of the world. The social, cultural, ethnic, and racial diversity of the U.S. Muslim population challenges the racialized archetype of the Muslim man as Arab, brown skinned, and bearded, and of the Muslim woman as Arab, brown skinned, submissive, and covered in some kind of oppressive garment.

In addition to this vast ethnic and racial diversity, U.S. Muslims in the United States follow a wide spectrum of "Islamic beliefs" or Islamic sects, from Sunnism, to Shi'ism, to Sufism, to Ahmadiyya, to the Nation of Islam, to name but a few. Like "American Christianity," with its variety of denominations, "American Islam" cannot be defined by a singular strand of Islamic thought. Sunni Muslims are the majority population among U.S. Muslims, but a significant Shi'a population also exists. The Sunni-Shi'a binary reflects the wider picture of Muslims around the world, with Sunnis amounting to approximately 85 percent of the *ummah*, while Shi'as amount to roughly 15 percent of the global population of Muslims. Within the Sunni tradition, several major sects are represented in the U.S. Muslim population. The same representation is true for followers of Shi'ism in the United States.

Some historians and scholars claim that Muslims arrived on modern-day U.S. soil long before the slave trade started in the 16th century, but the facts are flimsy to back up this claim. Human beings of African descent are widely recognized as the "first Muslims" in the history of the United States. Scholars estimate that up to 30 percent of all Africans enslaved during the transatlantic slave trade from the 16th to the 19th centuries came from Muslim backgrounds. The descendants of these African Muslims in the United States made invaluable contributions on several fronts to the betterment of U.S. society, including the building of the country's infrastructure and the struggle for civil rights during the 1950s and 1960s.

The U.S. Muslim population today, as a whole, is approximately one-third African American, one-third Arab American, and one-third Asian American. Arab Americans started immigrating to the United States in the 19th century. The majority of Arab Americans identify themselves as Christians, but a substantial Arab Muslim population lives across the country, especially in the cities of Detroit and Dearborn in Michigan. While small pockets of Asian Muslims lived in the United States in the 19th century, the majority of Asian Muslims living in the country today trace their immigrant history to the Immigration and Nationality Act of

1965, a piece of legislation that made it legal for thousands and thousands of Muslims to immigrate to the country. The passing of the Immigration and Nationality Act of 1965 had a major impact on the demographic composition of the U.S. Muslim population, which had previously been mostly African American.

Latin American Muslims, or Hispanic Muslims, are the fastest growing segment of the overall U.S. Muslim population. La Convivencia, the Spanish term for "living with difference," is sometimes used by Latin American Muslims to explain the way that they negotiate the various elements of their lived experiences as Latinos, Muslims, and Americans. La Convivencia is a sociological concept dating back to the time of "Islamic Spain," or the period (711–1492 CE) in which Muslims ruled and led a civilization on the Iberian Peninsula on the western edge of the European continent. This period in history is known for its religious pluralism and its intercultural identity. People of various religions, cultures, ethnicities, and races worked alongside one another in "Islamic Spain" to achieve remarkable feats in the realms of science, literature, architecture, and governance.

Some historians claim that Muslims from Al-Andalus, or "Islamic Spain," traveled by boat across the Atlantic Ocean to the modern-day United States as early as the 11th century. Other historians claim that Muslims were on board the *Niña,* the *Pinta,* and the *Santa Maria,* the fleet of ships navigated by Christopher Columbus in 1492. Regardless of the accuracy of these historical claims, Latin American Muslims have a long history on U.S. soil. Today, they trace their ancestry back to the modern-day countries of Colombia, Dominican Republic, Ecuador, Guatemala, Mexico, Puerto Rico, and Venezuela, among many others. Some of these U.S. Muslims are third- and fourth-generation, while others are newly arrived in the United States.

European American Muslims are linked to Latin American Muslims in the sense that many of these individuals trace their ancestry back to the European continent. European American Muslims, however, are distinguished from Latin American Muslims in the sense that they speak languages, and come from nations, outside of the Iberian Peninsula. The term "European American Muslims" is a broad term that encompasses Muslims on U.S. soil today who trace their ancestry back to nations across the European Union. While European American Muslims are a diverse group of people tracing their ancestry back centuries to the Islamic faith, many European American Muslims are recent converts from ethnic ancestries including English, French, Irish, Italian, and Scottish. The other segment of the current European American Muslim population includes descendants of Muslims who migrated to the United States in the 19th and 20th centuries. These U.S. Muslims include those of Albanian, Bosnian, and Polish descent, among other Eastern European nationalities.

Regardless of the fact that U.S. Muslims constitute a diverse population that is deeply rooted in the social, cultural, and political fabric of the United States, the monolithic understanding and representation of the Islamic faith and Muslims contribute to the rise of discriminatory acts and hate crimes against Muslims living on U.S. soil. A substantial number of U.S. Muslims experience discrimination in several areas of U.S. society, including school settings, employment processes, the workplace environment, airports, and other realms of traveling and transport. These experiences of discrimination, many of which are deemed by experts to be unconstitutional, are documented by entities responsible for protecting the civil rights of U.S. citizens and residents.

U.S. Muslim organizations, as well as their allies working for equality, are making earnest efforts to document and combat these discriminatory developments. These organizations, some of which are "Islamic," but others of which are secular, are working daily to combat hate crimes carried out against Muslims across the country. A simple Google search will reveal a plethora of hateful and sometimes deadly acts in recent years against U.S. Muslims. These crimes include cold-blooded murders, arson attacks against mosques or Islamic centers, graffiti on properties owned or regulated by U.S. Muslims, assault and battery against Muslims, and physical removal of the *hijab* from Muslim women.

Skewed media coverage of the Islamic faith and Muslims is frequently identified as a major reason that explains the rising tide of Islamophobia, and even the violent outbursts, against Muslims in the United States. Numerous studies have revealed that the Islamic faith and Muslims are widely depicted in mainstream media through the lenses of violence, terrorism, oppression of minority populations, government corruption, and mistreatment of women. Stories of "normal" Muslims or "everyday experiences of Muslims" are largely neglected for the more sensational stories, like those linked to "Islamic extremism" or the activities of militants like Daesh, better known as the Islamic State of Iraq and Syria (ISIS). Widescale media coverage of these issues and groups typically conflates the overwhelming majority of Muslims worldwide with the beliefs and actions of a fringe segment of the *ummah*. The entertainment industry, especially Hollywood films, also plays a significant role in exacerbating Islamophobia in the United States. Cinematic films and television programs typically misrepresent Muslims as violent religious fanatics, enemies of the United States, and people who generally oppose certain values including freedom of religion, freedom of speech, and women's rights

Muslims are positioned at the center of politically and emotionally charged questions over the meaning of U.S. national identity. Critics claim that the Islamic faith, and in turn Muslims, oppose the so-called "American values." The reason for this opposition, according to some commentators, is the *sharia,* a term that is generally recognized to mean "Islamic law." State governments around the country have pushed legislation that would effectively ban the *sharia* and thus prohibit Muslims from exercising their constitutional rights of freedom of religion and freedom of conscience. Leading politicians at the national level in Washington, DC have also issued grave warnings that U.S. Muslims and Islamic organizations on U.S. soil are seeking to install the *sharia* in order to dismantle the U.S. Constitution. These anti-*sharia* bills create an environment of suspicion and fear that fosters even more belief in the legitimacy of the "clash of civilizations."

An abundance of myths, half-truths, and outright lies have risen around the *sharia.* The fear of the *sharia* "creeping" into the U.S. political system, at the state and national levels, is oftentimes centered on the Council on American-Islamic Relations (CAIR), a leading civil rights and advocacy organization, and an ambiguous transnational movement commonly referred to as the "Muslim Brotherhood." Attempts have been made to designate CAIR and the Brotherhood as "terrorist organizations," because these groups allegedly work to infiltrate U.S. society and politics with a "radical jihadi" movement bent on instilling "political Islam."

Similarly to the *sharia,* the term *jihad* has generated fear of Muslims in the United States. The Arabic term *jihad* is commonly believed to mean "holy war" against Christians, Jews, and other "infidels" who oppose Islamic teachings. *Jihad,* however, is literally translated from Arabic to English to mean "to strive or to struggle." In the 7th century, the Prophet Muhammad explicitly declared that a defensive war, which he declared to be permissible in the eyes of Allah, is considered to be the "lesser *jihad*" in comparison to the "greater *jihad,*" which he defined as "the struggle against oneself" or against one's impulsive desires and ego. The term *jihad,* it should be noted, is not simply misunderstood by critics of the Islamic faith—it also is misused by "Muslim extremists." Wahhabism, a puritanical form of Sunni Islam, is repeatedly mentioned by experts as the cause of the radicalization of, extremism among, and use of violence by

Muslims. Some scholars even go as far as calling Wahhabism the main source of terrorism around the world.

Taqiyya, an Arabic term that is translated to mean "deception," is similar to the *sharia* and *jihad* in the sense that critics of the Islamic faith use it to "prove" that "Western civilization" and "Islamic civilization" are fundamentally at odds and incompatible with each other. *Taqiyya* is understood by critics as meaning "lying" or "deceiving," in a way that leads people to think that Muslims are not trustworthy. People in the United States who use the term *taqiyya* to dehumanize Muslims claim that the Qur'an commands followers of the Islamic faith to lie, cheat, and deceive people at any cost, in order to promote the *sharia* and infiltrate the foundations of U.S. society with an "Islamic supremacist" agenda. The truth of the matter is that many U.S. Muslims are not even well-schooled on the concept of *taqiyya,* which applies only when a Muslim's life is in danger, and many scholars as well as *imams* dismiss the accusation of lying and deceiving among Muslims in the United States as nothing more than an anti-Muslim campaign to marginalize and oppress Muslims on U.S. soil.

The alleged danger posed by Muslim extremists helped to fuel the anti-refugee campaign carried out largely by right-wing political forces during the 2016 U.S. presidential election. Refugees leaving Muslim-majority countries, particularly those from Syria, were deemed threats to U.S. national security. This framing of Muslim refugees as potential terrorists led to several "Muslim Bans" enacted by the Republican Party and ultimately approved by the Supreme Court of the United States. The "Muslim Ban" initiated by Donald Trump, however, is not the first immigration policy in U.S. history to deny Muslims entry into the United States or fair treatment in gaining access to U.S. residency. The U.S. government has a long track record of passing religiously and racially restrictive legislation banning entry to Muslims worldwide. The Immigration and Nationality Act of 1965 is the landmark piece of legislation that opened up the country's borders and drastically changed the religious and racial demographics of Muslims in the United States.

In summary, against the "clash of civilizations" is the "dialogue of civilizations," a political theory that sees "the West" and the "Muslim world" as two bodies that can live in peaceful coexistence. The "dialogue of civilizations" is rooted in the idea that stronger bridges of mutual understanding and genuine friendship can be built if groups of people engage in more intercultural and interreligious dialogue with one another. Mosques in the United States are often the sites of these kinds of activities and services. During Ramadan, the Islamic holy month, countless numbers of *masjids* across the country open their doors to neighbors, friends, and strangers of various cultural, ethnic, racial, and religious backgrounds. Ramadan is also the period when Muslims in the United States, and across the world, increase their charitable contributions to people in need of various resources. One of the Five Pillars of Islam—*zakat,* the Arabic term that translates to charity—is the giving of alms to the poor and needy, regardless of their cultural backgrounds, national origins, or religious traditions.

Religious pluralism, or the energetic pursuit of religious diversity, stands at the center of the "dialogue of civilizations." Developed over the years by leading sociologists, philosophers, and theologians on U.S. soil and beyond, religious pluralism is not merely the acceptance of religious diversity, a term commonly understood to mean "the different paths to the Creator." Religious pluralism is an active sociological process of working across religious boundaries and communities for the betterment of the whole society. Religious pluralism is the encounter of commitments between two or more religious communities toward a common goal. Religious pluralism is a state of mind and a type of society in which people of different religious and racial backgrounds are able to come together in dialogue in order to understand one another regardless of their various differences.

The Founding Fathers of the United States set these egalitarian principles in stone while envisioning their newly found country in the 18th century. The U.S. Founding Fathers, as many scholars have noted, envisioned Muslims as future citizens of the United States. Primary documents from the 18th century show that George Washington, the first U.S. president, and Thomas Jefferson, the co-author of the Declaration of Independence and third U.S. president, not only wrote about Muslims in light of U.S. society, but they also welcomed them to enjoy the same kind of freedoms that other U.S. citizens could enjoy under the U.S Constitution. These primary documents define U.S. identity in egalitarian and inclusive terms. The vision of the Founding Fathers is where future generations of U.S. citizens, and those living in the United States, must turn. "We hold these truths to be self-evident, that all men are created equal. That they are endowed by their Creator with certain inalienable rights, among them Life, Liberty, and the Pursuit of Happiness."

These universal and timeless words capture the best of the U.S. tradition. They also capture the best of the Islamic tradition, as the forthcoming pages will reveal.

Chronology

August 3, 1492—Christopher Columbus, the Catholic Italian navigator and explorer, left the Spanish port of Palos to lead his three ships—the *La Niña,* the *Pinta,* and the *Santa María*—westward to reach India. Columbus ended up landing in the Caribbean. Historians suggest that Muslims were likely on board the ships as part of Columbus's first exploration on behalf of the Spanish Crown.

December 25, 1522—Twenty enslaved Muslim Africans attacked their Christian masters on the island of Hispaniola, then governed by Diego Columbus, the eldest son of Christopher Columbus and the viceroy of the Indies for fifteen years.

May 27, 1586—Sir Francis Drake, the English privateer, besieged and captured the strategic Spanish settlement of St. Augustine in Florida. Indentured Muslim servants from Eastern Europe and Turkey are said to have been freed by Drake's forces.

March 9, 1753—A document shows that two men—Abel Conder and Mahamut—petitioned the South Carolina government for their freedom from indentured servitude. Abel and Mahamut are believed to have been Muslims of North African descent.

December 2, 1783—George Washington, the first U.S. president, wrote a letter to Joshua Holmes to address the religious persecution of Irish Catholic immigrants living in New York City. Washington wrote that the "bosom of America is open to receive not only the opulent and respectable Stranger, but the oppressed and persecuted of all Nations and Religions, whom we shall welcome to a participation of all our rights and privileges." Washington's "Letter to Irish Catholics" is often referenced by scholars discussing the pluralistic views of the U.S. Founding Fathers as they relate to the integration of Muslims into the fabric of U.S. society.

June 28, 1786—The U.S. government agreed to the Treaty of Peace and Friendship with the Barbary States, a set of nations in North Africa. The Treaty of Peace and Friendship officially established commercial and maritime rights for U.S. shipping vessels off the coast of North Africa. By signing the Treaty of Peace and Friendship, the Barbary States, the equivalent of a modern-day Muslim-majority country, became the first country in the world to recognize the independence of the United States.

November 11, 1800—Captain William Bainbridge and the USS *George Washington* visited Constantinople (modern-day Istanbul in Turkey). This was the first visit of a U.S. warship to the capital of the Ottoman Empire.

December 9, 1805—President Thomas Jefferson hosted the first presidential *iftar,* or breaking of the Ramadan fast, by inviting Sidi Soliman Mellimelli, a Tunisian diplomat, to Washington, DC. President Jefferson changed the time of dinner for Mellimelli from the usual "half after three" to "precisely at sunset" to accommodate Mellimelli's observance.

July 6, 1829—Abdul Rahman Ibrahim, an African Muslim slave from Timbuktu, Mali, who was enslaved and brought to the modern-day United States, died in Monrovia, Liberia, after obtaining his freedom from President John Quincy Adams. Abdul Rahman Ibrahim was a well-documented African Muslim slave of the 19th century.

September 1, 1837—The article "A Convert from Mohammedanism" appeared in the *Boston Reporter* detailing the life of Omar Ibn Said, an African American Christian and former slave. Born and raised in a wealthy Muslim Fula family on the border of the modern countries of Senegal and Gambia, Said escaped from slavery and ended up producing Arabic texts that shed light on the Islamic beliefs of the early years of his life.

March 9, 1841—The U.S. Supreme Court ruled that the African slaves, some of whom were Muslim, who seized control of the *Amistad* slave ship were free people because of the rights provided by the U.S. Constitution. Representative John Quincy Adams of Massachusetts, who had previously served as the sixth president of the United States, defended the Africans and their natural right to freedom before the U.S. Supreme Court.

July 22, 1862—President Abraham Lincoln and Ottoman Empire Sultan Abdülmecid agreed to the Treaty of Commerce and Navigation. The Treaty, in effect, served as the first official trade agreement between the United States and the Ottoman Empire.

June 13, 1881—Private Mohammed Kahn, formerly of Company E of the 43rd New York Infantry Regiment, appeared at the Pension Office in Washington, DC. Private Kahn submitted a written document to the Pension Office detailing his personal identity and his service in the Union Army during the Civil War. Kahn stated he was born in Persia, raised in Afghanistan, and immigrated to the United States in 1861, where he shortly thereafter enlisted.

February 5, 1917—The 64th U.S. Congress passed the Immigration Act of 1917, also referred to as the Asiatic Barred Zone of 1917. The Barred Zone, which included the South Asian subcontinent, Southeast Asia, and any modern-day Middle Eastern country, effectively banned the immigration of Muslims to the United States. Today, approximately 60 percent of the world's Muslim population reside in Asia, with roughly another 20 percent living in the Middle East and North Africa.

January 26, 1920—Mufti Muhammad Sadiq of the Ahmadiyya Muslim community set sail from England to Philadelphia, Pennsylvania. Once in the United States, Mufti Sadiq proceeded to convert hundreds of African Americans to the Islamic faith. He is widely recognized as one of the first Muslim missionaries ever to step foot on modern-day U.S. soil.

July 4, 1930—The founder of the Nation of Islam (NOI), Wallace Fard (W. F.) Muhammad, arrived in Detroit, Michigan. Fard was a mysterious figure who brought the teachings of the NOI to African American neighborhoods in the United States.

February 15, 1934—Arab Muslim immigrants, largely from Jordan, Lebanon, Palestine, and Syria, opened the doors of their mosque in Cedar Rapids, Iowa. Today, the mosque is referred to as the "Mother Mosque of America."

June 28, 1957—President Dwight D. Eisenhower attended the dedication ceremony of the Islamic Center in Washington, DC, making him the first U.S. president to give a speech at a *masjid*. In his speech, President Eisenhower said, ". . . under the American Constitution . . . this place of worship, is just as welcome and could be a similar edifice of any other religion. Indeed, America would fight with her whole strength for your right to have here your own church and worship according to your own conscience."

July 2, 1962—The U.S. District Court for the District of Columbia considered the case of *Fulwood v. Clemmer* and ruled that prisons are legally bound to provide facilities for religious services to Muslims.

February 21, 1965—Malcolm X, an African American and Muslim religious leader, was assassinated by rival Black Muslims while addressing his Organization of Afro-American Unity in Washington Heights, New York City.

October 3, 1965—President Lyndon B. Johnson signed into law the Immigration and Nationality Act of 1965, a piece of legislation that allocated more visas to people from Asia and the Middle East. The Act of 1965 declared that "no person shall receive any preference or priority or be discriminated against in the issuance of an immigrant visa because of the person's race, sex, nationality, place of birth or place of residence." Following the law's enactment, the U.S. Muslim population increased significantly, from 200,000 in 1951 to more than 1 million by 1971.

October 23, 1983—A U.S. Marine compound in Beirut, Lebanon, was attacked by a truck bomb in which 220 Marines and 21 other U.S. service personnel were killed. The U.S. intelligence community pointed the blame at Hezbollah, a political organization and militant group that originated in Lebanon.

June 25, 1991—Imam Siraj Wahhaj, spiritual leader of the Masjid Al-Taqwa in Brooklyn, New York, provided the opening prayer in the U.S. House of Representatives, becoming the first Muslim with the honor to do so.

February 6, 1992—Wallace D. (W. D.) Mohammed led the invocation at a session of the U.S. Senate, marking the first time a Muslim had done so. In his blessing, W. D. Mohammed prayed that Americans "continue to live as a prosperous nation of many in one and as a people of faith taking pride in human decency, industry, and service."

September 11, 2001—Also referred to as the 9/11 attacks, a series of airline hijackings carried out in New York City and Washington, DC, by 19 militants killed nearly 3,000 people and injured more than 6,000 people. The attacks triggered the "War on Terror," a foreign policy endeavor that caused extensive death and destruction in several Muslim-majority countries around the world.

September 17, 2001—Following the 9/11 attacks, President George W. Bush visited the Islamic Center of Washington, DC. In his speech there, President Bush stated, "The face of terror is not the true faith of Islam," and added that "Islam means peace." While President Bush's words rang true for many U.S. Muslims and Muslims around the world, they fell on deaf ears once the United States invaded Afghanistan in 2001 and Iraq in 2003.

October 7, 2001—The U.S. government invaded Afghanistan to attack the Taliban, a group that the United States believed to have provided material support for the 9/11 hijackers. The Afghan War is typically treated as the beginning of the so-called "War on Terrorism."

January 4, 2007—Representative Keith Ellison of Minnesota became the first Muslim member of the U.S. Congress to take his ceremonial oath to the U.S. Constitution with a Qur'an owned by Thomas Jefferson.

June 4, 2009—President Barack Obama gave a speech titled "A New Beginning," popularly referred to as the "Cairo Speech," at Cairo University in Egypt. President Obama's speech called for improved relations with Muslims and more cooperation between Western countries and Muslim-majority countries in the struggle against religious persecution and political extremism.

June 1, 2015—The Supreme Court of the United States ruled against Abercrombie & Fitch, the retail store chain, which refused to hire Samantha Elauf, a practicing Muslim and woman who observed *hijab* by wearing a headscarf pursuant to her perceived Islamic obligations. The Equal Employment Opportunity Commission (EEOC) filed suit on Elauf's behalf, alleging a violation of Title VII of the Civil Rights Act of 1964.

December 7, 2015—Republican presidential front-runner Donald Trump called for "a total and complete shutdown of Muslims entering the United States until our country's representatives can figure out what is going on." Trump's comment, widely condemned as anti-Muslim and Islamophobic, is seen as a precursor to his Executive Orders or "Muslim travel ban."

August 8, 2016—Sabre fencer and African American Muslim woman Ibtihaj Muhammad becomes the first U.S. athlete to observe *hijab* and compete in a headscarf for the United States during an Olympic competition. Muhammad left Rio de Janeiro, Brazil, the location of the Olympics, with a bronze medal in the team fencing event.

January 27, 2017—President Donald Trump signed Executive Order 13769, which banned foreign nationals from seven Muslim-majority countries from visiting the United States for 90 days. Executive Order 13769 also indefinitely suspended entry to all Syrian refugees, and barred all other refugees from entering the United States for a total of 120 days.

June 26, 2018—The U.S. Supreme Court ruled 5–4 in favor of Donald Trump's "Muslim travel ban" in the case *Trump v. Hawaii*. In her dissenting opinion, Justice Sonia Sotomayor issued a scathing rebuttal, stating that the U.S. Supreme Court failed to safeguard the fundamental principle of religious liberty and religious neutrality as commanded by the U.S. Founding Fathers. Sotomayor added that the "Muslim travel ban" "masquerades behind a façade of national-security concerns" and was driven primarily by "anti-Muslim animus."

November 6, 2018—Democratic politicians Ilhan Omar and Rashida Tlaib became the first two Muslim women elected to the House of Representatives of the U.S. Congress. Representative Omar won the election in Minnesota's 5th Congressional District, and Representative Tlaib won the election in Michigan's 13th Congressional District.

A

Abrahamic Tradition

The term "Abrahamic tradition" represents the shared monotheistic linkages between Jews, Christians, and Muslims, the three largest religious populations in the United States. The term "Abrahamic" is said to have been coined by Louis Massignon, a French Catholic scholar of Islam, pioneer of Christian-Muslim relations, and author of the influential paper "Three Prayers of Abraham." The term "Abrahamic" is named after Abraham, the Hebrew prophet as first mentioned in Genesis in the Torah and the first human being to declare the belief in one God. As such, Abraham, or *Ibrahim* in Arabic, is the common link for approximately 4 million followers of Judaism, 245 million followers of Christianity, and the 6 million Muslims living in the United States. The Abrahamic tradition is centered around several common theological roots including the belief in the oneness of God, the divine revelation of the prophets, the angels, the shared sacred history of God's encounter with humanity, and Judgment Day.

Abraham is considered to be the patriarch of the Torah, the spiritual forefather of the New Testament, and the architect of the Qur'an. He was called by God to leave the house of his father, Terah, and settle in the land of Canaan, which God subsequently promised to Abraham and his progeny. Muslims trace their origins back to Ishmael, the first-born son of Abraham and Hagar, the mistress of Abraham. Ishmael's second son, Kedar, is said to be the direct ancestor of Muhammad, the prophet of Islam. The Jewish people, on the other hand, are believed to be the direct descendants of Isaac, Abraham's second son.

According to the Islamic tradition, Muhammad came to reassert, in the seventh century, the primordial monotheistic religion of Abraham. Thus, the Islamic faith is not understood to be a "new religion" with new scripture, but rather the "original" and oldest religion that had been lost over centuries by Jews and Christians because of their human innovations, misguided interpretations, and incorrect practices. The Islamic faith is considered to be the final version of the Abrahamic tradition that reveals the same overarching truths revealed in the Torah and Gospels. Therefore, it is appropriate to understand the Islamic faith as one that is deliberately self-conscious of its relationship with the Jewish and Christian traditions. Muslims themselves are aware of these connections and often refer to scripture to explain the Abrahamic linkages.

The concept of the "Abrahamic tradition" notably emerged in the post-9/11 public discourse as a tool to counter anti-Muslim sentiments stoked by anti-Islam activists, media figures, and politicians. The word "Abraham" has itself effectively become "a counter-metaphor amidst interreligious quarrels" (Rosenhagen 2015). Some scholars, however, do not view Abraham as a unifying figure who transcends the differences among Jews, Christians, and Muslims. Jon Levenson, a Harvard University scholar and author of *Inheriting Abraham: The Legacy of the Patriarch in Judaism, Christianity, and Islam,* reveals how "the increasingly conventional notion of the three equally 'Abrahamic' religions derives from a dangerous misunderstanding of key Biblical and Qur'anic texts." Levenson believes that the "Abrahamic tradition" does not do justice to any of the monotheistic traditions; it is, he argues, "often biased against Judaism in subtle and pernicious ways" (Levenson 2012).

Nonetheless, the term "Judeo-Christian" has demonstrated far greater staying power in U.S. public discourse in comparison to the "Abrahamic tradition." In the 1930s, the term "Judeo-Christian" was used by the National Conference of Christians and Jews (NCCJ) to lay out a vision of the United States that relied on biblical prophets, traditions, and moral principles shared by Jews and Christians of varied denominations living on U.S. soil. According to the NCCJ, the "Judeo-Christian" narrative served as a kind of "national glue" that provided U.S. citizens with a moral compass amidst the challenges stemming from social, cultural, ethnic, racial, and religious diversity. These sentiments were echoed in a 1952 speech by Dwight D. Eisenhower, in which the president famously summarized the "American creed" a month before his inauguration. President Eisenhower claimed that the United States's democracy "has no sense unless it is founded in a deeply felt religious faith." Today, prominent Christian and conservative politicians regularly insist that the United States was founded as—and destined to be—a "Judeo-Christian" nation.

Peter L. Berger, a preeminent scholar of the sociology of U.S. religions, disagreed with these propositions and argued that the term "Abrahamic" is more constructive than "Judeo-Christian," considering that the United States is witnessing a growth of religious diversity.

The term "Abrahamic" is often used today by interfaith groups and organizations that are working in solidarity to end anti-Jewish, anti-Christian, and anti-Muslim discrimination on U.S. soil. The Abrahamic Alliance International (AAI), an organization based in San Jose, California, has a mission statement of "uniting Jews, Christians, and Muslims for active peacebuilding and poverty relief" (Abrahamic Alliance International n.d.). The AAI accomplishes its mission by holding seminars to build mutual respect, helping the marginalized through local community service, mentoring peacemakers according to sacred scriptures, and relieving poverty through generosity, educational empowerment, and compassionate service (Abrahamic Alliance International n.d.). The Tri-Faith Initiative, based in Omaha, Nebraska, also is made up of Jews, Christians, and Muslims who have chosen to be in a relationship together as neighbors on one campus, committed to practicing respect, acceptance, and trust. The mission of the Tri-Faith Initiative is to intentionally co-locate Jewish, Christian, and Muslim houses of worship on a single piece of land to promote dialogue, transcend differences, and build bridges of understanding. There also are academic initiatives like the Lubar Institute for the Study of the Abrahamic Religions at the University of Wisconsin and the Children of Abraham Institute at the University of Virginia, which are organizing research and public conversations between scholars and followers of the Abrahamic religions (Rosenhagen 2015).

Contemporary events also give hope for stronger bonds of "Abrahamic solidarity" among Jews, Christians, and Muslims. In the state of Texas in 2018, the Pakistani-born attorney Salman Bhojani became the first Muslim elected to the city council in Euless, a Fort Worth suburb. Republican opponents of Bhojani's candidacy raised fear of his Muslim faith as well as the alleged "anti-American" teachings found in the Qur'an (Brockman 2018). Not only were many Muslims outraged at these accusations, but so were Jewish and Christian clergy, who condemned the attacks on Bhojani's faith and ethnicity. Reverend Steve Heyduck, Senior Pastor of the First United Methodist Church of Euless, stated in a press release that "the church stands firmly in the tradition of Jesus being opposed to racism and hatred. We lament that some who claim the name of Christ treat those who do not as suspicious or less committed citizens" (Faith in Texas 2018).

Muslims and religious minority populations living in predominantly Muslim countries participated in a turning point at a conference entitled "Religious Minorities in Muslim Lands: Its Legal Framework and a Call to Action" in Marrakesh, Morocco, in January 2016. Held in conjunction with the High Patronage of His Majesty King Mohammed VI of Morocco and the Forum for Promoting Peace in Muslim Societies, the conference culminated in the signing of the Marrakesh Declaration, a treatise signed by hundreds of Muslim intellectuals, scholars, and politicians. The Marrakesh Declaration affirmed a commitment among Muslim leaders to build on the principles articulated in the Consitution of Medina, an interfaith document created by the Prophet Muhammad that contained a number of principles of contractual citizenship, such as "freedom of movement, property ownership, mutual solidarity and defense, as well as principles of justice and equality before the law" (Marrakesh Declaration 2016). Moreover, in response to the political issues dividing Christians and Muslims, Muslims are electing to join "The Covenants Initiative," following the publication of *The Covenants of the Prophet Muhammad with the Christians of the World* (Morrow 2013). The Covenants Initiative calls on all Muslims from all schools of jurisprudence and spiritual paths "to take a vigorous, proactive and public stance in support of peaceful Christians presently being attacked by some seriously misguided 'Muslims'" (Covenants Initiative 2015, 66–67).

See also: Dhimmi; Jesus and Mary; *Jizya*; *Ummah*

Further Reading

Abrahamic Alliance International. n.d. "About." San Jose, CA: Abrahamic Alliance International. Retrieved from http://www.abrahamicalliance.org/aai/about.

Considine, Craig. 2016. "Religious Pluralism and Civic Rights in a 'Muslim Nation': An Analysis of Prophet Muhammad's Covenants with Christians." *Religions* 7, no. 15: 1–22.

Covenants Initiative, The. 2015. *Six Covenants of the Prophet Muhammad with the Christians of His Time: The Primary Documents*. Edited by John Andrew Morrow. Tacoma, WA: Covenants Press/Angelico Press.

Dardess, George. 2005. *Meeting Islam: A Guide for Christians*. Brewster, MA: Paraclete Press.

Faith in Texas. 2018. "Clergy Unite Against Racism." Faith in Texas. Retrieved from https://faithintx.org/clergy-unite-against-racism/.

Feiler, Bruce. 2004. *Abraham: A Journey to the Heart of Three Faiths*. New York: Perennial.

Gaston, K. Healna. 2018. "The Judeo-Christian and Abrahamic Traditions in America." Oxford Research Encyclopedias. Last modified January 2018. Retrieved from http://religion.oxfordre.com/view/10.1093/acrefore/9780199340 378.001.0001/acrefore-9780199340378-e-425.

Levenson, Jon D. 2012. *Inheriting Abraham: The Legacy of the Patriarch in Judaism, Christianity, and Islam*. Princeton, NJ: Princeton University Press.

Marrakesh Declaration. 2016. "Marrakesh Declaration." Last modified January 27, 2016. Retrieved from http://www.marrakeshdeclaration.org/files/Bismilah -2-ENG.pdf.

Morrow, John Andrew. 2013. *The Covenants of the Prophet Muhammad with the Christians of the World*. Tacoma, WA: Angelico Press/Sophia Perennis.

Rosenhagen, Ulrich. 2015. "One Abraham or three? The conversation between three faiths." *The Christian Century,* November 24, 2015. Retrieved from https://www.christiancentury.org/article/2015-11/one-abraham-or-three.

Siddiqui, Mona, ed. 2013. *The Routledge Reader in Christian-Muslim Relations*. London: Routledge.

Tri-Faith Initiative. n.d. "About." Omaha, NE: Tri-Faith Initiative. Retrieved from https://trifaith.org/about/.

African American Muslims

People of African descent are generally recognized as the "first Muslims" to live on what is today referred to as "U.S. soil." While scholars of various academic disciplines do not know the exact number of African Muslims who were forcefully removed from the African continent, the general consensus among scholars is that approximately 20 to 30 percent of the Africans brought to the Western hemisphere during the transatlantic slave trade were Muslims. Most of these Muslims are believed to have been forcefully taken from the West African peoples known as Fulas, Fula Jallon, Fula Toro, and Massine. Large populations of these ethnic groups are currently residing in modern-day African nations like Cameroon, Central African Republic, The Gambia, and Senegal.

While a number of scholars suggest that Muslims arrived on modern-day U.S. soil as early as the 9th century, there are few hard facts to support this claim. Abubakari II and Mansa Musa, the African emperors who ruled modern-day Mali in the 14th century, are reported to have discovered "America" nearly 200 years before Christopher Columbus. In his book *The Saga of Abubakari II,* Malian scholar Gaoussou Diaware claimed that

Emperor Abubakari left with 2,000 boats to explore whether the Atlantic Ocean—like the great River Niger that swept through Mali—had another "bank." In 1311, he handed the throne over to his brother, Kankou Moussa, who also is said to have set off on an expedition into the unknown.

The presence of Muslims on U.S. soil between the 17th and 19th centuries is an area of increasing interest to historians and scholars of Islamic studies in the United States. Expert opinion suggests that the Islamic faith was often practiced by African Muslims in secret, but that some of these Muslims also reluctantly abandoned their faith for Christianity in order to appease their Christian slaveowners. In her book *Servants of Allah: African Muslims Enslaved in the Americas,* Sylviane A. Diouf sheds light on how the Islamic faith flourished on a large scale during the years of slavery in the United States. She details how, even while enslaved, many Muslims managed to follow most of the precepts of their religion by maintaining their distinctive lifestyles, material "Muslim culture," and faithfulness to Allah. Scholars also claim that a hybrid form of the Islamic faith emerged because African Muslims themselves mixed-and-matched their teachings and traditions with norms from other religions, particularly Christianity. On Sapelo Island, off the coast of Georgia, African American Muslim slaves are said to have been "Christians by day and Muslims by night." Local historian Cornelia Walker Bailey noted that churches on Sapelo Island were built facing east toward Mecca, that Christian women observed *hijab* when entering their place of worship, and that Christian worshippers removed their shoes when entering the prayer space, a custom that is observed by Muslims in mosques worldwide.

The lives of several prominent U.S. Muslim slaves have been documented over the years. Omar Ibn Said, who is said to have been born in present-day Senegal, had been captured by slave traders and brought to Charleston, South Carolina, in 1807. Said is best known for writing his own version of Qur'anic passages in Arabic on a jail cell wall after being arrested in Fayetteville, North Carolina, after attempting to escape from slavery in 1810. It was later reported that the walls of Said's prison cell "were covered in strange characters, traced in charcoal or chalk, which no scholar in Fayetteville could decipher." These "strange characters" were likely letters of the Arabic alphabet and teachings of the Qur'an. In addition to his autobiography, Said produced an Arabic translation of the 23rd Psalm, to which he wrote the very first words of the Qur'an (1:1): "In the name of God, the Most Gracious, the Most Merciful." Eventually, Said was bought and subsequently released from prison by a prominent

Christian family that persuaded him to convert to Christianity. In 1837 an article in the *Boston Reporter* referred to Said as a "convert from Mohammedanism," a 19th-century term that was often used as a synonym for "Muslim." Seventeen years later, a reporter wrote that Said had "thrown aside the blood-stained *Qur'an* and now worships at the feet of the Prince of Peace," a phrase used to denote Jesus of Nazareth.

Yarrow Mamout, an enslaved African Muslim of the Fulani people who died a free man in Georgetown, Washington, DC, is the center of James H. Johnston's book *From Slave Ship to Harvard: Yarrow Mamout and the History of an African American Family*. Mamout was an educated Muslim from Guinea who was brought to Maryland on the slave ship *Elijah* (Johnston 2012). He gained his freedom 44 years later. Mamout is known for being the center of a portrait painted by Charles William Peale, a prominent American artist of the U.S. Revolutionary period. Peale helped to distinguish Mamout by writing an obituary and sending it to newspapers. The *Gettysburg Compiler* was one of the papers that carried Mamout's obituary. Peale wrote that all people who knew Mamout recognized him as "industrious, honest, and moral" and that he was "never known to eat of swine, nor drink ardent spirits" (Oxford University Press 2012).

In the first decades of the 20th century, African Americans began to actively form communities that defined themselves as "Islamic." According to Amina Beverly McCloud, author of *African American Islam,* "[f]our sets of factors can be identified as the primary influences that set the stage for the implantation of Islam within African American communities: the social and political climate of [the United States] with regard to its citizens of African descent, the social and political climate in African America, Islamic retentions passed to generations through storytelling and naming, and Muslim immigration" (McCloud 1995, 9). The Moorish Science Temple (MST) of America, as McCloud points out, is considered to be one of the first homegrown Muslim movements and communities in the United States. Founded by Timothy Drew, known to his followers as Noble Drew Ali, in 1913 in Newark, New Jersey, the Moorish Science Temple taught that blacks were descendants of the ancient Moabites, a western Semitic ethnic group that is said to have inhabited the northwestern and southwestern shores of Africa. Noble Drew Ali claimed that blacks were Moors who had had their Muslim identity stripped away from them because of slavery and racial segregation in the United States. According to Patrick D. Bowen, an expert on the history of conversions to the Islamic faith in U.S. history, the Moorish Science Temple movement was a hybrid community in which

Muslims mixed MST teachings with other Islamic, political, and esoteric concepts, a tendency that left the larger Moorish community fractured (Bowen 2017).

The size of the African American Muslim population increased thanks to the arrival of missionaries working on behalf of the Ahmadiyya Muslim community in the early stages of the 20th century. Mufti Muhammad Sadiq, an Ahmadi Muslim missionary from Qadian, India, arrived in Philadelphia in 1920 to proselytize the Islamic faith. Upon his arrival, Sadiq is said to have befriended Marcus Garvey, the black nationalist leader, and to have started preaching the Islamic faith to African Americans in urban neighborhoods. Writing for *Religion & Politics,* Aysha Khan noted that Mufti Sadiq led the conversion of nearly 10,000 African Americans over the span of his first three years living in the United States. Following the emergence of Ahmadiyya, another movement—the Universal Islamic Society—emerged in Detroit, Michigan, in 1926. The founder of the Universal Islamic Society (UIS), Duse Muhammad Ali, established this organization with the motto, "One God, One Aim, One Destiny." The UIS also had success in reaching African American communities in urban neighborhoods in the United States. According to Moustafa Bayoumi, an award-winning author and scholar, the Islamic faith was perceived to be an attractive alternative to Christianity because Islam is a religion "in which Blacks had an alternative universal history to which to pledge allegiance." Bayoumi pointed to the contributions made by black people to the growth and progression of the Islamic faith, most notably Bilal Ibn Rabah, the Abyssinian slave freed by the Prophet Muhammad. Bilal rose to the prominent position of *muezzin,* the Arabic term that denotes the leader who calls the Muslim faithful to their daily prayers.

African American Muslim experiences also were significantly shaped by the emergence of the Nation of Islam (NOI), a community and organization that today represents a significant subset of the larger U.S. Muslim population. Although critics often argue that the NOI's principles of black racial superiority fall outside of the realm of the Prophet Muhammad's vision of racial equality, the organization maintains a loyal following among African Americans. The NOI emerged on U.S. soil in the early 1930s by successfully combining elements of the Islamic faith with values of the black nationalist movement that gained attention among African Americans in the 19th century.

The founder of the NOI, Wallace Fard (W. F.) Muhammad, arrived in Detroit on July 4, 1930. Fard is a mysterious figure who had over 50 aliases. Scholars who have studied him, as John Andrew Morrow noted in his book *Finding W. D. Fard,* suggest that he may have been an African American, an Arab from Syria, Lebanon, Algeria, Morocco, or Saudi Arabia, a Jamaican, a Turk, an Afghan, an Indo-Pakistani, an Iranian, an Azeri, a white American, a Bosnian, a Mexican, a Greek, or even a Jew (Morrow 2019). Before disappearing in 1933, W. F. Muhammad provided African Americans with an Islamic theology that outlined an innate racial superiority of black people over white people. He taught that black people descended from a superior race that lived in a paradise on earth over 6,000 years ago, only to be destroyed by a "white devil" named Yacub. W. F. Muhammad also claimed that he was both the Messiah and the Mahdi, two claims that are also heavily questioned by some U.S. Muslims.

W. F. Muhammad was replaced as a leader of the NOI by Elijah Muhammad, a convert to the Islamic faith who developed the NOI into a stronger organization that focused on empowering black people, promoting the self-sufficiency of black communities, combating white supremacy, and converting African Americans to a lifestyle based on Islamic teachings. Today, the Southern Poverty Law Center refers to the NOI as an extremist organization with "deeply racist, anti-Semitic and anti-LGBT rhetoric."

Following the emergence of the Nation of Islam, another predominantly African American group—the Five-Percent Nation—was founded in Harlem, New York City, by Clarence 13X around 1963. Clarence 13X, later known as "Allah the Father," was a former student of Malcolm X and member of the Nation of Islam. Also referred to as the "Five Percenters" or the "Nations of Gods and Earths," the Five-Percent Nation is named after the theory that 5 percent of human beings worldwide are "poor righteous teachers," whereas 85 percent of the population are "uncivilized" or lost. The other 10 percent of the global human population is considered "evil" and guilty of enslaving the poor. The Five-Percent Nation distanced itself from the NOI on the grounds that the group's founder, W. F. Muhammad, was "Allah" in the flesh. The Five-Percent Nation, however, used similar narratives as the NOI in the sense that they both draw on black nationalism, family unity, healthy living, and the self-sufficiency of communities.

Today, African American Muslims comprise approximately 20 to 30 percent of the overall Muslim population in the United States. According to a 2017 Pew Research Center survey, roughly one-fifth of all U.S. Muslims are black. The Pew Research Center also revealed that nearly 50 percent of black Muslims in the United States are converts to the Islamic faith. Around

60 percent of native-born U.S. Muslims are of African American descent. African American Muslims are more likely than other U.S. Muslims to be in the lowest income category (Mogahed and Chouhoud 2017, 9).

U.S.-born black Muslims stand out from the overall U.S. Muslim population in other ways. Fully two-thirds are converts to the Islamic faith, compared with just one in seven among all other U.S. Muslims (Pew Research Center 2017). "U.S.-born Black Muslims are less likely than other U.S.-born Muslims to say they have a lot in common with most Americans, and they are more likely than all other U.S. Muslims to say natural conflict exists between the teachings of [the Islamic faith] and democracy" (Pew Research Center 2017). U.S.-born African American Muslims are more likely than other U.S. Muslims to say it has become harder in recent years to "be Muslim" in the United States—nearly all U.S.-born black Muslims (96 percent) say there is a lot of discrimination against Muslims in the United States, almost identical to the share who say there is a lot of discrimination against black people in the United States (94 percent) (Pew Research Center 2017). Furthermore, African American Muslims do not share the optimism of the majority of U.S. Muslims about living in the United States. Only 28 percent of African American Muslims express a positive outlook, which echoes the views of the larger African American population of the United States (23 percent) (Mogahed and Chouhoud 2017, 5).

The African American Muslim population has decreased as an overall share of the total U.S. Muslim population since the passing of the Immigration and Nationality Act of 1965. This piece of immigration legislation increased the number of Muslim immigrants from the Middle East, South Asia, and Southeast Asia. As of 2018, U.S.-born people of African descent account for about 13 percent of the adult U.S. Muslim community, and among Muslims whose families have been in the United States for at least three generations, fully 50 percent are of African descent (Pew Research Center 2017).

The African American Muslim population today consists of some of the United States's most visible and influential leaders in the realm of politics, religious life, and entertainment. Keith Ellison holds the title as the first Muslim to ever serve in the U.S. Congress. Ellison represented Minnesota's 5th Congressional District in the U.S. House of Representatives from 2006 until 2018. During his tenure in the U.S. Congress, as noted on his official website, Ellison "founded the Congressional Consumer Justice Caucus and [belonged to] more than a dozen other caucuses that focus on issues like social inclusion [and] environmental protection. Ellison was elected co-chair of the Congressional Progressive Caucus for the 113th Congress, which promotes the progressive promise [of] fairness for all, [and served as] a member of the Congressional Black Caucus" (2019). He is perhaps best known for using a Qur'an owned by Thomas Jefferson to be sworn into the U.S. Congress on Capitol Hill in 2007.

African American Muslims hold other significant "first" honors in U.S. history. On February 6, 1992, Wallace D. Mohammed, the son of Elijah Muhammad, gave the invocation on the floor of the U.S. Senate, marking the first time a Muslim had ever done so (Harrington 1992). One year earlier, on June 25, 1991, Siraj Wahhaj, a respected *imam* of Masjid Al Taqwa in New York City, was the first Muslim to deliver a prayer in the House of Representatives (Abdal-Haqq 1998, 197). Nearly two decades later, at the 2016 Summer Olympics in Rio de Janeiro, Brazil, saber fencer Ibtihaj Muhammad became the first U.S. Muslim woman to observe *hijab* while competing for the United States in the Olympics competition.

African American Muslims have also been vocal critics of racial and religion-based injustices in U.S. society. Comedian Dave Chappelle, known for leading *Chapelle's Show* on the U.S. cable television network Comedy Central, is outspoken on issues pertaining to the social construction of race, experiences of African Americans, and racism at large in the United States. Hip-hop artist Wasalu Muhammad Jaco, better known as Lupe Fiasco, was raised Muslim and uses his platform to debunk anti-Muslim stereotypes that depict Muslims as violent and radicalized. Sports stars such as Muhammad Ali, the boxer, and Kareem Abdul Jabbar, the basketball super-star, also vocally criticized injustices carried out in the name of white su-premacy and religious bigotry in U.S. society. Ali, who converted to the Islamic faith in 1963 under the guidance of the NOI, is remembered for protesting the Vietnam War, which he argued was based on racism. Ali for-feited his boxing title and spent years in prison for his protest. Abdul Jabbar received the Presidential Medal of Freedom, the highest civilian award of the United States, from President Barack Obama in 2016.

See also: Slavery

Further Reading

Abdal-Haqq, Irshad. 1998. "The Muslim Invocation on Capitol Hill: Revisiting the Legality of Prayer in Congress." *Journal of Islamic Law* 3, no. 2 (Fall/Winter): 197–204.

Bayoumi, Moustafa. 2002. "East of the Sun (West of the Moon): The Harmony History of Islam Among Asian and African Americans." *Asian American/Asian Research Institute: The City University of New York.* Last modified May 16, 2002. Retrieved from http://aaari.info/02-05-16Bayoumi/.

Berg, Herbert. 2005. "Mythmaking in the African American Muslim Context: The Moorish Science Temple, the Nation of Islam, and the American Society of Muslims." *Journal of the American Academy of Religion* 73, no. 3: 685–703.

Bowen, Patrick D. 2017. "The Moorish Science Temple of America. In *A History of Conversion to Islam in the United States: White American Muslims before 1975.* Leiden, The Netherlands: Brill.

Curtis, Edward E., VI. 2006. *Black Muslim Religion in the Nation of Islam, 1960–1975.* Chapel Hill: University of North Carolina Press.

Diouf, Sylviane A. 2013. *Servants of Allah: African Muslims Enslaved in the Americas.* New York: New York University Press.

Flodin-Ali, Yasmine. 2018. "What Malcolm X Taught Me About Muslim America." *Religion & Politics,* May 22, 2018. Retrieved from http://religionandpolitics.org/2018/05/22/what-malcolm-x-taught-me-about-muslim-america/.

Ghanea Bassiri, Kambiz. 2010. *A History of Islam in America.* Cambridge, UK: Cambridge University Press.

Harrington, Linda M. 1992. "Muhammad Marks a First for Senate." *Chicago Tribune,* February 7, 1992. Retrieved from https://www.chicagotribune.com/news/ct-xpm-1992-02-07-9201120340-story.html.

Johnston, James H. 2012. *From Slave Ship to Harvard: Yarrow Mamout and the History of an African American Family.* New York: Fordham University Press.

Khan, Aysha. 2018. "Ahmadi Muslims Have a Storied American History—And a Legacy That Is Often Overlooked." *Religion & Politics,* November 20, 2018. Retrieved from https://religionandpolitics.org/2018/11/20/ahmadi-muslims-have-a-storied-american-history-and-a-legacy-that-is-often-overlooked/.

Library of Congress. n.d. "Omar Ibn Said Collection." Washington, DC: Library of Congress. Retrieved from https://www.loc.gov/collections/omar-ibn-said-collection/about-this-collection/.

McCloud, Aminah Beverly. 1995. *African American Islam.* New York and London: Routledge.

Mogahed, Dalia, and Youssef Chouhoud. 2017. *American Muslim Poll 2017: Full Report.* Washington, DC: Institute for Social Policy and Understanding. Retrieved from https://www.ispu.org/american-muslim-poll-2017/.

Morrow, John Andrew. 2019. *Finding W. D. Fard: Unveiling the Identity of the Founder of the Nation of Islam.* Newcastle upon Tyne, UK: Cambridge Scholars Publishing.

Miyakawa, Felicia. 2005. *Five Percenter Rap: God Hop's Music, Message, and Black Muslim Mission.* Bloomington: Indiana University Press.

Pew Research Center. 2017. "1. Demographic portrait of Muslim Americans." Washington, DC: Pew Research Center. Last modified July 26, 2017. Retrieved from http://www.pewforum.org/2017/07/26/demographic-portrait-of-muslim -americans/.

Ahadith

The term *ahadith*—literally translated to mean "news," "stories," or "reports"—is an Arabic word that popularly refers to the collection of oral narrative reports of the sayings and actions of Muhammad, the prophet of Islam and the last prophet of the monotheistic tradition according to the overwhelming majority of Muslims around the world. The *ahadith* (singular *hadith*) are stories and traditions that reveal Muhammad's approval, disapproval, or silence regarding specific matters that unfold or may unfold in a given society. The *ahadith* are considered to be an authoritative source of God's revelation and commandments, second only to the Qur'an in terms of providing Islamic guidance to Muslims. Muhammad himself stated, "I have left among you two matters by holding fast to which, you shall never be misguided: the Book of God [Qur'an] and my Sunna [*ahadith*]."

The *ahadith* shed extensive light on the *Sunna,* or Muhammad's daily practices, which cite responses that he had given to questions asked of him during his lifetime and address issues of conduct in day-to-day life. The *ahadith* were gathered, transmitted, and taught orally for two centuries after his death and then began to be presented in written form and codified (*Oxford Dictionary of Islam* n.d.). Validation of the sayings and stories of Muhammad has historically focused on the "chain of transmission," which records how the oral information was passed down from person to person. The six most authoritative collections are those of Al-Bukhari, Muslim, Al-Tirmidhi, Abu Daud Al-Sijistani, Al-Nasai, and Al-Qazwini (*Oxford Dictionary of Islam* n.d.). According to Jonathan A. C. Brown, author of *Misquoting Muhammad: The Challenge and Choices of Interpreting the Prophet's Legacy,* it is primarily over the *ahadith* and their contents that Islam's sects and schools of thought have diverged (Brown 2014, 8).

There is, of course, belief that there are some *ahadith* that are spurious (Nasr 2000, 71). Traditional Islamic scholars themselves developed an elaborate science to examine the text of the *ahadith* and the validity of the chains of prophetic transmission (Nasr 2000, 71). A basic rule for check-ing the authenticity of a *hadith* is that it should not contradict the messages or laws outlined in the Qur'an.

See also: Qur'an

Further Reading

Brown, Jonathan A. C. 2014. *Misquoting Muhammad: The Challenge and Choices of Interpreting the Prophet's Legacy*. London: Oneworld Publications.

Nasr, Seyyed Hossein. 2000. *Ideals and Realities of Islam*. Chicago: ABC International Group, Inc.

Oxford Dictionary of Islam. n.d. "Hadith." Oxford, UK: Oxford University. Retrieved from http://www.oxfordislamicstudies.com/article/opr/t125/e758.

Zamin, Muntasir. 2018. "Can We Trust Hadith Literature? Understanding the Processes of Transmission and Preservation." YaqeenInstitute.org. Last modi-fied October 30, 2018. Retrieved from https://yaqeeninstitute.org/muntasir -zaman/can-we-trust-hadith-literature-understanding-the-process-of -transmission-and-preservation/.

Ahmadiyya

According to its official website, the Ahmadiyya community is a dynamic, fast growing international revival movement within the *ummah* that spans over 200 countries with membership exceeding tens of millions (Al Islam n.d.). Its current headquarters are based in London, United Kingdom. Ah-madiyya Muslims consist of those Muslims who believe that the appear-ance of the "Promised Messiah" took place in 1889 in the person of Mirza Ghulam Ahmad of Qadian, India, a town in the Gurdaspur District of Pun-jab. Ahmadis believe that Mirza Ghulam Ahmad had fulfilled the prophe-cies made by the Prophet Muhammad about the second coming of the *mahdi*, or "messiah," and advent of the Promised Mahdi. The word *mahdi* is Arabic for "divinely guided one" and can be viewed as the "figure who Muslims believe will usher in an era of justice and true belief just prior to the end of time." *Mahdi* also is an honorific title applied to the Prophet Muhammad and the first four caliphs by the earliest Muslims. The concept of *mahdi* was developed primarily by the Shi'as into a divine bringer of deliverance who would come back to support them. The Ahmadiyya community is the only "Islamic organization" in the world to believe that the long-awaited Messiah has come in the person of Mirza Ghulam Ahmad, whose prophecy as the long-awaited Messiah is controversial in the *ummah* because he came after the Prophet Muhammad, whom the overwhelming majority of Muslims worldwide consider the final prophet or "seal of the prophets" of the Abrahamic tradition.

Mirza Ghulam Ahmad wrote more than 70 books and pamphlets on Islamic topics like *jihad,* freedom of conscience, freedom of speech, freedom of religion, the *sharia,* and women's rights (Hanson 2007, 78). According to a pamphlet published in 1889 by the Ahmadiyya community—entitled *Who Are Ahmadi Muslims?*—Mirza Ghulam Ahmad founded the Ahmadiyya Muslim *jamaat,* the Arabic word for "assembly," under "divine guidance." The main objective of Mirza Ghulam Ahmad's life work was to reestablish "the original purity and beauty of Islam." He called on his followers to engage in the *jihad bil qalam,* or the "jihad by the pen," and encouraged Muslims worldwide to use the pen, a symbol of education and knowledge, as a constructive tool to dispel misinformation and allegations toward Muslims as peddled by critics. By replacing *"jihad* by the sword" with *"jihad* of the pen," Mirza Ahmad Ghulam taught his followers to wage a peaceful, bloodless, and intellectual battle. His teaching mirrored the example given by the Prophet Muhammad, who is said to have told his companions, "The ink of the scholar is more sacred than the blood of the martyr."

Alongside the emphasis on searching for *ilm,* the Arabic word for "knowledge," Mirza Ghulam Ahmad encouraged nonviolent action and peace over physical aggression and militarism. He believed that senseless violence was not only prohibited according to the teachings of the Prophet Muhammad, but was a great misfortune for the *ummah.* The fourth leader of the Ahmadiyya Muslim community, Mirza Tahir Ahmad, stated that the Islamic faith "categorically rejects and condemns every form of terrorism" and that the Islamic faith "does not provide any cover of justification for any act of violence, be it committed by an individual, a group or a government" (Ahmad 1989). The official website of the Ahmadiyya Muslim community claims that it is the only Islamic organization to categorically reject terrorism in any form. The Ahmadiyya Muslim community also claims that it is the only Islamic organization in the world to endorse a separation of religion and state (Al Islam n.d.).

The Ahmadiyya community has endured repression throughout history, especially in Pakistan. The Pakistani Constitution declares Ahmadis to be *kafir,* the Arabic word for "infidel" or "unbeliever" that is sometimes used to describe non-Muslims at large. The Pakistani Penal Code subjects Ahmadis to severe legal restrictions, making it a criminal offense for Ahmadis to define themselves as Muslims, preach, refer to their places of worship as mosques, or disseminate materials on the Ahmadiyya faith. In 1953 an "Islamist" group called Jamaat e Islami engaged in anti-Ahmadiyya riots that had to be squashed by the Pakistani government; riots also followed the adoption in 1974 of the Second Amendment of the Constitution of Pakistan. In that year Pakistani President Zulfiqar Ali Bhutto approved the Second Amendment, which formally declared members of the Ahmadiyya community as "non-Muslims." Moreover, in 1984 the Pakistani President Muhammad Zia Ul-Haq signed an ordinance that prohibited Ahmadis from saying or implying they were Muslims. Punishment for doing so is a three-year prison sentence.

Since 2002 the U.S. Commission on International Religious Freedom (USCIRF) has named Pakistan as a "country of particular concern" for its "systematic, ongoing, and egregious" violations against Ahmadis and attacks against freedom of religion within Pakistan in general (United States Commission on International Religious Freedom 2016). The repression of the Ahmadiyya Muslim community in Pakistan forced the Ahmadi *caliph*, the Arabic word for the civil and religious ruler and successor of the Prophet Muhammad, to move the Ahmadi headquarters from Qadian to the Fazl Mosque in London, a shift introduced by Mirza Tahir Ahmad, the fourth head of the Ahmadiyya movement.

Anti-Ahmadi Muslim efforts have also been reported in the United States. Several Muslim leaders from Pakistan called for violent *jihad* in November 2017 at an event called Final Prophet Conference in Springfield, Virginia. A spokesperson for the Ahmadiyya community in the United States, Qasim Rashid, told *Newsweek* that "free speech doesn't mean the freedom to promote violence" and that the people invited to speak at the conference are "as bad as the Nazis [that marched] in Charlottesville," Virginia, in August 2017 (Maza 2017).

The Ahmadi community has a history of missionary activity in the United States. Mufti Muhammad Sadiq is widely recognized as the first Ahmadi missionary in U.S. history. A companion of Mirza Ghulam Ahmad, Sadiq arrived in Philadelphia in 1920 "but was immediately seized by authorities upon them finding out he was a Muslim, as they believed Islam to be a religion of polygamy," a practice that was outlawed in the United States (Bowen 2010, 401). In 1921 he established the Ahmadi headquarters in Chicago and soon thereafter launched a journal, *Review of*

Religions, and a newspaper, *Moslem Sunrise. Review of Religion* and *Moslem Sunrise* were circulated throughout the United States and Canada as part of the Ahmadi missionary work of converting people to Ahmadiyya. *Moslem Sunrise* "contained information about events concerning the [Ahmadis] worldwide, histories of the movement, Ahmadiyya leaders' writings, prescriptions for proper Islamic practices, updates on the progress of his mission in the U.S., reprints of newspaper articles discussing Ahmadiyya activities, [and] letters from converts and those who praised his efforts" (Hanson 2010, 401).

Today, an estimated 15,000 to 20,000 Ahmadi Muslims live in the United States. The largest populations of Ahmadis in the United States are located in Baltimore, Chicago, Los Angeles, New York City, and Washington, DC. One of the current National Spokesperson's for the Ahmadiyya community in the United States, Qasim Rashid, is a politician, best-selling and critically acclaimed author, practicing attorney, and former visiting scholar fellow at the Prince Al-Waleed bin Talal Islamic Studies Program at Harvard University. Rashid publishes regularly in major media publications including *Time, The Independent,* and *Washington Post.* He also regularly speaks at a variety of universities and houses of worship, and interviews in a variety of media including the *New York Times,* FOX News, CNN, Muslim Television Ahmadiyya International, Huff Post Live, Al Jazeera, NBC, among several other national and international outlets (Ahmadiyya Muslim Community n.d.). In June 2019, Rashid became the first U.S. Muslim to win the Democratic primary for the Virginia state senate. He also received national attention in July 2019 when several news organizations like the *New York Times,* NBC News, and ABC News reported on a threatening tweet he received, which resulted in a federal indictment.

Despite facing discrimination on multiple levels in many countries, fostering better relations with people of various communities is a priority for Ahmadi communities across the United States. The purpose of their outreach is to break down walls—whether real or perceived—that stand between people, faith communities, and humanity. In the face of the discrimination they experience inside and outside of the United States, Ahmadis maintain their resolve by promoting religious pluralism. According to many Ahmadis, that is the best way to improve relations between Ahmadis and the wider U.S. population. Today, countless Ahmadis live by the community's official motto, "Love for all, hatred for none." Since 2011 members of the Ahmadiyya movement have held an annual blood drive on 9/11 in order to honor the people who lost their lives on that day.

Further Reading

Ahmad, Mirza Tahir. 1989. *Murder in the Name of Allah*. Cambridge, UK: Lutter-worth Press.
Ahmadiyya Muslim Youth Association. n.d. "Who We Are." MuslimYouth.org. Retrieved from http://muslimyouth.org/about.php.
Al Islam. n.d. "Ahmadiyya Muslim Community." AlIslam.org. Retrieved from https://www.alislam.org/library/ahmadiyya-muslim-community/.
Hanson, John H. 2007. "Jihad and the Ahmadiyya Muslim Community: Nonviolent Efforts to Promote Islam in the Contemporary World." *Nova Religio: The Journal of Alternative and Emergent Religions* 11, no. 2: 77–93.
Maza, Cristina. 2017. "Radical Islamic Groups Call for Jihad at Meeting near Washington, D.C." *Newsweek*, November 22, 2017. Retrieved from https://www.newsweek.com/radical-islam-pakistan-muslims-jihad-washington-in fidels-ahmadi-719537.
Rashid, Qasim. 2013. *The Wrong Kind of Muslim: An Untold Story of Persecution & Perseverance*. Amazon Digital Services LLC.
United States Commission on International Religious Freedom. 2016. "Pakistan: USCIRF Condemns Egregious Treatment of Ahmadis." Washington, DC: United States Commission on International Religious Freedom. Last modified December 9, 2016. Retrieved from http://www.uscirf.gov/news-room/press -releases/pakistan-uscirf-condemns-egregious-treatment-ahmadis.
Zafar, Harris. 2014. *Demystifying Islam: Tackling the Tough Questions*. Lanham, Boulder, New York, and London: Rowman & Littlefield.

Apostasy

Apostasy, or *riddah* in the Arabic language, is a religious concept that relates to the act of leaving the Islamic faith or rejecting Islamic teachings in both word and action. Apostasy is emerging as a topic of controversy especially in discussions on freedom of religion in the Islamic tradition and the perceived in compatibility between "Western civilization" and "Islamic civilization." Critics of the Islamic faith claim that Muslims follow a religion that forces people to embrace or convert to Islam, even against people's own will. These critics point to the *sharia,* the Arabic word for "Islamic law," as a body of laws that legally prescribe harsh penalties against any Muslim who engages in apostasy. Muslim jurists and Islamic scholars, however, interpret the *sharia* in diverse ways and, therefore, find no consensus on whether harsh penalties should be issued for apostates.

In the Qur'an there is no mention of the death penalty for apostates. To the contrary, several verses of the Qur'an unequivocally state, "There shall be no compulsion in religion: true guidance has become distinct from error" (Qur'an 2:256) and, "Say, 'This is the truth from your Lord. Let him who will, believe in it, and him who will, deny it'" (Qur'an 18:29). Both of these verses clearly support the idea of freedom of religion and, therefore, the right of an individual to either leave the fold of the *ummah* or believe in a religion other than Islam.

Nevertheless, there are several verses of the Qur'an that could be used to legitimize the killing of apostates. The first of these verses concerns the Prophet Muhammad's time in Medina in which his enemies were attempting to discredit his prophethood and leadership of the *ummah*. The Qur'an refers to these individuals as "apostates." Secondly, the Qur'an describes Muslims who had rejected the Islamic faith and then returned to it, only to reject it for a second or even a third time, as "apostates." The Qur'an does not suggest the death penalty in either of these cases but specifies a punishment for the apostates, almost certainly in the afterlife (Saeed 2011).

There is scarce evidence in the *ahadith,* the collection of the Prophet Muhammad's sayings, to indicate that he had ever imposed or called for the death penalty of people that left the fold of Islam or converted to another faith, or no faith. Abdullah Saeed, a leading scholar on apostasy, noted that the *ahadith* collection of Bukhari details the story of a man who came to the city of Medina and converted to the Islamic faith. Shortly thereafter, he wanted to return to his former religion and asked Muhammad for permission to do so. Muhammad let him go free, without imposing the death penalty or, indeed, any punishment (Saeed 2011).

Leaving the fold of the *ummah* and the Islamic faith and converting to another faith or no faith is a challenge and perhaps even a traumatic experience for ex-Muslims. Some people never publicly "come out" as an ex-Muslim because they fear that family members may disown them or that Muslims within their communities may separate themselves from them. To help and provide support for ex-Muslims, a nonprofit organization named Ex-Muslims of North America (EXMNA) was founded in 2013 by Sarah Haider and Muhammad Syed. According to its website, EXMNA envisions a world where every person is free to follow their conscience and advocates for acceptance of religious dissent and secular values (Ex-Muslims of North America n.d.). EXMNA also claims to be "the first organization of its kind to establish communities exclusive to ex-Muslims in order to foster a sense of camaraderie and offer a space free of judgment for lack of religiosity."

See also: Freedom of Religion; Freedom of Speech

Further Reading

Al-Alwani, Taha Jabir. 2011. *Apostasy in Islam: A Historical and Scriptural Analysis*. Herndon, VA: International Institute of Islamic Thought.

Baker, Man. 2018. "Capital Punishment for Apostasy in Islam." *Arab Law Quarterly* 32, no. 4: 439–61.

Ex-Muslims of North America. n.d. "About Us." ExMuslims.org. Retrieved from https://exmuslims.org/about-us/.

Saeed, Abdullah. 2011. "Hadith and Apostasy." Princeton, NJ: The Witherspoon Institute. Last modified April 4, 2011. Retrieved from https://www.thepublic discourse.com/2011/04/3082/.

Arab American Muslims

Arab American Muslims are one of the largest ethnic groups within the overall U.S. Muslim population. The U.S. Census Bureau estimates that nearly 2 million U.S. citizens are of Arab descent. Estimates made by the Arab American Institute (AAI) claim that the population is closer to 3.7 million. The majority of Arab Americans, as the AAI notes, were born on U.S. soil, and nearly 82 percent of Arab Americans are citizens of the United States. Although there is a tendency to view all Arab Americans as Muslims, the majority of Arab Americans actually identify themselves as Christian.

Historians typically locate the origins of Arab American experiences in the 19th century. Most of the Arab immigrants that arrived in the United States in the 19th century immigrated from Jordan, Lebanon, Palestine, and Syria. The majority of Arab immigrants who came to the United States in this century had worked in professions like mining, manufacturing, and shopkeeping. These Arab immigrants were classified as "Turks," a term used to identify Muslims as early as the 17th century, and were neither quite "white enough" to be classified as "white," nor quite "dark enough" to be classified as "black." These "Turks" also were not quite "Asian enough" to be classified alongside Asian groups like the Chinese and

Japanese. Today, Arab immigrants and their children have no explicit option to identify themselves as Arab, or to identify with a particular place of origin in the Middle East region when filling out details for the U.S. Census Bureau. In the census, "respondents who specify a country or region of origin in the Middle East region instead of a specific racial or ethnic category generally are counted as 'White'; historically, the U.S. government has classified people as 'White' if they have origins in any of the original peoples of the Middle East, North Africa, or Europe" (Pew Research Center 2017).

Syrian and Lebanese Muslims are said to have founded one of the first *masjids,* the Ross Masjid in North Dakota, in U.S. history. Erected in 1929, the Ross Masjid served as a place of worship for an enclave of Arabic speakers with family surnames like Abdallah, Juma, and Omar. According to *Prairie Peddlers,* a book about the Syrian and Lebanese immigrants of North Dakota by William Sherman, the Arab Muslims of the area were sometimes called "black" or demonized as "disloyal" because they were originally from the Ottoman Empire, a political entity generally treated as an enemy of the United States in the early 20th century.

One Arab American Muslim from the U.S. Midwest, Abdullah Igram, was a World War II veteran and community leader of Cedar Rapids, Iowa. In 1953, *Time* magazine reported that Igram, a 30-year-old grocery store owner and president/founder of the International Moslem Society, had written to the Secretary of the Army about allowing U.S. Muslim soldiers to wear religious-identification dog tags (*Time* 1953). While he had served in the Army, Igram saw that Protestants had dog tags labeled "P," Catholics had dog tags labeled "C," and Jews had dog tags labeled "J." Igram had written a letter to President Dwight D. Eisenhower to request that the military formally recognize Islam and allow service members to print "I" or "M" on their dog tags (Rothman 2016). Igram's request was successful when the "I" for Islamic was added to the military identification tags after consideration by President Eisenhower.

The perception of Arab American Muslims in the modern context is heavily influenced by the depictions and racialized characterizations of these Muslims in the entertainment industry. According to Jack Shaheen, author of the book *Reel Bad Arabs: How Hollywood Vilifies a People,* the overwhelming majority of Hollywood films throughout history have depicted Arabs as "brute murderers, sleazy rapists, religious fanatics, oil-rich dimwits and abusers of women" (Shaheen 2004). The popular movie *Back to the Future* (1985), for example, presents an antagonist as a Libyan terrorist who shouts

Arabic gibberish as he guns down the film's protagonist. Another well-known film—*True Lies* (1994)—frames Arnold Schwarzenegger against fanatical and incompetent Palestinian terrorists who detonate a nuclear device in Florida. In more recent years, the Clint Eastwood–directed film *American Sniper* (2014) has been widely denounced by U.S. Muslim activists for its depiction of Iraqi Muslims and its glorification of the movie's main character, Chris Kyle, a Navy SEAL who wrote a memoir in which he described the killing of Iraqi Muslims as "fun." Kyle also wrote in his memoir, "I hate the damn [Muslim] savages. . . . I couldn't give a flying f— about the Iraqis."

Despite the sensational characterizations in the entertainment industry, Arab American Muslims are increasingly active in the realm of political engagement and U.S. civic life. The Arab American Institute (AAI) is the leading voice for political issues pertaining to Arabs on U.S. soil. Established in 1985 and based in Washington, DC, the AAI is "a non-profit, nonpartisan national leadership organization . . . created to nurture and encourage the direct participation of Arab Americans in political and civic life in the United States" (Arab American Institute n.d.a). The AAI has been a valuable resource for members of the government, the media, the political sphere, and community organizations.

Voting preferences among Arab Americans during the presidential election of 2016 highlighted the diversity of the overall Arab population in the United States. Despite controversial comments by Donald Trump for "a total and complete shutdown" of Muslims entering the country, 12 percent of Arab American Muslims said they would vote for the Republican nominee, according to a Zogby Analytics survey. Sixty-seven percent said they would vote for Democrat Hillary Clinton (Taylor 2015).

Rashid Tlaib, a Democratic Representative of the 13th Congressional District of Michigan, is one of the main Arab American Muslim leaders in the United States. A member of the Democratic Socialists of America, Tlaib is the first women to have ever served in the Michigan legislature and is one of the first two Muslim women—alongside Representative Ilhan Omar—to serve in the U.S. Congress. Tlaib is nationally recognized, especially by U.S. Muslims, for her criticism of the Saudi Arabian government and its human rights violations, oppression of minority populations, and intervention in Yemen.

See also: Ummah

Further Reading

Al-Deen, Aminah. 2018. *History of Arab Americans: Exploring Diverse Roots*. Santa Barbara, CA: Greenwood.

Alsultany, Evelyn. 2012. *Arabs and Muslims in the Media: Race and Representation after 9/11*. New York: New York University Press.

Arab American Institute. n.d.a. "About the Institute." Washington, DC: Arab American Institute. Retrieved from http://www.aaiusa.org/about-institute.

Arab American Institute. n.d.b. "Demographics." Washington, DC: Arab American Institute. Retrieved from http://www.aaiusa.org/demographics.

Bayoumi, Moustafa. 2009. *How Does It Feel to Be a Problem?: Being Young and Arab in America*. London: Penguin Group.

Haddad, Yvonne Yazbeck. 2012. *Becoming American?: The Forging of Arab and Muslim Identity in Pluralist America*. Waco, TX: Baylor University Press.

Pew Research Center. 2017. "1. Demographic portrait of Muslim Americans." Washington, DC: Pew Research Center. Last modified July 26, 2017. Retrieved from http://www.pewforum.org/2017/07/26/demographic-portrait-of-muslim -americans/.

Rothman, Lily. 2016. "The Khan Family and American History's Hidden Muslim Soldiers." TIME.com, August 3, 2016. Retrieved from http://time.com/4432865 /khan-muslim-american-soldiers-history/.

Salaita, Steven. 2006. *Anti-Arab Racism in the USA: Where It Comes From and What It Means for Politics Today*. London: Pluto Press.

Shaheen, Jack. 2004. *Reel Bad Arabs: How Hollywood Vilifies a People*. Petaluma, CA: Olive Branch.

Taylor, Jessica. 2015. "Trump Calls For 'Total and Complete Shutdown of Muslims Entering' U.S." NPR, December 7, 2015. Retrieved from https://www.npr .org/2015/12/07/458836388/trump-calls-for-total-and-complete-shutdown-of -muslims-entering-u-s.

Time. 1953. "Welcome to the Time Vault." TIME.com, July 13, 1953. Retrieved from http://time.com/vault/issue/1953-07-13/page/78/.

Asian American Muslims

The term "Asian American" is given to U.S. residents who trace their ancestry back to the Asian continent, spanning from Pakistan in the west to the Pacific islands east of the Asian landmass. According to the Pew Research Center (2017), approximately three in ten U.S. Muslims are of Asian descent (28 percent), including those from South Asia. Muslim immigrants are significantly more likely than U.S.-born Muslims to describe their race as "Asian" (41 percent vs. 10 percent) (Pew Research Center 2017). Among Muslims in the third generation or higher—people born in the United States and whose parents also were born in the United States—very few identify themselves as Asian (2 percent) (Pew Research Center 2017). Around two-thirds of Asian American Muslims are Sunni, many fewer are Shi'a, and about 20 percent identify themselves as simply "Muslim" without specifying any Islamic sect. In terms of Asian American Muslims as a whole, approximately 54 percent express a "positive outlook" of the United States in general, a number that is nearly twice that of African American Muslims (28 percent) (Mogahed and Chouhoud 2017, 5). During the 2016 presidential election, Asian American Muslims (78 percent) were the most likely ethnic group to have cast a ballot (Mogahed and Chouhoud 2017, 6).

People of Pakistani descent represent the largest group within the larger Asian American Muslim population. According to the U.S. Census of 2010, approximately 370,000 Pakistanis are living in the United States. The Migration Policy Institute estimates that the Pakistani population is higher at approximately 453,000 Pakistanis living in the United States (Migration Policy Institute 2015, 1). In terms of their levels of educational attainment, Pakistanis living on U.S. soil are, on average, more likely to have obtained a higher education degree. Pakistanis in the United States also are, on average, more likely to have higher household incomes in comparison to the overall U.S. population (Migration Policy Institute 2015, 1). The Pakistani diaspora in the United States "has established numerous, well-funded, and professionally managed organizations throughout the country. These groups take a broad range of forms, including professional and business networks, advocacy organizations, [societies] that raise money in support of universities [and] hospitals, and organizations contributing to economic and human development in the homeland" (Migration Policy Institute 2015, 2). These figures show that Pakistanis are significant contributors to U.S. society and have been giving back to their fellow U.S. citizens for decades (Considine 2017).

The immigration of Asian Muslims to the United States was not always a possibility or reality due to legislation that is widely regarded as xenophobic. The Chinese Exclusion Act, passed by the U.S. Congress in 1882, prevented Muslims that may have fallen under the ethnic category of "Chinese" from immigrating to the United States. In 1917, the U.S. Congress passed the Asiatic Barred Zone, which completely banned Muslims from modern-day countries like Afghanistan, Jordan,

India, Indonesia, Iran, Iraq, Oman, Saudi Arabia, Turkey, and Yemen. Nevertheless, Asian American Muslims were already present in the United States prior to the passing of the Barred Zone. Asian American Muslims started to establish religious organizations in the period just before and after World War I. Starting in 1907, the Tatars from Central Asia settled in Brooklyn, New York, and helped to establish the American Mohammedan Society. The Tatars are a predominantly Sunni Muslim and Turkic-speaking people who trace their ancestral roots to countries including Russia, Uzbekistan, Ukraine, Kazakhstan, Turkey, and several Eastern European countries of the former Soviet Union.

In 1920 the Ahmadiyya Muslim missionary Mufti Muhammad Sadiq of Qadian, India (now located in Pakistan), moved to Philadelphia, Pennsylvania. Upon his arrival, Mufti Sadiq was arrested on the grounds that Muslims condoned polygamy, which was illegal in the United States. He was subsequently detained and spent several months in confinement. Eventually, Mufti Sadiq lived in New York, Michigan, and finally Illinois, where he founded a mosque in Chicago and worked largely to convert African Americans to the Islamic faith. Mufti Sadiq was so admired by his contemporaries for his emphasis on knowledge, peace, and racial equality that Lincoln-Jefferson University in Jefferson City, Missouri, granted him an honorary doctorate.

Uyghur Muslims, a population that is culturally and ethnically close to Central Asian nations, also live in the United States. The Uyghur are the largest Turkic ethnic group living in Xinjiang, a western province of China, and are predominantly Muslim. Approximately 10 million Uyghurs live in China. An alarmingly large number of Uyghur Muslims are currently being held in "re-education" camps created by the Chinese government. Critics claim that these re-education camps are more like concentration camps or internment camps for Muslims. The purpose of these camps is to force the Uyghurs to renounce their Islamic faith in favor of a secular Chinese nationalist identity. International organizations that monitor human rights and human rights violations are referring to the crackdown on Uyghurs with words and phrases including "ethnic cleansing" as well as "cultural genocide." These organizations claim that up to 2 million Uyghurs are currently being held in Xinjiang.

A growing number of Uyghur Muslims in the United States have had family members detained by the Chinese authorities. Nury Turkel, the chairman of the Board for the Uighur Human Rights Project, told the U.S. House Committee on Foreign Affairs in September 2018 that over a million Uyghurs have been mass interned by the Chinese government. Scholar Rian Thum suggested that "mass murder and genocide do not look like impossible outcomes" of China's treatment and depiction of Uyghur Muslims as "terrorists." The strategic shift by the Chinese government in labeling Uyghurs a threat to national security accelerated after the 9/11 attacks. According to Turkel, Chinese authorities introduced the term "terrorism" into political and public discourse in order to legitimize their repression of the Uyghur people (Turkel 2018).

Today, it is estimated that up to 15,000 Uyghurs live in the United States. The majority of Uyghur Muslims currently live in Washington, DC, which has been described by the online news outlet The Middle East Eye as "the political nerve center of the East Turkistan movement." Washington, DC, also is home to the Uyghur American Association (UAA), a nonprofit organization that "works to promote the preservation and flourishing of a rich humanistic and diverse Uyghur culture, and to support the right of the Uyghur people to use peaceful, democratic means to determine their own political future," according to the UAA website.

Indonesian American Muslims are U.S. citizens and residents who trace their ancestry back to Indonesia, the country with the largest Muslim population in the world. The Indonesian Muslim Society in America, or IMSA, is a religious, charitable, scientific, literary, educational, and nonprofit organization based in Champaign, Illinois. To assist the Indonesian Muslim community in the United States to advance its intellectual and spiritual capacities, IMSA organizes discussions, undertakes social and charitable causes, coordinates the material resources of the Indonesian Muslim community, and promotes understanding and friendly relations between Muslims and people of various faiths. Shamsi Ali, an Indonesia-born *imam* based in Queens, New York City, is one of the leading Indonesian Muslim voices working to bridge the gap between Jews, Christians, and Muslims in the United States. In an interview with the BBC, he stated that Islam, to him, stands for "justice, equality, tolerance, freedom, giving to others, respecting the human rights" (Rasmussen 2013). Within the Indonesian Muslim community in the United States, Imam Ali serves as an advisory board member to IMSA and to the Indonesian Muslim Intellectual Society in America (ICMI). Alongside Rabbi Marc Schneier, Imam Ali co-authored the memoir *Sons of Abraham: A Candid Conversation about the Issues That Divide and Unite Jews and Muslims,* which aims to show that Jews and Muslims are not enemies, but friends who are united in monotheism and their shared forefather, Abraham. Imam

Ali also is the president of the Nusantara Foundation, a nonprofit organization that is working to foster the dialogue of civilizations and improve relations across perceived religious divides and differences.

Afghans, the term referring to a person from the South and Central Asian country of Afghanistan, also live in the United States. Afghan people have been immigrating to the United States longer than most of the Asian Muslim populations discussed in this entry. The National Archives of the United States holds a document referred to as "Approve Pension File" for Private Mohammed Kahn (alias John Ammahail) of Company E for the 43rd New York Infantry Regiment of the U.S. Army. Raised in Afghanistan, Private Kahn immigrated to the United States in 1861 and fought in the famous Battle of Gettysburg in 1863. The website of the National Archives notes that Kahn was separated from Company E shortly after the Battle of Gettysburg and arrested in Hagerstown, Maryland, by a Union guard, who did not believe Kahn when he said he was part of Company E. Eventually, Kahn made his way back to Company E in Spotsylvania, Virginia.

The U.S. Census Bureau estimates that roughly 66,000 people of Afghan descent live in the United States. Wallace Fard Muhammad, the Muslim missionary credited for founding the Nation of Islam in the United States, is reported to have been born in Shinka, Afghanistan, in the late 19th century. A small number of Afghan families moved to the United States between the 1930s and 1970s. The Afghan people who migrated to the country during these decades are believed to be educated and belonging to a relatively higher socio-economic grouping. The Afghan American population increased significantly following the Soviet Union's invasion of Afghanistan in 1979. The Soviet-Afghan War resulted in a refugee crisis wherein Afghan people fled to the United States and the European Union, as well as neighboring countries such as Pakistan and Iran.

See also: Ummah

Further Reading

Considine, Craig. 2017. *Islam, Race, and Pluralism in the Pakistani Diaspora*. London and New York: Routledge.

Migration Policy Institute. 2015. "The Pakistani Diaspora in the United States." Washington, DC: Migration Policy Institute. Last modified June 2015. Retrieved from file:///Users/craigconsidine/Downloads/RAD-Pakistan.pdf.

Mogahed, Dalia, and Youssef Chouhoud. 2017. *American Muslim Poll 2017: Full Report*. Washington, DC: Institute for Social Policy and Understanding. Retrieved from https://www.ispu.org/american-muslim-poll-2017/.

National Archives. 2017. "Private Mohammed Kahn: Civil War Soldier." Washington, DC: National Archives. Last modified June 23, 2017. Retrieved from https://narations.blogs.archives.gov/2017/06/23/private-mohammed-kahn -civil-war-soldier/.

Pew Research Center. 2017. "1. Demographic portrait of Muslim Americans." Washington, DC: Pew Research Center. Last modified July 26, 2017. Retrieved from http://www.pewforum.org/2017/07/26/demographic-portrait-of-muslim -americans/.

Rasmussen, Sune Engel. 2013. "Shamsi Ali: The rise and fall of a New York imam." BBC, November 3, 2013. Retrieved from https://www.bbc.com/news /magazine-24468337.

Turkel, Nury. 2018. "China's Repression and Internment of Uighurs: U.S. Policy Responses." House Committee on Foreign Affairs. Washington, DC. Last modified September 26, 2018. Retrieved from https://docs.house.gov/meetings/FA /FA05/20180926/108718/HHRG-115-FA05-Wstate-TurkelN-20180926.pdf.

Uyghur American Association. n.d. "About UAA." Washington, DC: UAA. Retrieved from https://uyghuramerican.org/about_uaa.

C

Civil Rights

Civil rights as they pertain to U.S. Muslims may be explored in light of two realms. The first realm explores how U.S. Muslims have served as invaluable leaders in the quest for civil rights in the United States. The second realm examines the experiences of U.S. Muslims through the lens of civil rights violations that are currently unfolding in U.S. society.

The rise of the Nation of Islam (NOI) and the conversion of Muhammad Ali and Malcolm X to the Islamic faith put Muslims on the map for opposing white supremacy and fighting for racial as well as social justice. Muhammad Ali, as scholar Michael Ezra pointed out in his opinion article on Al Jazeera, influenced the leading black organizers who formed the backbone of the Civil Rights Movement in a distinctly positive and broad-based way. Ali's criticism of the Vietnam War and his resistance to the U.S. Army draft in 1966 led to his ban from professional boxing by U.S. authorities, the stripping of his boxing title, and his eventual imprisonment. Ali said of his opposition to the Vietnam War: "My conscience won't let me go shoot my brother, or some darker people—some poor hungry people in the mud—for big powerful America. They never called me a n*****." Following the 9/11 attacks, Ali had denounced terrorism carried out by Muslims and spoke out against Islamophobia in the United States and beyond. He said in 2001: "I am angry that the world sees a certain group of Islam followers who caused this destruction, but they are not real Muslims. They are fanatics who call themselves Muslims, permitting this murder of thousands."

Alongside Ali, Malcolm X is recognized as one of the leaders of the Civil Rights Movement in the 1950s and 1960s. In his teenage years, Malcom X was involved in criminal activities, which led to his imprisonment from 1946 to 1952 and his subsequent conversion to the NOI while

29

in prison. Once he was released, Malcolm X helped to push the NOI into mainstream public discourse and founded *Muhammad Speaks,* the NOI's successful newspaper. He also gave many public lectures in which he promoted black supremacy and criticized the Civil Rights Movement, led by Martin Luther King Jr., for its emphasis on black integration into the white-dominant society. Malcolm X had originally rejected King's call for nonviolence and urged people to defend themselves "by any means necessary." These positions held by Malcolm X influenced the emergence and growth of the Black Power and Black Consciousness movements in the late 1960s. Malcolm X, however, ended up breaking from the NOI in 1964 to create the Organization of Afro-American Unity (OAAU), a Pan-African secular organization intended to empower and unite all people of African origin.

Prior to the creation of the OAAU, Malcolm X had made the pilgrimage, or *hajj* in Arabic, to Mecca where he observed the racial harmony among Muslims, a harmony that he did not experience in the United States. His "Letter from Mecca" captured his views of the *hajj* as well as racial equality: "Never have I witnessed such sincere hospitality and overwhelming spirit of true brotherhood as is practiced by people of all colors and races here in this ancient Holy Land. . . . There were tens of thousands of pilgrims, from all over the world. They were of all colors, from blue-eyed blondes to black-skinned Africans. But we were all participating in the same ritual, displaying a spirit of unity and brotherhood that my experiences in America had led me to believe never could exist between the white and non-white." Malcom X was assassinated in 1965 by three members of the NOI that were upset with his transformation from racial exclusivist to racial inclusivist.

Several U.S. Muslims today are taking up the causes of Ali and Malcolm X by serving as civil rights activists. Linda Sarsour, a Palestinian Muslim woman born and raised in Brooklyn, New York, is one of the foremost civil rights and political activists in the United States. She is the former executive director of the Arab American Association of New York and co-chair of the 2017 Women's March in Washington, DC. Sarsour's activism spans a number of areas including police brutality, immigration policy, and mass incarceration, and her support extends to movements and campaigns such as Black Lives Matter as well as Boycott, Divestment and Sanctions (BDS). Following the killing of Michael Brown, a young African American, in Ferguson, Missouri, Sarsour co-founded "Muslims for Ferguson" in an attempt to garner support from U.S. Muslims in the struggle against police brutality in the United States. President Barack Obama's "Champions of Change" campaign, as noted in the Obama White House archives, referred to Sarsour as an ambitious and independent community activist who shatters stereotypes of Muslim women while also treasuring her religious and ethnic heritage (The White House—President Barack Obama n.d.). One of Sarsour's more recent initiatives, MPower Change, is "the largest Muslim led social and racial justice organization in the United States," according to its website.

Omar Suleiman is a New Orleans, Louisiana–born civil rights activist and founder/president of the Yaqeen Institute for Islamic Research. Currently based in Dallas, Texas, Suleiman has advocated for racial equality and protecting the lives of vulnerable migrants in the United States. In March 2018, Suleiman was arrested after engaging in an act of civil disobedience in Washington, DC, during a protest that demanded protection for recipients of DACA, officially known as the Deferred Action for Childhood Arrival, which protects undocumented immigrants who came to the United States before the age of sixteen. A July 2018 interview with the *Guardian* provides insight into Suleiman's views on social justice, which he described as "welcoming people to the table in the fullness of their traditions. I believe one's commitment to faith can be to the benefit of all humanity."

Today, the Council on American-Islamic Relations (CAIR), a nonprofit organization with offices around the country, has a civil rights department that counsels, mediates, and advocates on behalf of Muslims and others who have experienced religious discrimination, defamation, or hate crimes (Council on American-Islamic Relations n.d.). CAIR works to protect and defend the constitutional rights of U.S. Muslims, thereby supporting the rights of all people in the United States. Since its founding in 1994, CAIR has sought with some success to position itself as the go-to U.S. Muslim civil rights organization (Anti-Defamation League n.d.).

CAIR's recent reports are showing a steady rise in anti-Muslim hate crimes. CAIR's quarterly reports from April to June 2018 indicate that anti-Muslim hate crimes were up 21 percent, as compared to the first quarter of 2018 (Council on American-Islamic Relations 2018). Hate crimes against U.S. Muslims in the previous year totaled 300 incidents, according to CAIR, a number that was up from 260 in 2016. Experts believe that the rise in anti-Muslim hate crimes may in part be due to the misinformation in public discourse as it pertains to the nature of the *sharia*. Anti-Islam activists oftentimes take to mainstream news outlets to denounce the *sharia* as an "anti-American" system of laws that is fundamentally incompatible with the values of "Western civilization." Since 2010, politicians across the United States have introduced over 201 bills in 43 states that are deemed to be anti-*sharia* (Southern Poverty Law Center 2018). Legal scholars conclude that enforcing a ban on the *sharia* would violate many elements of the First and Fourteenth Amendments of the U.S. Constitution.

Negative public perceptions of U.S. Muslims also has led to job discrimination and workplace environment discrimination. The Carnegie Mellon survey published in 2013 found that job applicants who self-identify "as Muslim on their social media profiles were called back at a lower rate nationwide by prospective employers than Christians with the [same] exact names and qualifications" (Greenberg 2013). The Carnegie Mellon study also uncovered that only 2 percent of Muslim applicants in Republican-leaning states received interview invitations from employers, compared to 17 percent for the Christian candidates with the same qualifications.

Racial profiling of U.S. Muslims also has emerged as a consequence of Islamophobic sentiments in the U.S. public sphere. In an article titled "Racial Profiling of Arabs and Muslims in the US," scholar Chrystie Flournoy Swiney (2018) found that the civil rights and civil liberties of U.S. Muslims, as guaranteed in the U.S. Constitution and U.S. legal system, have gradually been eroding since the 9/11 attacks. The surveillance of U.S. Muslims, an institutionalized process that is linked to racial profiling in that it racializes Muslim identity, led to a major lawsuit by Muslim leaders and lawyers in New York City. The New York City Police Department (NYPD) was accused of illegally spying on U.S. Muslims by surveilling mosques, infiltrating Muslim student groups, putting spies and informants inside of mosques, and collecting intelligence on Muslim-owned restaurants (Pilkington 2018). The NYPD had admitted in court that the surveillance scheme did not produce any credible evidence of "terrorist" or "extremist" activity. The unlawful policing and blatant discrimination against Muslims in New York City and New Jersey ended up being settled in court. As a result of the settlement, the NYPD had to create a new set of guidelines for intelligence gathering and submit new "counter-radicalization" training policies to the Muslim plaintiffs in the case.

See also: Countering Violent Extremism (CVE); Hate Crimes; Islamophobia; LGBTQ; Social Justice Activism; U.S. Founding Fathers

Further Reading

Anti-Defamation League. n.d. "The Council on American Islamic Relations (CAIR)." Washington, DC: ADL. Retrieved from https://www.adl.org/education/resources/profiles/the-council-on-american-islamic-relations-cair.

Council on American-Islamic Relations. n.d. "About Us." Washington, DC: CAIR. Retrieved from https://www.cair.com/about_us.

Council on American-Islamic Relations. 2017. "The Empowerment of Hate: The Civil Rights Implications of Islamophobic Bias in the U.S. 2014–2016." Washington, DC: CAIR. Retrieved from http://www.islamophobia.org/reports/188-the-empowerment-of-hate.html.

Council on American-Islamic Relations. 2018. "CAIR Report: Anti-Muslim Bias Incidents, Hate Crimes Spike in Second Quarter of 2018." Washington, DC: CAIR. Last modified July 12, 2018. Retrieved from https://www.cair.com/cair_report_anti_muslim_bias_incidents_hate_crimes_spike_in_second_quarter_of_2018.

Ezra, Michael. 2016. "How Muhammad Ali Influenced the Civil RightsMovement." AlJazeera.com, June 5, 2016. Retrieved from https://www.aljazeera.com/indepth/features/2016/06/muhammad-ali-influenced-civil-rights-movement-160605055700822.html.

Greenberg, Allen. 2013. "Muslim job candidates may face greater discrimination." BenefitsPro.com. Last modified December 2, 2013. Retrieved from https://www.benefitspro.com/2013/12/02/muslim-job-candidates-may-face-greater-discriminat/?slreturn=20190401093302.

Malcolm X. n.d. "Malcolm X's (Al-Hajj Malik El-Shabazz) Letter from Mecca." University of Georgia. Retrieved from http://islam.uga.edu/malcomx.html.

Malcolm X. 1964. "Malcolm X—By Any Means Necessary—Organization for Afro American Unity." YouTube. Retrieved from https://www.youtube.com/watch?v=WBS416EZsKM.

Malcolm X. 1987. *The Autobiography of Malcolm X: As Told to Alex Haley*. New York: Ballantine Books.

Muhammad, Elijah. 2006. *Message to the Blackman in America*. Phoenix: Secretarius MEMPS.

Pilkington, Ed. 2018. "NYPD settles lawsuit after illegally spying on Muslims." TheGuardian.com, April 5, 2018. Retrieved from https://www.theguardian.com/world/2018/apr/05/nypd-muslim-surveillance-settlement.

Southern Poverty Law Center. 2018. "Anti-Sharia law bills in the United States." Montgomery, AL: SPLC. Last modified February 5, 2018. Retrieved from https://www.splcenter.org/hatewatch/2018/02/05/anti-sharia-law-bills-united-states.

Swiney, Chrystie Flournoy. 2006. "Racial Profiling of Arabs and Muslims in the US: Historical, Empirical, and Legal Analysis Applied to the War on Terrorism."

Muslim World Journal of Human Rights 3, no. 1. DOI: https://doi.org/10.2202
/1554-4419.1053.

Clash of Civilizations

The "clash of civilizations" is a concept deployed and popularized by Harvard University scholar Samuel P. Huntington in the early 1990s. Writing after the collapse of the Berlin Wall and the fall of Soviet Union communism, Huntington argued that "the fundamental source of conflict in this new world will not be primarily ideological or primarily economic. The great divisions among humankind and the dominating source of conflict will be cultural" (Huntington 1993, 22). Huntington added that "the fault lines between civilizations will be the battle lines of the future" (Huntington 1993, 22). He identified the Muslim world as the primary "alien civilization" that must be confronted if necessary and claimed that "Muslim culture" is fundamentally incompatible with "Western culture." To drive home the point, Simon & Schuster, the publishers of the first paperback of Huntington's book *The Clash of Civilizations and the Remaking of World Order,* "had two flags juxtaposed on the cover, one representing the stars and stripes of the United States and the other a white crescent and star against a green background," symbolizing the Islamic tradition (Huntington 2003). Huntington used the clash of civilizations to establish a binary worldview in which "the West" and the "Muslim world" are diametrically opposed in terms of "us versus them," "good vs. evil," "civilized versus uncivilized," and "secular versus non-secular" (Considine 2016, 2).

The roots of the perceived clash of civilizations are dated back to the 8th century when St. John of Damascus, the Syrian monk and one of the founding fathers of the Eastern Christian Church, described the Islamic faith as a heresy derived from Christian sources. By the end of the 10th century, as scholar Tamarra Sonn (2004, 67) pointed out, the story of a battle between Charlemagne, the medieval French emperor who ruled much of Europe from 768 to 814, and the Basques at Roncesvalles in the 8th century had been used by Christian scholars as proof that the Muslims of Spain were the enemies of both Europe and Christendom. Centuries later, in 1095, Pope Urban II issued a papal call to arms at the Council of Clermont to call on Christians to join the "holy war" against Muslims. Pope Urban II told Christians that killing Muslims in wars declared "just" by the Church was not a sin. Thus, it became both a Christian duty and a quick route to "present and eternal glory" to join in the holy war against Muslims (Sonn 2004, 68). This war was played out in the Holy Land as Christians invaded Muslim lands and killed Jews and Christians as well as their main target, Muslims (Sonn 2004, 68–69).

According to Bernard Lewis, the author of *What Went Wrong: The Clash Between Islam and Modernity in the Middle East,* the status of women is the most profound single difference between the two civilizations (Lewis 2002, 67). Further, Lewis (1990) maintained that a violent intolerance is at the core of Islam, and that contemporary violent behavior among Muslims is the result of such a core. Many of Huntington's and Lewis's views on the clash of civilizations were adopted by the Republican Party by the end of the 1990s. According to Rebecca Shimoni Stoil, a contributor to the website FiveThirtyEight, the most profound turning point in Republican voters' views on the clash of civilizations came after 9/11, "as increased U.S. military involvement in the Middle East resulted in more pro-Israel policies percolating into the Republican agenda." Many influential Republicans saw new relevance in Huntington's model for a clash of civilizations as Israel was struggling with its own upswing in terrorist attacks. The narrative immediately following the 9/11 attacks centered on the idea that Israel and the United States were aligned as members of "the Judeo-Christian West," in opposition to other cultures—in this case, "Islam" (Shimoni Stoil 2017).

The presidential election of 2016 provided new life to the clash of civilizations theory, thanks largely to the campaign of Republican nominee Donald Trump and his team of advisers. In February 2015, Michael Flynn, who had served as President-elect Trump's national security advisor, tweeted, "Fear of Muslims is RATIONAL." A year earlier, Steve Bannon, the one-time chief strategist of President Trump, told BuzzFeed News that the "Judeo-Christian West is in a crisis" and that Western civilization is entering "the very beginning stages of a very brutal and bloody conflict . . . an outright war against jihadist Islamic fascism" (Feder 2016). President Trump himself also appeared to reiterate the validity of the clash of civilizations theory in March 2016 during an interview on CNN with Anderson Cooper. Trump told Cooper, "I think Islam hates us."

The clash of civilizations theory has been widely discredited for overlooking the confluence of world civilizations as well as the dialogue of civilizations. The dialogue of civilizations has been defined as "a post–Cold War approach to international politics that acknowledges the

importance of religious and cultural diversity in international society"
(Kayaoglu 2012, 129). The dialogue of civilizations also "claims to promote the role of culture and religion in conflict prevention and global
peace" (Kayaoglu 2012, 129). Speaking at a United Nations roundtable
summit on the "Dialogue among Civilizations," Mohammad Khatami, the
former Iranian president, claimed that there are two ways to realize the
dialogue of civilizations. First, to engage in "an interaction and interpen-
etration of cultures and civilizations with each other, involving a variety of
factors" (Khatami 2001, 26). Second, to engage in a dialogue among civilizations that could also mean "a deliberate dialogue among representative
members of various civilizations such as scholars, artists and philosophers
from disparate civilizational domains" (Khatami 2001, 26). In a 1998 interview with CNN, Khatami referred to the dialogue of civilizations as a
process that can benefit from the achievements and experiences of all nations, Western and Islamic, by holding dialogue with them. Specifically, he
recommended the exchange of professors, writers, scholars, artists, journalists, and tourists in order to enhance dialogue and understanding between diverse nations of the world (CNN 1998).

Despite accusations that followers of the Islamic faith have historically excluded the diversity of world cultures and failed to integrate these
cultures into the fabric of Islamic life, Muslims themselves have typically
considered the wisdom of traditions and have not been shy about borrowing from them or transforming them into elements of their own worldview
(Nasr 2000, 25). During the Middle Ages, as scholar Tamara Sonn pointed
out, the unique system of freedom of religion and administrative flexibility
under Muslim rule produced a period of "stability, growth, peace, and
prosperity in which the sciences and arts were brought to new levels of
perfection" (Sonn 2004, 46). Indeed, Western civilization is in many ways
indebted to Muslims for retrieving the philosophical works of Greek philosophers such as Aristotle and Ptolemy (Ahmed 2007, 220). "Muslim
scholars who discovered long-forgotten Greek texts in Egyptian libraries
worked with Christian scholars who could translate them into their native
Syriac and then into Arabic" (Sonn 2004, 46). Islamic empires such as the
Abbasids, Ottomans, Safavids, and Mughals all encouraged scholarship
along with the growth of literature, dialogue, and understanding (Ahmed
2007, 220).

The narrative of the clash of civilizations brings up an image of two
mutually exclusive entities. Islam, however, is a "Western" religion that
shares deep roots with Judaism and Christianity. Islam is the second

largest religious population in the United States. Rather than viewing Muslims as a separate entity, scholar John Esposito suggests viewing Muslims as part and parcel of U.S. society. He argued that "any talk of Islam *and* the West must be complemented by our recognition of Islam *in* the West" (Esposito 1998, 203).

Writing in *Islam Under Siege: Living Dangerously in a Post-Honor World,* scholar Akbar Ahmed counters the clash of civilizations theory by stating, "We can no longer accept the notion of a world divided between opposing halves—Islam versus the West" (Ahmed 2003, 17).

See also: Freedom of Religion; Freedom of Speech; Islamophobia; *Jihad*; Pluralism; The Prophet Muhammad; *Sharia*; U.S. Founding Fathers

Further Reading

Ahmed, Akbar. 2003. *Islam Under Siege: Living Dangerously in a Post-Honor World.* Cambridge, UK: Polity.

Ahmed, Akbar. 2007. *Journey into Islam: The Crisis of Globalization.* Washington, DC: Brookings Institution.

Considine, Craig. 2016. "Religious Pluralism and Civic Rights in a 'Muslim Nation': An Analysis of Prophet Muhammad's Covenants with Christians." *Religions* 7, no. 15: 1–21.

Esposito, John. 1998. *Islam: The Straight Path.* Oxford, UK: Oxford University Press.

Feder, J. Lester. 2016. "This Is How Steve Bannon Sees the Entire World." BuzzFeed News, November 16, 2016. Retrieved from https://www.buzzfeednews.com /article/lesterfeder/this-is-how-steve-bannon-sees-the-entire-world#.slm3 NNPQ5.

Huntington, Samuel P. 1993. "The Clash of Civilizations?" *Foreign Affairs* 72, no. 3: 22–49.

Huntington, Samuel P. 2003. *The Clash of Civilizations and the Remaking of World Order.* New York: Simon & Schuster.

Kayaoglu, Turan. 2012. "Constructing the dialogue of civilizations in world politics: a case of global Islamic activism." *Islam and Christian-Muslim Relations* 23, no. 2: 129–47.

Khatami, Mohammad. 2001. *Dialogue among Civilizations: The Round Table on the Eve of the United Nations Millennium Summit.* Paris, France: UNESCO. Retrieved from http://unesdoc.unesco.org/images/0012/001238/123890E.pdf.

Lewis, Bernard. 1990. "The roots of Muslim rage." *Atlantic Monthly,* September 1990: 47–60.

Lewis, Bernard. 2002. *What Went Wrong? The Clash Between Islam and Modernity in the Middle East.* New York: Perennial.

Nasr, Seyyed Hossein. 2000. *Ideals and Realities of Islam*. Chicago: ABC International Group, Inc.
Shimoni-Stoil, Rebecca. 2017. "How the GOP Became a 'Pro-Israel' Party." FiveThirtyEight, December 8, 2017. Retrieved from https://fivethirtyeight.com/features/how-the-gop-became-a-pro-israel-party/.
Sonn, Tamarra. 2004. *A Brief History of Islam*. Hoboken, NJ: Wiley-Blackwell.

Converts

The Islamic faith is one of the fastest growing faith traditions in the United States, thanks in part to the number of people who are converting or "reverting" to the faith. Many of these converts are Caucasian and Latin people who were born and raised in Protestant or Catholic households. People convert to the Islamic faith for a variety of reasons, and there is no single life experience or trajectory that all Muslim converts follow on their path to the faith. Scholars attribute the conversion or reversion to the Islamic faith to a number of factors like intellectual curiosity, the faith of their partner, meaning or purpose in life, and a close affiliation with another Muslim prior to conversion (Younis and Hassan 2017, 31).

Converting to the Islamic faith is actually quite simple. An individual has to take the *shahada,* an Arabic word meaning "confession" or "profession" of faith. The *shahada* consists of the proclamation that "There is no god but Allah, and Muhammad is his Prophet/Messenger." The emphasis placed on a singular God reaffirms the monotheistic outlook of the Islamic tradition and commands Muslims to worship none other than God.

Conversion to Islam also is referred to as "reversion." The distinction between the two concepts is largely a semantic issue, but there are interesting perspectives on which term is best to describe the process of "switching" from one religion (or no religion) to the Islamic faith. Those preferring "reversion" do so based on the claim that each and every human being is born, naturally, into a state of purity and innocence that is referred to as *fitrah,* the Arabic term for the natural state that all people are born with. According to this theory, the original "natural state" means that every single human being is born as a Muslim regardless of whether they are conscious of the state. Thus, to "revert" to the Islamic faith means that a person is effectively returning to the "original" and "true" religion of God. The words of the *shahada* are whispered into the ears of each newborn Muslim regardless of the geographic location of the birth.

Some of the earliest stories of U.S. citizens converting to the Islamic faith date back to the Barbary Wars between the U.S. government and the Barbary States of Algiers, Tripoli, Morocco, and Tunis. The Barbary Wars had occurred over the period of 1785 to 1815. During the conflict, it is said that several captured U.S. sailors had converted to the Islamic faith, or had "turned Turk," a derogatory and racialized slur used in the 18th century to refer to Muslims. According to historian Edward E. Curtis IV, editor of the *Encyclopedia of Muslim-American History* (2010), approximately five out of 300 sailors from the USS *Philadelphia,* which ran aground outside of Tripoli in 1803, became Muslims (Curtis 2010, 553). Curtis also recollected the story of a sailor named Walker from Baltimore who, sometime between 1810 and 1813, "abandoned 'his country, his family, and religion' to live with the Muslim 'horde of barbarians,' according to a U.S. diplomat in Algiers" (Curtis 2010, 553).

According to Patrick D. Bowen, author of *A History of Conversion to Islam,* thousands of white U.S. citizens embraced Islam between 1800 and 1965. One of the early Anglo-American converts to the Islamic faith is George Bethune English, an adventurer, diplomat, Harvard University alum, native Bostonian, and soldier. Bethune, a Marine officer, was commissioned as a second lieutenant by President James Madison on March 1, 1815, shortly after the end of the War of 1812. After the war, English moved to Egypt, where he later resigned his commission with the Marines and eventually converted to the Islamic faith. As a Muslim, English traveled extensively and became known for his travels along the Nile River with an Egyptian expeditionary unit, a role that led to accusations that he was a secret agent of the Egyptian state. English ended up changing his name to Mohammed Afendi, learning the Arabic language, studying the Qur'an, and publishing a book entitled *Narrative of the Expedition to Dongola and Sennaar* in 1822.

Another notable early U.S. convert to the Islamic faith is Alexander Russell Webb, a U.S. Muslim who achieved public renown in the 19th century. Webb was a journalist, editor, and civil servant who served as U.S. consult to the Philippines in 1887. Raised a Presbyterian, he converted to the Islamic faith in 1888, changed his first name to Mohammed, and later wrote numerous books to introduce the Islamic faith to English-speaking people in the United States. Webb also started the first Islamic press in the country by publishing a journal entitled *The Moslem World.* At the Parliament of the World's Religions in 1893, he gave a speech in which he discussed the reasons why the Islamic faith is misunderstood in the United States and Europe. He pointed specifically to biased media coverage of Muslims: "If a Mohammedan, Turk, Egyptian, Syrian or African commits a crime the newspaper reports do not tell us that it was committed by a Turk, an Egyptian, a Syrian or an African, but by a Mohammedan" (Webb 1893, 523). Later in his speech he reminded the audience that the Islamic faith is part of the larger Abrahamic tradition: "We [Muslims] firmly believe that the teachings of Moses, Abraham, Jesus and Mohammed were substantially the same" (Webb 1893, 525). In 1901, he was appointed Honorary Turkish Consul General in New York and was invited to Turkey, where he received two Ottoman medals of merit (Abd-Allah 2006).

In the 20th century, U.S. society witnessed the conversion of many African Americans to the Islamic faith. The large number of conversions among African Americans is generally attributed to several movements including the Moorish Science Temple, led by Noble Drew Ali, and Ahmadiyya missionaries, mainly Mufti Muhammad Sadiq. Following the lead of Noble Drew and Mufti Sadiq, Wallace Fard (W. F.) Muhammad appeared on U.S. soil in the early 1930s and also started his missionary work of converting African Americans from Christianity to the Islamic faith, primarily through the Nation of Islam (NOI). W. F. Muhammad's teaching of the racial superiority of African Americans and self-sufficiency enticed many African Americans in light of the racial discrimination and segregation between whites and blacks in the United States. Elijah Muhammad, a convert to the Islamic faith and successor to W. F. Muhammad as leader of the NOI, led the Nation into a period of growth in terms of followers and influence. Two notable converts to the Islamic faith in the mid-20th century—Muhammad Ali and Malcolm X—are widely recognized as two of the more influential U.S. Muslims in history. In his autobiography, Malcolm X explained, "I found Allah and the religion of Islam [while in prison] and it completely transformed my life." U.S. converts to the Islamic faith are still influenced today by many of the conditions that led African Americans to convert in the 20th century. Scholars Tarek Younis and Ghayda Hassan found that the socio-political experiences of discrimination and racial inequality are significantly implicated in the process of conversion and Muslim identity development in the "Western context" (Younis and Hassan 2017, 30).

Today, Latin or Hispanic Muslims are typically understood to be the fastest growing segment of the U.S. Muslim population. Approximately

6 percent of U.S. Muslims are said to be of Latin or Hispanic origins, and as many as a fifth of new converts to the Islamic faith nationwide identify with the Latin or Hispanic Muslim American category. According to Harold Daniel Morales, author of *Latino Muslim by Design,* Latinos convert to the Islamic faith for many reasons, among them being similarities between "Islamic values" and "Latin culture." Morales found that converts cite such similarities as respect for social justice, strong family values, and the importance of faith and religion. Most of the Latin American converts to the Islamic faith were born and raised in Catholic families. Some Latin American Muslims also note that they are returning or "reverting" to their true Islamic heritage as rooted in "Muslim Spain," the period when Muslims ruled over much of the Iberian Peninsula between 711 and 1492 CE.

Scholars also note that the Islamic faith is the fastest growing religion among incarcerated people in the United States. According to SpearIt, a professor of law at Texas Southern University, approximately 15 percent of the U.S. prison population is Muslim, many of whom convert in prison. Basia Spalek and Salah El-Hassan's research on Muslim converts in U.S. prisons revealed that the Islamic faith offers these prisoners a moral framework for rehabilitation and positive reasons to avoid violence and other forms of criminality. Muslim chaplains are also active in correctional facilities to offer faith-based guidance for Muslims. Muslim prison chaplains focused on *da'wah,* the Arabic word for "outreach," around the time in which Malcolm X was serving time. Today, as the Association of Muslim Chaplains notes on its website, Muslim chaplaincy in the United States has moved beyond *da'wah* toward efforts that offer more Islamic-based support and pastoral care. The Association of Muslim Chaplains and the Muslim Chaplain's Association are two national organizations leading the way in terms of offering support for U.S. Muslims serving prison terms. Organizations at the state level are also active in the realm of Muslim chaplaincy. The Muslim Chaplain Services of Virginia, a non-profit Islamic-based organization, was awarded a $25,000 grant by the Virginia government in 2000 to invest in the possibilities for greater engagement of Muslim chaplains in the United States, as the Harvard Pluralism Project website notes.

The topic of converts *from* Islam also deserves attention. About a quarter of U.S. adults who were raised Muslim (23 percent) no longer identify as Muslims, a number that is on par with the share of U.S. citizens who were raised Christian and no longer identify with Christianity

(22 percent) (Mohamed and Sciupac 2018). A 2017 Pew Research Center survey of U.S. Muslims found a similar estimate (24 percent) of the share of those who were raised Muslim but left Islam (Pew Research Center 2017). Among this group, 55 percent no longer identify with any religion (Pew Research Center 2017).

See also: Apostasy

Further Reading

Abd-Allah, Umar F. 2006. *A Muslim in Victorian America: The Life of Alexander Russell Webb*. Oxford, UK: Oxford University Press.

Bowen, Patrick D. *A History of Conversion to Islam in the United States: White American Muslims before 1975*. Leiden, The Netherlands: Brill Publishers.

Curtis, Edward E., IV, ed. 2010. *Encyclopedia of Muslim-American History*. New York: Facts on File.

Mohamed, Besheer, and Elizabeth Podrebarac Sciupac. 2018. "The share of Americans who leave Islam is offset by those who become Muslim." Washington, DC: Pew Research Center. Last modified January 26, 2018. Retrieved from http://www.pewresearch.org/fact-tank/2018/01/26/the-share-of-americans-who-leave-islam-is-offset-by-those-who-become-muslim/.

Morales, Harold Daniel. 2012. "Latino Muslim by Design: A Study of Race, Religion and the Internet in American Minority Discourse." UC Riverside Electronic Theses and Dissertations: University of California–Riverside. Retrieved from https://escholarship.org/uc/item/877902gr.

Pew Research Center. 2017. "U.S. Muslims Concerned about Their Place in Society, but Continue to Believe in the American Dream." Washington, DC: Pew Research Center. Last modified July 26, 2017. Retrieved from http://www.pewforum.org/2017/07/26/findings-from-pew-research-centers-2017-survey-of-us-muslims/.

Spalek, Basia, and Salah El-Hassan. 2007. "Muslim Converts in Prison." *The Howard Journal of Crime and Justice* 46, no. 2: 99–114.

SpearIt. 2012. "Raza Islamica: Prisons, Hip Hop & Converting Converts." *Berkeley La Raza Law Journal* 22, no. 1: 175–201.

SpearIt. 2012. "Religion as Rehabilitation? Reflections on Islam in the Correctional Setting." *Whittier Law Review* 34: 763–87.

Younis, Tarek, and Ghayda Hassan. 2017. "Changing Identities: A Case Study of Western Muslim Converts Whose Conversion Revised Their Relationship to Their National Identity." *Journal of Muslim Minority Affairs* 37, no. 1: 30–40.

Webb, Mohammed Alexander Russell. 1893. "Transcript of Speech made by Mr. Mohammed Alexander Russell Webb at the 1893 Parliament." Parliament

ofReligions.org. Retrieved from https://parliamentofreligions.org/content/tran
script-speech-made-mr-mohammed-alexander-russell-webb-1893-parliament.

Countering Violent Extremism (CVE)

Muslim radicalization, in various forms, is generally understood to be a
process that encourages a militant and politically activist ideology whose
ultimate goal is to unify the *ummah,* or global Muslim population, under
the caliphate by means of violence. The violent threat posed by "radical
Muslims" on U.S. soil is a political issue that has yielded intense debate
in the U.S. Congress and around the country. During a Republican debate
in New Hampshire in February 2016, Senator Marco Rubio of Florida
stated that "radical Muslims" linked to Daesh, commonly referred to as
ISIS (Islamic State of Iraq and Syria), are "a sophisticated network" that
radicalized people "here in the homeland and around the world. . . . We
face a very significant threat of homegrown violent extremism" (Dick
2016). Senator Rubio's claims were challenged in an academic article,
"Muslim 'Homegrown' Terrorism in the United States: How Serious Is
the Threat?" by scholar Risa Brooks, who found that on both analytical
and empirical grounds, "there is not a significant basis for anticipating
that Muslim Americans are increasingly motivated or capable of successfully engaging in lethal terrorist attacks in the United States" (Brooks
2011, 7).

The U.S. government's "Countering Violent Extremism" (CVE) program, which began in 2014 under President Barack Obama's administration as a "anti-terrorism initiative," has been criticized by U.S. Muslims
and U.S. civil rights organizations for stigmatizing Muslims and casting
unwarranted suspicion on innocuous activity, as noted by the American
Civil Liberties Union (ACLU). According to the Brennan Center for
Justice at the New York University School of Law, the aim of the CVE
program is to "deter U.S. residents from joining 'violent extremist' groups
by bringing community and religious leaders together with law enforcement, health professionals, teachers and social service employees"
(Brennan Center 2018). The series of programs initiated by the CVE program "call on law enforcement, social service providers, teachers, and
members of religious communities to identify individuals who might have
extreme or 'radical' views, under the assumption that they are at risk of

committing violence. To many, that's known as spying" (American Civil Liberties Union n.d.). The administration of President Donald Trump tossed out the term "violent extremism" and the Countering Violent Extremism (CVE) agenda of President Barack Obama. Instead, the Trump administration renamed it "countering Islamic extremism" or "countering radical Islamic extremism" (Stengel 2017).

Research carried out by the Brennan Center for Justice noted that there are several myths surrounding the CVE program. The first myth is that "there is a predictable process by which individuals become terrorists, and that there are visible signs that law enforcement, families, and teachers can identify." The Brennan Center noted in its report that this model "rests on false premises" and that "all serious empirical studies—included those funded by the U.S. government—have concluded that there is no typical trajectory that a person follows to become a terrorist." A second myth is that CVE programs do not specifically target U.S. Muslims. According to documents dated to February 2015 from the White House CVE summit, "Muslim communities are the principal—if not sole—target of CVE programs."

Muslim communities across the United States have demonstrably proven that they are key players in the struggle to combat radicalization. U.S. Muslims have provided significant levels of cooperation with law enforcement, proving that they are part of the solution to radicalization rather than merely the problem. Law enforcement agencies, as the Brennan Center again noted, have acknowledged time and again that U.S. Muslims have "an exemplary record of cooperation in counterterrorism efforts."

Aside from the efforts of U.S. Muslims to cooperate with law enforcement in the struggle against radicalization, there is sufficient evidence that Muslims in the United States condemn the views and actions of groups like Daesh or Al-Qaeda. A 2017 poll carried out by the Pew Research Center found that more than eight in ten U.S. Muslims (82 percent) say that they are either very concerned (66 percent) or somewhat concerned (16 percent) about radicalization among Muslims. The same 2017 Pew poll found that 73 percent of U.S. Muslims say there is little or no support for radicalization among their fellow Muslims. On the matter of suicide bombings, as a 2013 Pew poll revealed, more than eight in ten (81 percent) of U.S. Muslims said that this form of violence against civilians is never justified. Similarly, an earlier 2009 Pew poll found that less than 1 percent of U.S. Muslims believed that suicide bombings can ever be justified. These findings are striking in light of the anti-Islam comments made by

U.S. leaders. For example, in an op-ed for *USA Today* in July 2016, Franklin Graham, the prominent U.S. evangelical leader, wrote that "tens of thousands of Muslims in America . . . are not bashful about justifying suicide bombings in the name of Islam."

See also: Civil Rights; Freedom of Religion; Islamophobia; Racialization

Further Reading

American Civil Liberties Union. n.d. "Anti-Muslim Discrimination." New York: ACLU. Retrieved from https://www.aclu.org/issues/national-security/discriminatory-profiling/anti-muslim-discrimination.

Brennan Center for Justice. 2018. "Countering Violent Extremism (CVE): A Resource Page." New York University: Brennan Center for Justice. Last modified October 4, 2018. Retrieved from https://www.brennancenter.org/analysis/cve-programs-resource-page.

Brooks, Risa. 2011. "Muslim 'Homegrown' Terrorism in the United States: How Serious Is the Threat?" *Quarterly Journal: International Security* 36, no. 2 (Fall): 7–47.

Dick, Jason. 2016. "The Threat, and the Politics, of Homegrown Terrorism." Rollcall .com. Last modified February 8, 2016. Retrieved from http://www.rollcall.com/news/home/the-threat-and-the-politics-of-homegrown-terrorism.

Pew Research Center. 2013. "Appendix A: U.S. Muslims—Views on Religion and Society in a Global Context." Washington, DC: Pew Research Center. Last modified April 30, 2013. Retrieved from https://www.pewforum.org/2013/04/30/the-worlds-muslims-religion-politics-society-app-a/.

Pew Research Center. 2017. "U.S. Muslims Concerned about Their Place in Society, but Continue to Believe in the American Dream." Washington, DC: Pew Research Center. Last modified July 26, 2017. Retrieved from https://www.pewforum.org/2017/07/26/findings-from-pew-research-centers-2017-survey-of-us-muslims/.

Stengel, Richard. 2017. "Why Saying 'Radical Islamic Terrorism' Isn't Enough." NYTimes.com, February 13, 2017. Retrieved from https://www.nytimes.com/2017/02/13/opinion/why-saying-radical-islamic-terrorism-isnt-enough.html.

D

Dhimmi

The Islamic concept of *dhimmi* is an Arabic term relating to the treatment of religious minority populations living in a Muslim-majority society or under what may be called an "Islamic state." The term translates to "non-Muslims living under the protection of the *sharia*," or Islamic law. Anti-Islam critics and polemicists claim that *dhimmi* is a permanent, oppressive status in which Jews, Christians, and groups of various faiths are forced to accept an unjust tax or face conversion, slavery, or death. Additional critics use the term "dhimmitude" in alleging that groups like Jews and Christians are forced to appease and surrender to the *sharia* in Muslim-majority countries, and when describing the parlous state of religious minority populations who refuse to convert to the Islamic faith.

The notion of *dhimmi* dates back to the 7th century. The Arabian Peninsula at the time was populated by Jews, Christians, Zoroastrians, and the pagan religions that once dominated cities like Mecca. After receiving revelations from God, the Prophet Muhammad started his mission of welcoming people to the Islamic faith and establishing a state based on teachings received through God. One of Muhammad's goals as leader of the nascent Muslim community was to ensure the safety of those individuals and communities that did not identify themselves as "Muslim." To achieve the goal of creating a community and state that transcended tribal, racial, or religious divisions, Muhammad designated Jews and Christians, the "People of the Book," as "protected subjects," or *dhimmis*. The protected status placed on Jews and Christians meant that Muslims could not raid their properties for wealth or attack their communities in any form or manner. Jews and Christians under the *dhimmi* status also received complete protection by the "Muslim army" if they were attacked by forces outside of the first Islamic state created by the Prophet Muhammad. In addition to these protections, Jews and Christians were guaranteed freedom of religion, freedom of worship in sacred spaces, freedom of speech, and freedom to be judged by their own religious laws.

Nonetheless, the Islamic concept of *dhimmi* is often used by anti-Islam activists to represent the Islamic faith as one that enables a political system that is inherently biased against Jews, Christians, and people of diverse faiths. These activists often turn to the Qur'an to justify their arguments. One verse of the Qur'an (9:29), if taken literally, may appear to be oppressive toward the *dhimmi:* "Fight those from among the People of the Book who believe neither in God, nor in the Last Day, nor hold as unlawful what God and His Messenger have declared to be unlawful, nor follow the true religion, until they pay the tax willingly and agree to submit." This Qur'anic verse, however, stresses that certain conditions have to be met to fight against "People of the Book." Religious minority populations who are not hostile toward Muslims, who do not oppress them or try to convert them to another religion, are to be defended and protected by a "Muslim nation." Another verse of the Qur'an (8:55–56) is frequently taken out of context to imply that the *sharia* demands the subjugation and oppression of groups like Jews and Christians: "The worst creatures in the sight of God are those who reject Him and will not believe; those with whom you have made a covenant, and who break their covenant on every occasion and have no fear [of God]." This verse refers to "non-believers" as the "worst of creatures" in the sight of God because they allegedly "conceal the truth." This Qur'anic passage, however, goes on to clarify that the cause of the condemnation of the "non-believers" or non-Muslims is that they violated a treaty they had agreed to, which resulted in the deaths of many Muslims.

Scholars such as Anver E. Emon argue that the *sharia* leads to "dhimmi rules" or the "dhimmi system" that subject people of various religious backgrounds to inequalities in terms of freedom of religion. Critics claim that Jews and Christians are subjected to a system that treats them as second-class citizens. The Prophet Muhammad explicitly mentioned the treatment of the *dhimmi* as documented in the *ahadith*. Muhammad stated, "Whoever oppresses a *dhimmi* or burdens a weight over him more than he can carry, I will be his enemy." Similarly, Muhammad stated, "I am claimant of anyone who oppresses a dhimmi. The one who I am claimant of (in this world), I am also claimant on the Day of Judgment."

Historically, as scholar Bernard Lewis notes in *The Multiple Identities of the Middle East*, the *dhimmi* were not always treated with respect as commanded by the Prophet Muhammad. Forced conversions to the Islamic faith among Jews, Christians, and people of diverse faiths were sometimes attempted by newly installed, hardline "Islamist" regimes or by militant reformers (Lewis 1998, 124). Broadly speaking, however, the use of force or violence against the *dhimmi* has been rare and atypical in Islamic history, as Lewis concluded. Specific cases of mistreatment of the *dhimmi* are often attributed to corrupt rulers and poor governance.

In the present-day U.S. context, Muslims themselves rarely address the notion of the *dhimmi;* minority religious populations in the United States are already protected, at least in theory, by the U.S. Constitution. Muslims do not have the ability—and the overwhelming majority do not even have the desire—to enact special rules or laws for the treatment of Jews, Christians, and people of various faiths. Nevertheless, the anti-Islam activists in the country are claiming that the *sharia* followed by U.S. Muslims calls for the *dhimmi* status. After the U.S. Congress passed the Patient Protection and Affordable Care Act (PPACA), commonly referred to as "Obamacare," anti-Islam activists claimed that the PPACA specifically exempted Muslims from health insurance requirements. One activist argued: "ObamaCare allows the establishment of Dhimmitude and Sharia Muslim diktat in the United States. Muslims are specifically exempted from the government mandate to purchase insurance, and also from the penalty tax for being uninsured. Islam considers insurance to be 'gambling,' 'risk-taking,' and 'usury' and is thus banned. Muslims are specifically granted exemption based on this" (Holan 2013).

Anti-Islam websites also circulated rumors in which the word "dhimmitude" was included to describe how religious groups were exempted from the health insurance mandate provision of the PPACA. Writing for the Snopes website, journalist David Mikkelson dispelled the rumors. He noted that U.S. Muslims would not qualify for an exemption from U.S. health insurance requirements because they "do not have a tradition of spurning Social Security (which is viewed more as a form of caring for those who are unable to meet their own needs than as something which involves elements of uncertainty, gambling, and interest payments) . . . [and] no Muslim group has ever qualified for an exemption under the guidelines which define which religious groups would be exempt from the health care law." Mikkelson added, "The fact is that the PPACA legislation does not specifically exclude any particular religious groups from its provisions. . . . The word 'dhimmitude' does not appear anywhere in the PPACA, and it has no application to U.S. health care legislation."

Fact-checkers at Factcheck.org dug even deeper into the question of religious exemptions in the PPACA. Fact-check.org concluded: "The Muslim faith does not forbid purchasing health insurance, and no Muslim group has ever been considered exempt under the definitions used in the health care law" (Henig 2010).

See also: Abrahamic Tradition; Freedom of Religion; Jesus and Mary; *Jizya*; Pluralism

Further Reading

Considine, Craig. 2016. "Religious Pluralism and Civic Rights in a 'Muslim Nation': An Analysis of Prophet Muhammad's Covenants with Christians." *Religions* 7, no. 15: 1–21.

Emon, Anver M. 2012. "Religious Minorities and Islamic Law: Accommodation and the Limits of Tolerance." In *Islamic Law and International Human Rights*. Edited by Anver M. Emon, Mark Ellis, and Benjamin Glahn. Oxford, UK: Oxford University Press.

Henig, Jess. 2010. "'Dhimmitude' and the Muslim Exemption." Factcheck.org. Last modified May 20, 2010. Retrieved from https://www.factcheck.org/2010/05/dhimmitude-and-the-muslim-exemption/.

Holan, Angie Drobnic. 2013. "'Dhimmitude' on page 107 of the health care law exempts Muslims, claims chain email." Politifact.com, May 30, 2013. Retrieved from https://www.politifact.com/truth-o-meter/statements/2013/may/30/chain-email/dhimmitude-page-107-health-care-law-exempts-muslim/.

Lewis, Bernard. 1998. *The Multiple Identities of the Middle East*. New York: Schocken Books.

Mikkelson, David. 2010. "Dhimmitude Exempts Muslims from Obamacare Requirements." Snopes.com, April 13, 2010. Retrieved from https://www.snopes.com/fact-check/health-insurance-exemptions/.

E

European American Muslims

While the term "European American Muslims" is not one that has gained a lot of traction in the overall discourse of Muslims living in the United States, it is used here to refer to U.S. Muslims who can trace their ancestry to the European continent, excluding Turkey and Russia. In this sense, European American Muslims may be viewed as white or Caucasian people. European American Muslims may be second-, third-, or fourth-generation U.S. Muslims, or they may be recent converts to the Islamic faith. Instead of detailing the lives and experiences of the range of U.S. Muslims who have claimed European descent, this entry focuses instead on specific European Muslim communities with decades-old footprints on U.S. soil.

There is evidence that Albanian Muslims living in Biddeford, Maine, built one of the first mosques on U.S. soil in 1915. The second-floor meeting room of the Pepperell Counting House on Main Street is reported to have served as a "mosque" for the Albanian Muslims (Butler 2003). Evidence of the community in Biddeford is found in the Woodlawn Cemetery on West Street in Biddeford. Some of the tombstones in the cemetery have an engraving of the star and crescent, symbolizing the Islamic faith, while other grave markers note that the deceased was an "Albanian Muhamedan"—meaning a follower of Muhammad, or a Muslim. Today, the American Albanian Islamic Center of Kenosha, Wisconsin, which was established in 1979, serves as a religious and cultural center to serve the people of the Islamic faith throughout Southeastern Wisconsin (American Albanian Islamic Center of Wisconsin n.d.). Albanian Muslims in Harper Woods, Michigan, also built the Albanian Islamic Center in 1963. The Center's founder and first *imam,* Vehbi Ismail, arrived in Detroit in 1949. Today, the Albanian Islamic Center holds classes to teach Arabic, Albanian, and English.

Bosnian Muslims, or Bosniacs, are said to have established a community, the Dzemijetul Hajrije Islamije (The Benevolent Society), in Chicago, in 1906, which is arguably one of the oldest Islamic communities on U.S. soil. The majority of Bosnian Muslims in the United States today immigrated during the war in Bosnia and Herzegovina, between 1992 and 1995. On May 6, 1999, the United States received its first airlifted refugees from Kosovo. In total, the United States had agreed to take in 20,000 or so refugees; the vast majority of these people (if not all) were Muslims (Taylor 2015). For many Bosnian Muslims, their light skin and hair, along with other "European features," means many have managed to avoid the lingering effects of anti-Muslim racism that is attributed to brown skin and Arab ancestry (Parvini 2016). Bosnian Muslims have thus been described as having "the right skin color, but the wrong religion." St. Louis has emerged as one of the epicenters of Bosnian life in the United States. There are currently an estimated 70,000 Bosnian immigrants living in the St. Louis area, the vast majority of whom arrived as refugees in the 1990s.

The Islamic Community of North America Bosniacs (ICNAB), the premier umbrella organization representing the cross section of over 200,000 Bosnian Muslims living in the United States and Canada, was officially formed in 2003 (Islamic Community of North American Bosniacs n.d.). Bosnian Muslims also have organized locally in cities such as Boston, where they have founded the New England Friends of Bosnia and Herzegovina (NEFBiH), a 501(c)3 nonprofit organization started in 2012. The purpose of NEFBiH is to promote Bosnian-Herzegovinian heritage through cultural, educational, and festive programs. The group also safeguards the Bosnian language, raises awareness of genocide through human rights campaigns, and fosters partnerships and collaborations with like-minded organizations (New England Friends of Bosnia and Herzegovina n.d.).

One of the United States's oldest European diasporic communities is the Lipka Tatars, a predominantly Turkic and Muslim ethnic group with roots in what are now the countries of Belarus, Lithuania, and Poland. The term "Lipka" is derived from the Tatar word for Lithuania. Hundreds of Lipka Tatars immigrated to the United States at the turn of the 20th century, at which point they founded the first Muslim organization in Brooklyn, New York City, in 1907, called the American Mohammedan Society (Schuessler 2017). In the 1920s, they purchased a church building and turned it into a mosque, which is today one of the oldest surviving mosques in North America (Schuessler 2018). The official membership of the Lipka community in Brooklyn today is around 200 families, a small dot out of an estimated 6 million Muslims living in the United States (Schuessler 2018). The shifting demographics of the Muslim population around the mosque present some challenges including the risk of losing its unique cultural foundation and remaining an insular community with a dwindling membership (Schuessler 2018).

Considering that these Muslim populations living on U.S. soil happen to be of Caucasian descent, the issue of the racialization of Islam, and the experiences of white U.S. Muslims, should be articulated. White Muslims are reported to be "invisible Muslims" because they do not fit the racialized stereotype of the brown, Middle Eastern, Arab person. Thus, white, European-origin Muslims in the United States may not face the same intensity of anti-Muslim racism and hate crimes as other Muslims who fit the racial stereotype of Muslim identity. At the same time, European American Muslims may lose their white privilege afforded to them by the dominant white culture of the United States as soon as they reveal their "Muslim sounding name" or their Muslim identity as a whole. Such scenarios draw attention to the fact the whiteness, and race in general, is a fluid concept that has no fixed meaning. Regardless, the European American Muslim communities, with deep roots on U.S. soil, prove that whiteness, Islam, and U.S. national identity are certainly compatible.

See also: Racialization

Further Reading

Albanian Islamic Center. n.d. "Albanian Islamic Center: Description." Retrieved from http://biid.lsa.umich.edu/FM_Albanian_Islamic_Center.html.

American Albanian Islamic Center of Wisconsin. n.d. "About Us." Kenosha, WI. Retrieved from http://aaicw.org/?page_id=10.

Butler, Charles L. 2003. *Biddeford (ME) (Images of America)*. Mount Pleasant, SC: Arcadia Publishing.

Islamic Community of North America Bosniacs. n.d. "About ICNAB." United States. Retrieved from http://icnab.com/index.php/english/about-icnab.

New England Friends of Bosnia and Herzegovina. n.d. "Who We Are." Cambridge, MA: New England Friends of Bosnia and Herzegovina. Retrieved from http://nefbih.org/who-we-are/.

Parvini, Sarah. 2016. "Bosnian Muslims in Southern California may not fit the stereotype but they feel the prejudice." LATimes.com, July 4, 2016. Retrieved from http://www.latimes.com/local/lanow/la-me-bosnian-muslims-20160704 -snap-story.html#.

Schuessler, Ryan. 2017. "America's oldest Muslim families on the Trump presidency: 'This can't deter us.'" TheGuardian.com. Retrieved from https://www.theguardian.com/us-news/2017/jan/18/muslim-american-families-donald-trump.

Schuessler, Ryan. 2018. "How 16 Americans found family, faith and their immigrant roots—generations after their parents left their homelands." PRI.org. Retrieved from https://www.pri.org/stories/2018-11-22/how-16-americans-found-family-faith-and-their-immigrant-roots-generations-after.

Taylor, Adam. 2015. "That time the United States happily airlifted thousands of Muslim refugees out of Europe." WashingtonPost.com, November 17, 2015. Retrieved from https://www.washingtonpost.com/news/worldviews/wp/2015/11/17/that-time-the-united-states-happily-airlifted-thousands-of-muslim-refugees-out-of-europe/?utm_term=.34f387f4f5c1.

Zurcher, Anthony. 2016. "America's 'invisible' Muslims." BBC.com, October 30, 2016. Retrieved from https://www.bbc.com/news/magazine-37663226.

F

Foreign Policies

The U.S. government has an extensive history of engaging with Muslim-majority governments around the world. The first interaction occurred at the twilight of the U.S. Revolutionary War period when the United States made contact with the Barbary States, which at the time were autonomous provinces of the Ottoman Empire on the coast of North Africa. These states consisted of Algiers, Morocco, Tripoli, and Tunis. What is today referred to as the country of Morocco was the first nation in the world to recognize the independence of the United States.

The Treaty of Peace and Friendship between the U.S. government and the Sultan of Morocco, Mohammed Ibn Abdullah, was ratified by the U.S. Founding Fathers on July 18, 1787. The Treaty of Peace and Friendship allowed U.S. commercial and maritime entities to engage in trade on the coast of North Africa. Years later, in 1796, the Sultan of Morocco and the U.S. Founding Fathers reaffirmed the Treaty of Peace and Friendship, also referred to as the Treaty of Tripoli. In addition to reaffirming many of the policies outlined in the 1787 treaty, the Treaty of Tripoli of 1796 explicitly laid out the relationship between the United States and the North African nations in terms of the relationship between religion and national identity.

Article 11 of the 1796 treaty stated, "The United States of America is not in any sense founded on the Christian religion, as it has in itself no character or enmity against the laws, religion, or tranquility of [Muslims], and as the said States never have entered into any war or act of hostility against any Muslim nation, it is declared by the parties that no pretext arising from religious opinions shall ever produce an interruption of the harmony existing between two countries" (Avalon Project n.d.).

The Treaty of Tripoli of 1796 broke down after maritime and trading disagreements between the U.S. government and the Barbary States occurred. As a result, the Barbary Wars of the late 18th century represent one of the first foreign policy encounters between the U.S. government and Muslim-majority countries. The Barbary Wars were a 33-year period of tension between the United States and the Barbary States that included two wars in the Mediterranean Sea: the Tripolitan War (1801–1805) and the Algerine War (1815–1816) (Lambert 2005, 7). From 1785 to 1815, as historian Edward E. Curtis IV notes, the Barbary States captured 35 U.S. ships and took more than 700 sailors captive (Curtis 2010, 553).

Scholars who have examined the historical background of the Barbary Wars disagree with the popular claim among today's anti-Islam critics that the wars broke out because of fundamental differences between "Western civilization" and "Islamic civilization." Critics claim that the Barbary states were acting in the name of "radical Islam" and that they were engaged in a "holy war" against the *kafir* the Arabic term for infidels, thus making them the historical equivalent of modern "radical Islamic" groups such as Daesh or al-Qaeda. According to Frank Lambert, author of *The Barbary Wars: American Independence in the Atlantic World,* "evidence abounds that neither the pirates nor the Americans considered religion central to their conflict" (Lambert 2005, 8). Rather, the Barbary Wars were primarily about trade and the emerging United States's concern over its natural rights including liberty and equality.

The U.S. government's policies toward and relationship with the Palestinian people has long been a source of disappointment among U.S. Muslims. In the late-19th and early-20th centuries, the Zionist movement, a Jewish political movement that called for the establishment of a Jewish homeland in Palestine, engaged in a nation-state–building project that resulted in the *Nakbah,* an Arabic term for "catastrophe." The *Nakbah* forcefully displaced approximately 750,000 Palestinians, a refugee crisis that is still not resolved today. Yvonne Yazbeck Haddad of Georgetown University argued that "Islamists" created a stereotype of a "crusader-Zionist conspiracy" bent on subjugating Muslims and eradicating Islam. Islamism, Haddad contends, is a reaction to Zionism, which is perceived as Israeli aggression aimed at enthralling Palestinians and defying United Nations resolutions, with the aid of U.S. intervention at the United Nations. Islamists see that the United States and its Western allies maintain a clear double standard that supports Jews' having a Jewish state, but demonizes Muslims who want an Islamic state (Haddad 2012).

The post–World War II climate allowed the U.S. government to re-engage with Muslim-majority countries around the world. In 1955, the U.S. government entered into the Baghdad Pact with Britain, Iran, Iraq, Pakistan, and Turkey. The Baghdad Pact, which later became officially known as the Central Treaty Organization (CENTO), ensured the cooperation of all countries that entered into the agreement against the Soviet Union. Nuri Al-Sa'id, the Iraqi leader, was a leading proponent of the Pact, but nearby Arab leaders, like Egyptian President Gamal Abdel Nasser, viewed the agreement as another case of Western imperialism in the Middle East region.

The Cold War conflict between the U.S. government and the Soviet Union sometimes spilled over into the territories controlled by Muslim-majority governments. The Soviet War in Afghanistan between 1979 and 1989 is a case in point. The Soviet Union invaded Afghanistan in 1979 in order to establish a pro-communist and pro-Soviet regime in the capital of Afghanistan as well as destroy the *mujahideen* (the plural term of *mujahid,* the Arabic word for a person who engages in *jihad*) and Afghan troops, which were supported financially and militarily by the U.S. government. After the *mujahideen* and Afghan rebels defeated the Soviet forces, the United States withdrew its support and direct influence, after which a civil war ensued in Afghanistan. The civil war set the stage for the rise of the Taliban government, the group that the U.S. government believed to have played a role in the coordination of the 9/11 attacks.

The Iranian Revolution of 1979 was followed by the Iran-Iraq War between 1980 and 1988. The U.S. government sided with the Ba'athist regime of Saddam Hussein. According to a *New York Times* article written in 1992 by internationally recognized journalist Seymour M. Hersh, President Ronald Reagan's administration secretly decided to provide highly classified intelligence and arms sales to help Hussein defeat Iran. According to investigative journalists Shane Harris and Matthew M. Aid's article in *Foreign Policy,* the U.S. government knew that Hussein was launching some of the worst chemical attacks in history and still maintained a working relationship with his Ba'athist regime. Harris and Aid's research of Central Intelligence Agency (CIA) files revealed that "the Iraqis used mustard gas and sarin prior to four major offensives in early 1988 that relied on U.S. satellite imagery, maps, and other intelligence. These attacks helped to tilt the war in Iraq's favor and bring Iran to the negotiating table, and they ensured that the Reagan administration's long-standing policy of securing an Iraqi victory would succeed."

The Reagan administration also had to respond to the Beirut Marine barracks truck bombing that the U.S. intelligence community blamed on Hezbollah, the political organization and militant group that originated in Lebanon. On October 23, 1983, militants attacked the Marine barracks with a truck bombed that killed 220 U.S. Marines and an additional 21 U.S. service personnel. The Marines had been sent to Lebanon by President Reagan in 1982 on a peacekeeping mission.

The U.S. government ended up turning against Saddam Hussein, its onetime ally during the Iran-Iraq War (1980–1989), after Hussein invaded and attempted to annex Kuwait, an oil-rich country, during the presidency of George H. W. Bush. Referred to as the Persian Gulf War, the Gulf War, or the First Iraq War and codenamed Operation Desert Shield, the invasion of Iraq in 1991 was waged by over 35 nations, with the United States, Egypt, the United Kingdom, and Saudi Araba being the more significant contributors.

The United States and the United Kingdom, alongside support from countries like Australia, Canada, France, and Germany, led the invasion of Afghanistan following the 9/11 attacks in 2001. The purpose of the invasion of Afghanistan was to defeat the Taliban, which the U.S. government and intelligence agencies believed to have provided support for the 9/11 hijackers. Officially named "Operation Enduring Freedom," the Afghan War was intended to destroy the capabilities of Osama Bin Laden and Al-Qaeda and prevent the Taliban government from maintaining a stronghold over the Afghan people. Bin Laden responded to the invasion by calling on Muslims worldwide to engage in a global war against Western civilization in an Al Jazeera Arabic interview. As of 2019, the United States is still engaged in the Afghan War by continuing its fight against guerilla-style militants. The Afghan War is officially the longest war in U.S. history, having recently surpassed the Vietnam War.

The Afghan War was followed by the Iraq War, or the Second Iraq War. Along with coalition forces, the United States invaded Iraq in 2003 in order to take out Iraqi president Saddam Hussein, who the U.S. intelligence community claimed possessed weapons of mass destruction. After the collapse of his government, Hussein retreated into isolation and was found by U.S. soldiers in the Iraqi city of Tikrit. He was arrested and tried in court for war crimes against the Iraqi people on November 6, 2006. The Iraqi National Assembly, which had been established following Hussein's retreat, was seen by a large number of people worldwide as a puppet government for U.S. interests in the Middle East. Weapons of mass destruction were never found in Iraq. Also arising out of the Iraq War were human rights violations by U.S. military personnel at Abu Ghraib, a U.S. military prison in Iraq. Photographs revealed to the U.S. public showed these violations, and as a result, several members of the U.S. Army were charged with conspiracy, dereliction of duty, cruelty toward prisoners, maltreatment, assault, and indecent acts (Hersh 2004).

Pakistan, a country that borders Afghanistan, also became the target of the George W. Bush and Barack Obama administrations. Starting in 2004 under the Bush administration, the U.S. government embarked upon a controversial drone war that targeted the Taliban and other Pashtun militants mainly in the Khyber Pakhtunkhwa province along the Pakistan-Afghanistan border. According to the Bureau of Investigative Journalism (BIJ), the United States has executed a minimum of 430 confirmed strikes in Pakistan. As of 2019, between 2,515 and 4,026 people have died in the drone war campaign. The BIJ added that between 424 and 969 civilians have been killed and between 172 and 207 children have been killed as of 2019. In his book *Counter Jihad: America's Military Experience in Afghanistan, Iraq and Syria,* Brian Glyn Williams stated that President Obama expanded President's Bush's drone campaign in Pakistan—Obama, Williams noted, launched more than seven times as many bombs from drones as Bush.

The rise of Daesh, popularly known as the Islamic State of Iraq and Syria (ISIS), resulted from the "War on Terror" across the Middle East and South Asia. Emerging from the remnants of Al-Qaeda, Daesh came to the forefront in June 2014 when it attacked the cities of Mosul and Tikrit in Iraq. Two weeks after the invasion of these two cities, as the Wilson Center noted, Abu Bakr Al-Baghdadi, the leader of Daesh, announced the formation of a caliphate stretching from Aleppo in Syria to Diyala in Iraq. The Obama administration had taken action against Daesh in the late summer of 2014 by carrying out a set of airstrikes as part of "Operation Inherent Resolve." The Wilson Center revealed that the Obama administration conducted more than 8,000 airstrikes in Iraq and Syria, a campaign that significantly impacted the amount of territory controlled by Daesh. In February 2019, President Donald Trump declared that the United States "just took over 100 percent" of the last territories controlled by Daesh in Syria (Rogers, Callimachi, and Cooper 2019). Soon thereafter, President Trump declared the "100 percent" defeat of Daesh. However, John Bolton, the U.S. national security advisor, admitted on television that "the ISIS threat will remain" (Lister 2019). Indeed, in April 2019, Daesh leader Abu

Bakr Al-Baghdadi, recently believed to have been killed in U.S.-led airstrikes, reappeared in an 18-minute propaganda video after a five-year absence from public view (Hennigan 2019).

The U.S. foreign policy approach to the "Muslim world" today is largely centered around the seemingly endless war against "radical Islam." The Trump administration has claimed that the United States has defeated Daesh (ISIS), but experts push back on that claim due to the de-territorialized nature of Daesh's influence and its ability to recruit new members on the Internet and through social media. The Trump administration has also moved the U.S. Embassy in Israel from Tel Aviv to Jerusalem, a diplomatic move that was denounced by many U.S. Muslims as well as the United Nations General Assembly by a vote of 128–9. In addition to its continued alliance with the Israeli government, the U.S. government appears to be edging itself closer to a deeper alliance with Saudi Arabia. The Saudi Arabian government has become the proponent of Wahhabism, a development that is frowned upon by the majority of U.S. Muslims. Judging from recent foreign policies adopted by the Trump administration, the U.S. government has appeared to embrace Saudi Arabia while pursuing an aggressive rhetorical stance against the ayatollahs, the Shi'a religious leaders of Iran.

See also: Clash of Civilizations; Islamophobia; *Jihad*

Further Reading

Avalon Project. n.d. "The Barbary Treaties (1786–1816)—Treaty of Peace and Friendship, Signed at Tripoli (November 4, 1796)." Hartford, CT: Lillian Goldman Law Library at Yale Law School. Retrieved from http://avalon.Law .yale.edu/18th_century/bar1796t.asp.

Bureau of Investigative Journalism. 2019. "Drone Strikes in Pakistan." Bureau of Investigative Journalism. Retrieved from https://www.thebureauinvestigates .com/projects/drone-war/pakistan.

CNN Library. 2019. "Beirut Marine Barracks Bombing Fast Facts." CNN.com, March 21, 2019. Retrieved from https://www.cnn.com/2013/06/13/world /meast/beirut-marine-barracks-bombing-fast-facts/index.html.

Curtis, Edward E., IV, ed. 2010. *Encyclopedia of Muslim-American History.* New York: Facts on File.

Haddad, Yvonne Yazbeck. 2012. "Islamist Perceptions of U.S. Policy in the Middle East." In *The Contemporary Middle East: A Westview Reader,* edited by Karl Yambert. New York: Routledge.

Harris, Shane, and Matthew M. Aid. 2013. "Exclusive: CIA Files Prove America Helped Saddam as He Gassed Iran." ForeignPolicy.com, August 26, 2013. Retrieved from https://foreignpolicy.com/2013/08/26/exclusive-cia-files-prove-america-helped-saddam-as-he-gassed-iran/.

Hennigan, W. J. 2019. "The Most-Wanted ISIS Leader Is Still Alive. Here's How the U.S. Is Using Drones to Hunt Him Down." TIME.com, April 30, 2019. Retrieved from http://time.com/5577364/abu-bakr-al-baghdadi-isis-military-hunt/.

Hersh, Seymour M. 1992. "U.S. Secretly Gave Aid to Iraq Early in Its War Against Iran." NYTimes.com, January 26, 1992. Retrieved from https://www.nytimes.com/1992/01/26/world/us-secretly-gave-aid-to-iraq-early-in-its-war-against-iran.html.

Hersh, Seymour M. 2004. "Torture at Abu Ghraib." *The New Yorker*, April 30, 2004. Retrieved from https://www.newyorker.com/magazine/2004/05/10/torture-at-abu-ghraib.

Lambert, Frank. 2005. *The Barbary Wars: American Independence in the Atlantic World*. New York: Hill & Wang.

Lister, Charles. 2019. "Trump Says ISIS Is Defeated. Reality Says Otherwise." Politico.com, March 18, 2019. Retrieved from https://www.politico.com/magazine/story/2019/03/18/trump-isis-terrorists-defeated-foreign-policy-225816.

Rogers, Katie, Rukmini Callimachi, and Helene Cooper. 2019. "Trump Declares ISIS '100%' Defeated in Syria. '100% Not True,' Ground Reports Say." NYTimes.com, February 28, 2019. Retrieved from https://www.nytimes.com/2019/02/28/world/middleeast/trump-isis-territory.html.

Taylor, Alan. 2014. "The Soviet War in Afghanistan, 1979–1989." TheAtlantic.com, August 4, 2014. Retrieved from https://www.theatlantic.com/photo/2014/08/the-soviet-war-in-afghanistan-1979-1989/100786/.

Williams, Brian Glyn. 2016. *Counter Jihad: America's Military Experience in Afghanistan, Iraq, and Syria*. Philadelphia: University of Pennsylvania Press.

Wilson Center. 2019. "Timeline: The Rise, Spread, and Fall of the Islamic State." Washington, DC: Wilson Center. Last modified April 30, 2019. Retrieved from https://www.wilsoncenter.org/article/timeline-the-rise-spread-and-fall-the-islamic-state.

Freedom of Religion

The First Amendment of the U.S. Constitution acknowledges that freedom of religion is a fundamental civil and human right for all people living inside the United States. The amendment unequivocally states: "Congress shall make no law respecting an establishment of religion, or prohibiting the free exercise thereof; or abridging the freedom of speech. . . ." Everyone in the United States has the right to practice his or her religion, or no religion at all. The First Amendment guarantees that the U.S. government cannot penalize a person because of their religious beliefs. U.S. Supreme Court Justice Sonia Sotomayor captured the spirit of freedom of religion and its inextricable link to U.S. national identity when she argued in her opposition to the "Muslim travel ban": ". . . the United States of America is a Nation built upon the promise of religious liberty. Our Founders honored that core promise by embedding the principle of religious neutrality in the First Amendment" (Sotomayor 2018, 9).

Muslims in the United States are frequently chastised by U.S. citizens for their alleged intolerance of Jews, Christians, and atheists, among many other religious populations. As a result of this perception of the Islamic faith, an alarming number of U.S. citizens, in fact, do not think that Muslims should be granted the same constitutional protections on freedom of religion as other citizens. This view is in part shaped by the persecution of religious minority populations in Muslim-majority countries around the world. Many of these Muslim-majority countries, like Pakistan and Saudi Arabia, are unreceptive to, if not downright intolerant of, freedom of religion for Jews, Christians, or even minority sects of the Islamic tradition. U.S. residents and citizens, however, must be careful to avoid conflating the "Muslim world" with the Muslim population of the United States. There are significant differences between these two spheres, especially pertaining to freedom of religion.

U.S. Muslims overwhelmingly believe that freedom of religion is a foundational element of any notion of U.S. national identity. As a whole, U.S. Muslims overwhelmingly want to protect the U.S. Constitution and its granting of liberty in terms of religious belief and practice. The Qur'an, the Islamic holy text, is clear and firm on the idea that God has intended for human beings to openly and freely believe in and practice their own faith and religion. The Qur'an provides for complete freedom of religion in several verses: "There shall be no compulsion in religion: true guidance has become distinct from error" (Qur'an 2:256) and "Had your Lord pleased, all the people on earth would have believed in Him, without exception. So will you compel people to become believers?" (Qur'an 10:99).

Critics of the Islamic faith in the United States take offense to the idea that the Qur'an grants freedom of religion to all human beings. These critics often turn to the Arabic term *kafir* which literally means "infidel" or "ingrate," and is oftentimes understood as simply "unbeliever." The term *kafir* has been linked to the idea that Jews and Christians, alongside all minority religious populations, are rejected human beings in the Qur'an. While the Qur'an is clear in its respect and reverence for Jews and Christians, in the term *Ahl al-Kitab,* or "People of the Book," the Islamic holy text also extends freedom of religion to all "idolaters," as seen in the Qur'an (9:6): "If any one of the polytheists seeks asylum with you, grant him asylum so that he may hear the word of God; then convey him to a place of safety. That is because they are a people who have no knowledge." While this verse calls on idolaters to recognize the legitimacy of the Islamic tradition, it does not call for force or persuasive conversions. The Qur'an urges Muslims to deal with all human beings, regardless of religious preference or background, with respect, as long as they extend respect to Muslims as well.

Muslims in the United States often point to the vision of the U.S. Founding Fathers in justifying their belief in freedom of religion and the idea that Muslims were imagined as future U.S. citizens during the Revolutionary period. One of the most important declarations on freedom of religion came in the words of President George Washington's 1790 letter to the Hebrew Congregation of Newport, Rhode Island:

> . . . the Government of the United States . . . gives to bigotry no sanction, to persecution no assistance . . . they who live under its protection should demean themselves as good citizens. . . . May the children of the Stock of Abraham, who dwell in this land, continue to merit and enjoy the good will of the other Inhabitants; while everyone shall sit in safety under his own vine and figtree, and there shall be none to make him afraid. May the father of all mercies scatter light and not darkness in our paths, and make us all in our several vocations useful here, and in his own due time and way everlasting happy.

The U.S. Founding Fathers' democratic and egalitarian spirit is said to mirror the teachings and example of Muhammad, the prophet who lived over 1,100 years before the drafting and signing of the U.S. Constitution. In 632 CE, Muhammad created the Constitution of Medina, a political treatise that granted Jews in the city of Medina, Saudi Arabia, full autonomy and allowed them to keep their forms of worship and other distinctive Jewish practices. The Constitution of Medina states in no uncertain terms: "Whosoever among the Jews follows us shall have help and equality; they shall not be injured nor shall any enemy be aided against them. . . . The

Jews shall maintain their own religion and the Muslims theirs." The remarkable similarity between the U.S. Constitution and the Constitution of Medina suggests that these two political documents share a spirit of freedom, equality, and justice for all.

Nonetheless, the Constitution of Medina is used by critics of the Islamic faith to argue that Muhammad acted in an anti-Jewish or anti-Semitic manner. These U.S. citizens claim that Muhammad basically scrapped the Constitution of Medina and became increasingly hostile toward Jews. Scholars of the life and legacy of Muhammad, however, note that the Jewish tribes that agreed to the Constitution of Medina with Muhammad became increasingly hostile to his form of leadership and eventually scolded and denied his prophethood (Watt 1961, 99–100). After the Jewish tribes of Medina turned against Muhammad and the early Muslim community, Muhammad decided to move against the Jewish population because the tribes were actively working with—and supported by—the Meccan people, who were the main enemies of Muhammad and the first Muslim community. While critics refer to the attacks on the Medinan Jews by Muhammad as proof of the latter's anti-Jewish views, a more compelling argument is that the hostility between the Jewish tribes and early Muslims had been motivated more by political issues over the leadership of Medina rather than racial or religious disagreements between Jews and Muslims.

More recently, as the American Civil Liberties Union revealed, Muslim communities in the United States have faced a disturbing wave of bigotry and outright hostility ranging from discrimination and attacks to opposing the construction of mosques. The current environment suggests that the nation's commitment to freedom of religion is conditional and that the security and protections that the Constitution guarantees to people do not apply equally to individuals who call themselves Muslim. The backlash against U.S. Muslims is due in part to the resurgence of ethnonationalism, a form of national identity that opposes both cultural and religious pluralism.

Christians across the United States have rejected Islamophobia by standing for the human and constitutional rights of freedom of religion for Muslims. Amidst a wave of anti-Muslim rhetoric and comments by U.S. politicians, leaders in one of the most Republican states in the Union—Utah—stood in solidarity with Muslims. Utah's senior senator, Orrin Hatch, stated that he'd be "the first to stand up for their rights" (Seitz-Wald 2010). He also called Islam "a great religion." Utah's other Republican senator, Mike Lee, said he did not vote for Donald Trump in part because he saw the "Muslim travel ban" as a "religious test" (Canham 2017). Hatch and Lee, both Mormons, have drawn comparisons between the U.S. government's historic persecution of Mormons and the current treatment of U.S. Muslims. Mormon politicians, as Asma Uddin pointed out in the *New York Times,* "seem to understand better than many of their fellow Republicans that if another's freedom of faith is under attack, so, too, is their own" (Uddin 2018).

See also: Apostasy; Civil Rights; U.S. Founding Fathers

Further Reading

Ali, Abdullah Bin Hamid. 2011. "Preserving the Freedom for Faith: Reevaluating the Politics of Compulsion." *The Review of Faith & International Affairs* 9, no. 2 (Summer): 3–8.

Arjomand, Saïd Amir. 2009. "The Constitution of Medina: A Sociological Interpretation of Muhammad's Acts of Foundation of the 'Umma.'" *International Journal of Middle East Studies* 41, no. 4: 555–75.

Canham, Matt. 2017. "Mike Lee, critical of a Muslim ban, wants more info on Trump's refugee executive order." *Salt Lake Tribune,* January 30, 2017. Retrieved from https://archive.sltrib.com/article.php?id=4875807&itype=CMSID.

Considine, Craig. 2016. "Religious Pluralism and Civic Rights in a 'Muslim Nation': An Analysis of Prophet Muhammad's Covenants with Christians." *Religions* 7, no. 15: 1–21.

Constitution of Medina. n.d. "Ibn Ishaq's Record of the *Constitution of Medina*." RogerLouisMartinez.com. Retrieved from http://www.rogerlouismartinez .com/wp-content/uploads/2015/01/Constitution-of-Medina.pdf.

Esack, Farid. 2002. *Qur'an, Liberation and Pluralism: An Islamic Perspective of Interreligious Solidarity against Oppression.* Oxford, UK: Oneworld.

Isaacson, Walter. 2005. "Benjamin Franklin's Gift of Tolerance." In *After Terror: Promoting Dialogue among Civilizations.* Edited by Akbar Ahmed and Brian Forst. Cambridge and Malden: Polity.

Saeed, Abdullah. 2011. "Ambiguities of Apostasy and the Repression of Muslim Dissent." *The Review of Faith & International Affairs* 9, no. 2 (Summer): 31–37.

Seitz-Wald, Alex. 2010. "Sen. Orrin Hatch: 'I'd Be The First To Stand Up For Their Rights' To Build A Mosque Near Ground Zero." ThinkProgress.org, August 30, 2010. Retrieved from https://thinkprogress.org/sen-orrin-hatch -id-be-the-first-to-stand-up-for-their-rights-to-build-a-mosque-near-ground -zero-e0a6b5544676/.

Sotomayor, Sonia. 2018. *Donald J. Trump, President of the United States, Et Al., Petitioners v. Hawaii, Et Al.* 17 U.S. 965. Washington, DC: U.S. Supreme

Court. Last modified June 26, 2018. Retrieved from https://www.supreme court.gov/opinions/17pdf/17-965_h315.pdf.

Uddin, Asma. 2018. "What Islamophobic Politicians Can Learn from Mormons." NYTimes.com, May 22, 2018. Retrieved from https://www.nytimes.com /2018/05/22/opinion/mormons-islamophobia-utah.html.

Watt, William Montgomery. 1961. *Muhammad: Prophet and Statesman*. Oxford, UK: Oxford University Press.

Freedom of Speech

Anti-Islam activists oftentimes claim that the Islamic faith is incompatible with "U.S. values." These activists believe that the Qur'an and the teachings of the Prophet Muhammad command Muslims to stifle freedom of speech and punish individuals or groups that engage in blasphemy against the Islamic holy text or Muhammad himself. The facts, however, paint a more positive picture of how Muslims living in the United States support freedom of speech.

U.S. Muslims as a whole believe in the importance of freedom of speech not only as followers of the Islamic faith, but as U.S. citizens. Research carried out by several top civil rights organizations and research organizations shows that a high percentage of U.S. Muslims support the First Amendment of the U.S. Constitution, which reads: "Congress shall make no law . . . abridging the freedom of speech, or of the press; or the right of the people peaceably to assemble." For example, the CATO Institute, a libertarian think tank based in Washington, DC, carried out a joint study with YouGov, a marketing research firm based in London, England, that surveyed the views of 2,300 Muslims living in the United States. The study found that U.S. Muslims (37 percent) are less likely to favor laws banning "offensive speech" than people who identified themselves as African American (46 percent), Jews (41 percent), and Hispanics (39 percent) (Ekins 2017). U.S. Muslims were also found to be more likely than African Americans (54 percent), Jews (59 percent), and Hispanics (61 percent) to oppose laws banning "offensive free speech" in the United States (Ekins 2017).

U.S. Muslim leaders, Islamic organizations, and pro-Muslim advocacy groups consistently speak out in favor of freedom of speech in the United States. Over 200 prominent U.S. Muslims along with their Canadian counterparts signed a statement in May 2015 that "unconditionally condemned any intimidation or threats of violence directed against any individual or group exercising" the constitutional right "of freedom of speech, even when that speech may be perceived as hurtful or reprehensible." Those who signed the statement added that they uphold the First Amendment because it provides protections that are fundamental to defending minorities from the whims of the majority. These facts, as revealed through polling and the actions of U.S. Muslims themselves, mirror the claims made by scholar Wahiduddin Khan, author of *Principles of Islam*. In his book, Khan noted that the Islamic faith grants human beings "total intellectual freedom" and "independent expression" of views, whether they be related to social, cultural, religious, or political matters. He also stressed the importance of freedom of speech because without it an honest and open society cannot flourish.

Despite these facts, anti-Islam activists continue to represent the Islamic faith as a faith that stifles freedom of speech. In May 2015 the anti-Islam group American Freedom Defense Initiative held the "First Annual Muhammad Art Exhibit and Contest," popularly referred to as the "Draw Muhammad Contest," in Garland, Texas. Led by anti-Islam activist Pamela Geller, the "Draw Muhammad Contest" offered a prize of $10,000 for the "best drawing" of Muhammad. Critics of the event claimed that the American Freedom Defense Initiative's intention was to push Muslims into denouncing the event, which could then be used as "proof" that U.S. Muslims are not in favor of freedom of speech. Two young U.S. Muslim men turned up to the "Draw Muhammad Contest" and opened fire on security guards. Anti-Islam activists like Geller then used this act of violence to argue their point.

A few years earlier, on September 11, 2012, the matter of freedom of speech was the center point of worldwide protests in Muslim-majority countries over the posting of an obscure YouTube video titled *Innocence of Muslims,* which represented the Prophet Muhammad as a terrorist and pedophile. Egyptian protesters reacted to the video by overrunning the U.S. Embassy in Cairo. Muslim leaders at the United Nations in New York City claimed that Western countries hide behind the defense of freedom of speech in order to promote an "anti-Islam" agenda. Reports also revealed that Muslims worldwide held the U.S. government responsible for the posting of the video because the film was produced by a filmmaker residing in California. The administration of President Barack Obama officially denounced the video, but the U.S. government also insisted that freedom of speech and freedom of expression are rights protected by the U.S. Constitution.

Blasphemy laws upheld by Muslim-majority countries around the world are another target of anti-Islam activists in the United States. Blasphemy refers to an action or comment that may be deemed overly insulting or offensive to a group of people or showing contempt for God or religion as a whole. Blasphemy laws, on the other hand, are pieces of legislation that "sanction insulting or defaming religion and seek to punish individuals for allegedly offending, insulting, or denigrating religious doctrines, deities, symbols or 'the sacred,' or for wounding or insulting religious feelings" (U.S. Commission on International Religious Freedom 2017, 5).

Critics of the Islamic faith often turn to Pakistan to justify their criticism of Muslims as being "anti-freedom of speech." Sections 295–298 of the Pakistani Penal Code, titled "Of Offense Related to Religions," rule that comments or statements intended to "insult religion," or deliberate and malicious acts to offend religious people, are punishable by either fine or imprisonment. Section 295C of the Pakistani Penal Code goes as far as punishing any person who makes derogatory remarks about the Prophet Muhammad with either life imprisonment or the death penalty. Indonesia, the country with the largest Muslim population in the world, is often cited by critics as further proof that Muslims are "anti-freedom of speech." Article 156(a) of the Indonesian Criminal Code targets those who are "expressing feelings of hostility, hatred or contempt against religions" and "disgracing a religion." Both of these offenses are punishable by up to five years in jail.

The U.S. Commission on International Religious Freedom (USCIRF) claims that blasphemy is detrimental to freedom of religion because people have the right to embrace "a full range of thoughts and beliefs" and "the right to speak or write about them publicly." The USCIRF follows the lead of the United Nations Universal Declaration of Human Rights, adopted in 1948, which provides the following statement in Article 19: "Everyone has the right to freedom of opinion and expression; this right includes freedom to hold opinions without interference and to seek, receive and impart information and ideas through any media and regardless of frontiers." The blasphemy laws adopted across the world stand in direct contrast to the USCIRF and U.N.'s position on freedom of speech.

Blasphemy is another issue that arises in discussions over the amount of freedom of speech prescribed by the Qur'an. In the 7th century, the concept of blasphemy was centered on the prohibition of foul language with respect to the Prophet Muhammad (Saeed 2008, 32). Blasphemy, however, was later extended to include foul language with reference to God, any of the angels, and any other prophets (Saeed 2008, 32). Today, a number of Muslim-majority countries around the world have blasphemy laws that effectively criminalize speech that is considered to be insulting toward Muslims, especially on matters pertaining to the life of Muhammad himself. Again, however, the norms and policies of Muslim-led governments around the world should not be conflated with the U.S. Muslim population's views and beliefs. While Muslims may share a religious identity, they do not always share the same interpretation of the Qur'an and *ahadith* as they pertain to sensitive issues like freedom of speech.

See also: Civil Rights

Further Reading

Aaronson, Trever. 2016. "FBI Had Undercover Agent at Scene of 'Draw Muhammad' Shooting in Texas." TheIntercept.com. Retrieved from https://theintercept.com/2016/08/04/fbi-had-undercover-agent-at-scene-of -draw-muhammad-shooting-in-garland/.

Ekins, Emily. 2017. "The State of Free Speech and Tolerance in America." Washington, DC: CATO Institute. Retrieved from https://www.cato.org /survey-reports/state-free-speech-tolerance-am%C3%A9rica.

Irish, John. 2012. "At U.N., Muslim world questions Western freedom of speech." Reuters.com, September 28, 2012. Retrieved from https://www.reuters.com /article/us-un-assembly-islam/at-u-n-muslim-world-questions-western-free dom-of-speech-idUSBRE88R1JI20120929.

Khan, Wahiduddin. 2004. *Principles of Islam.* New Delhi, India: Goodword Books.

Saeed, Abdullah. 2011. "Ambiguities of Apostasy and the Repression of Muslim Dissent." *The Review of Faith & International Affairs* 9, no. 2 (Summer): 31–37.

Uddin, Asma T. 2011. "Blasphemy Laws in Muslim-Majority Countries." *The Review of Faith & International Affairs* 9, no. 2 (Summer): 47–55.

U.S. Commission on International Religious Freedom. 2017. "Respecting Rights? Measuring the World's Blasphemy Laws." Washington, DC: USCIRF. Retrieved from https://www.uscirf.gov/sites/default/files/Blasphemy%20Laws%20Report .pdf.

H

Hate Crimes

Hate crimes are defined as "crimes committed against persons or property that are motivated by the perpetrator's hatred or prejudice against the racial, ethnic, religious, or sexual identity of the victim" (Boyd et al. 1996, 819). These kinds of crimes oftentimes include "words or actions intended to harm or intimidate an individual because of his or her perceived membership in or association with a particular group" (Craig and Waldo 1996, 113). The term refers not simply to acts of violence but also to crimes involving the destruction of property, harassment, or trespassing (Green, McFalls, and Smith 2001, 481). "Hate crimes" was coined during the 1980s, as U.S. journalists and policy advocates searched for new terminology to describe the bigoted violence directed against Jews, blacks, and gays (Green, McFalls, and Smith 2001, 480).

Hate crimes against U.S. Muslims have skyrocketed in recent years. According to a study released in 2018 by the Council on American-Islamic Relations (CAIR), hate crimes targeting U.S. Muslims rose 15 percent in 2017, the second year of increases. In 2017, CAIR documented 300 hate crime incidents against U.S. Muslims, following a total number of 260 in 2016 and 180 in 2015 (Council on American-Islamic Relations 2018, 11). The FBI released a report that echoed the findings from the 2018 CAIR study. Hate crimes motivated by religion were the biggest category of hate crimes documented by the FBI in 2016, making up more than 20 percent of reported incidents (Federal Bureau of Investigation 2017). Muslim and Jewish people were the two most common targets in this category, with more than 24 percent and nearly 54 percent, respectively, of religiously motivated hate crimes committed against them. It also should be noted that hate crimes against U.S. Muslims are likely to be higher than the reported figures collected by anti–hate crime organizations. "While law enforcement

71

agencies in 49 states submit hate crime data to the FBI, and 38 states publish hate crime statistics in their own annual reports, the lack of state-level requirements for reporting, data collection, and law enforcement training contribute to systemic underreporting" (Arab American Institute 2018). U.S. Muslims are also said to underreport hate crimes because of a reluctance to interact directly with law enforcement.

Nationwide, anti-mosque activity in the United States is a form of hate crime experienced by U.S. Muslims. According to the American Civil Liberties Union (ACLU), at least 300 anti-mosque incidents have occurred across the country since 2005 (American Civil Liberties Union 2019). The states with 11 or more incidents since 2005 are California, Florida, Michigan, New Jersey, New York, Ohio, Texas, Virginia, and Washington. From January to July 2017, CNN mapped 63 publicly reported incidents in which mosques were targets of threats, vandalism, or arson. Several arson attacks on mosques were high-profile cases in the news. In January 2017 an arsonist set fire to the Victoria Islamic Center in Houston, Texas. The arsonist was convicted by the U.S. Department of Justice of using fire to commit a federal felony and sentenced to over 24 years in prison. In February 2017, a man who posted anti-Muslim rants before setting fire to a mosque in Fort Pierce, Florida, on the anniversary of the 9/11 attacks, was sentenced to 30 years in prison (Morlin 2017). Another arsonist was found guilty by the U.S. Department of Justice in March 2010 of vandalizing and burning down the Islamic Center of Columbia, Tennessee. According to the U.S. Department of Justice news release, the arsonist "committed the arson because of the religious character of the property" and "painted swastikas and the phrase 'White Power' on the mosque in the course of the arson." The news release also quoted Thomas E. Perez, the Assistant U.S. Attorney General for the Civil Rights decision: "The right to worship without fear of this kind of violent interference is among our most fundamental civil rights." These three incidents in Texas, Florida, and Tennessee are only scratching the surface of the number of attacks on U.S. Muslims' places of worship (Southern Poverty Law Center n.d.).

One of the more notable hate crimes perpetrated against U.S. Muslims occurred in Chapel Hill, North Carolina, on February 10, 2015. Three young U.S.-born Muslims—Deah Barakat (23), Yusor Abu-Salha (21), and Razan Abu-Salha (19)—were murdered "execution style" by Craig Stephen Hicks. Barakat was in his second year at the University of North Carolina–Chapel Hill School of Dentistry. His wife, Yusor Abu-Salha, also had plans to attend the School of Dentistry. Yusor's sister, Razan, was enrolled in the School of Design at North Carolina State University at the time of the hate crime. According to reports, Hicks committed the murders over repeated arguments relating to parking spots at an apartment complex in Chapel Hill, but social media posts were later revealed and showed that Hicks opposed all religions, particularly Islam. He had been charged with three counts of first-degree murder, but no federal charge on the grounds of "hate crimes" was brought against him. Since the murder of Barakat and the Abu-Salha sisters, Suzanne Barakat, the sister of Deah, has worked to "counter Islamophobia with her message of inclusivity, while sounding the alarm that unless we can stem the tide of hate, anyone labeled as 'other' faces the risk of violence" (National Public Radio 2016).

See also: Civil Rights; Islamophobia

Further Reading

American Civil Liberties Union. 2019. "Nationwide Anti-Mosque Activity." New York: ACLU. Retrieved from https://www.aclu.org/issues/national-security /discriminatory-profiling/nationwide-anti-mosque-activity.

Arab American Institute. 2018. "AAI Issue Brief: Hate Crimes." Washington, DC: Arab American Institute. Retrieved from http://www.aaiusa.org/aai_issue _brief_hate_crimes.

Boyd, Elizabeth A., Richard A. Berk, and Karl M. Hamner. 1996. "Motivated by Hatred or Prejudice: Categorization of Hate-motivated Crimes in Two Police Divisions." *Law & Society Review* 30, no. 4: 819–50.

Coleman, Nancy. 2017. "On average, 9 mosques have been targeted every month this year." CNN.com, August 7, 2017. Retrieved from https://www.cnn.com /2017/03/20/us/mosques-targeted-2017-trnd/index.html.

Council on American-Islamic Relations. 2018. "Targeted: 2018 Civil Rights Report." Washington, DC: Council on American-Islamic Relations. Retrieved from https://www.cairoklahoma.com/wp-content/uploads/2018/04/CAIR_2018 _Civil_Rights_Report.pdf.

Craig, Kellina M., and Craig R. Waldo. 1996. "'So, What's a Hate Crime Anyway?' Young Adults' Perceptions of Hate Crimes, Victims, and Perpetrators." *Law and Human Behavior* 20, no. 2 (April): 113–29.

Federal Bureau of Investigation. 2017. "2016 Hate Crime Statistics Revealed." Washington, DC: Federal Bureau of Investigation. Last modified November 13, 2017. Retrieved from https://www.fbi.gov/news/stories/2016-hate-crime -statistics.

Green, Donald P., Laurence H. McFalls, and Jennifer K. Smith. 2001. "Hate Crime: An Emergent Research Agenda." *Annual Review of Sociology* 27: 479–504.

Levin, Brian. 2016. "FBI: Hate Crime Went Up 6.8 Percent in 2015; Anti-Muslim Incidents Surge to Second Highest Ever." HuffPost.com, November 13, 2016. Retrieved from https://www.huffpost.com/entry/fbi-hate-crime-up-68-in-2_b _12951150.

Morlin, Bill. 2017. "Florida Man Gets 30 Years for Hate-Arson at Mosque." Birmingham, AL: Southern Poverty Law Center. Last modified February 2, 2017. Retrieved from https://www.splcenter.org/hatewatch/2017/02/07/florida -man-gets-30-years-hate-arson-mosque.

National Public Radio. 2016. "After a Horrible Hate Crime, How Do You Not Hate Back?" NPR.com, December 16, 2016. Retrieved from https://www.npr .org/2016/12/16/505579486/after-a-horrible-hate-crime-how-do-you-not -hate-back.

Southern Poverty Law Center. n.d. "Search Results: Arson Mosque." Birmingham, AL: SPLC. Retrieved from https://www.splcenter.org/search?keyword=arson +mosque.

Talbot, Margaret. 2015. "The Story of a Hate Crime." NewYorker.com, June 22, 2015. Retrieved from https://www.newyorker.com/magazine/2015/06/22/the -story-of-a-hate-crime.

Hijab

The Arabic term *hijab*, which translates roughly to "veil," refers to something that conceals, covers, or protects against penetration between two things. In the Qu'ran, the term *hijab* refers to a curtain used to separate the Prophet Muhammad and his wives from wedding guests, and thus the term refers to a boundary that creates space to protect one's honor (Mernissi 1987). As a Muslim woman's code of dress, *hijab* refers to a loose cloth or head-covering scarf worn by some women in public to cover her *'awrah,* an Arabic term denoting the parts of the body that should be covered (Solihu 2009, 26).

Muslim women are offered many types of *hijab* as the concept pertains to specific styles of Islamic clothing, as the BBC noted. The *hijab* is the most common type of headscarf worn by U.S. Muslim women. This garment covers the head and neck, but leaves the entirety of a women's face clear. The *shayla,* a garment that is wrapped around the head and pinned in place around the shoulders, is popular among Muslim women living in the Arabian/Persian Gulf. The *abaya,* a full-length garment, covers the entire body except the head, feet, and hands. The *niqab,* also a full-length garment, covers the entire body except for the area around a woman's eyes. The *burqa,* the most concealing of all *hijabs,* is a full-length garment the covers the entire body, including the eyes, which are covered by see-through mesh.

Hijab, too, is not an Islamic concept exclusive to women. Muslim men are obliged to observe *hijab* in their interactions with women and their clothing choices. As author and human rights activist Qasim Rashid noted in the *Independent,* the Qur'an addresses men first in relation to *hijab.* The Qur'an "commands men to not stare at women and not to be promiscuous." The Qur'an (24:30) obliges men to observe modesty: "Tell believing men to lower their gaze and remain chaste. That is purer for them. God is aware of what they do."

Today, *hijab* serves as part of the battleground for the perceived "clash of civilizations" between Western Christians and Muslims. *Hijab* is considered by some U.S. citizens to be a dangerous symbol that challenges a way of behaving that is considered normal in a contemporary secular society like the United States. *Hijab,* in this light, is considered to be a manifestation of inequality, because women wear it and men do not. This perception is influenced by the U.S. media and the stories it presents about the oppression of Muslim women around the world, including cases like the mistreatment of women in countries such as Saudi Arabia and Pakistan. Sociological research, however, shows that observing *hijab* is a practice that allows young U.S. Muslim women to create an autonomous cultural space for themselves with a public symbol that visibly repudiates the overly individualized culture of U.S. society. *Hijab* is, therefore, part of a larger identity construction process for U.S. Muslim women to negotiate their multiple identities as Americans and Muslims (Williams and Vashi 2007, 272). U.S. Muslim women also have been said to adopt *hijab* as a means to resist U.S. society's sexualized culture (Williams and Vashi 2007, 277).

Hijab is also adopted by Muslim women in the United States to achieve some distance from assimilating or "Westernizing" (Williams and Vashi 2007, 283). In a study of thirteen veiled U.S. Muslim women, participants inscribed *hijab* with various meanings, like functioning to define Muslim identity, performing "a behavior check, resisting sexual objectification, affording more respect, preserving intimate relationships, and providing freedom" (Droogsma 2007, 294). U.S. Muslim youth also are said to understand *hijab* as a public affirmation of trust in the U.S. political system that guarantees freedom of religion and freedom of speech (Haddad

2007, 253). Simultaneously, *hijab* also has become a symbol of anti-colonial solidarity and resistance to Islamophobic efforts to marginalize U.S. Muslims (Haddad 2007, 253).

Muslim women on U.S. soil have faced discrimination for observing *hijab* in the workplace. In 2008, the retail clothing chain Abercrombie & Fitch refused to hire Samantha Elauf because her headscarf violated the company's "look policy," which at the time prohibited employees from wearing head coverings (Levine 2015). The U.S. Supreme Court ruled in favor of Elauf in May 2015. Justice Antonin Scalia defended her by referring to Title VII of the Civil Rights Act of 1964, which demands that U.S. employers must reasonably accommodate a potential employees' religious beliefs without undue hardship to the employee (Levine 2015).

See also: Clash of Civilizations; Women's Rights

Further Reading

BBC. 2018. "What's the difference between a hijab, niqab and burka." BBC.com, August 7, 2018. Retrieved from https://www.bbc.co.uk/newsround/24118241.

Droogsma, Rachel Anderson. 2007. "Redefining Hijab: American Muslim Women's Standpoints on Veiling." *Journal of Applied Communication Research* 35, no. 3: 294–319.

Haddad, Yvonne Yazbeck. 2007. "The Post-9/11 Hijab as Icon." *Sociology of Religion* 68, no. 3: 253–67.

Levine, Marianne. (2015). "Supreme Court rules against Abercrombie in hijab case." Politico.com, June 1, 2015. Retrieved from https://www.politico.com /story/2015/06/ambercrombie-fitch-hijab-case-supreme-court-ruling-118492.

Mernissi, Fatima. 1987. *Women & Islam: An Historical and Theological Enquiry.* Oxford, UK: Basil Blackwell.

Rashid, Qasim. 2017. "Muslim men need to understand that the Quran says they should observe hijab first, not women." Independent.co.uk, March 29, 2017. Retrieved from https://www.independent.co.uk/voices/muslim-men-hijab -forcing-women-islam-teaching-mohammed-quran-modesty-a7655191.html.

Solihu, Abdul Kabir Hussain. 2009. "Making Sense of Hijab and Niqab in Contemporary Western Societies." *Intellectual Discourse* 17, no. 1: 25–41.

Williams, Rhys H., and Gira Vashi. 2007. "*Hijab* and American Muslim Women: Creating the Space for Autonomous Selves." *Sociology of Religion* 68, no. 3: 269–87.

Integration

Sociologists define the term "integration" as the state in which immigrants, migrants, and minority populations in a given community are incorporated into the larger social fabric and norms of the given society. Integration may be broken down further by describing it as a relational process in which various groups in a community or nation are able to harmoniously live side-by-side because of their cross-cultural and interreligious efforts to accommodate diversity, coordinate with one another, and unify under civic national principles.

Data from a 2017 Pew Research Center survey show that U.S. Muslims overwhelmingly embrace both the "American" and "Muslim" elements of their identity. The vast majority of U.S. Muslims told the Pew Research Center that they are proud to be American (92 percent), while nearly all of the survey respondents said they are proud to be Muslim (97 percent) (Pew Research Center 2017). About nine in ten (89 percent) polled also said they are proud to be *both* American and Muslim. Muslims, furthermore, are generally content with living in the United States. Four in five U.S. Muslims say they are satisfied with the way things are going in their lives, and six in ten say they have "a lot" in common with most U.S. citizens (Pew Research Center 2017).

Integration of U.S. citizens also is measured by levels of educational attainment and contributions made in the realm of higher learning. U.S. Muslims are one of the most educated minority religious populations in the country. On average, U.S. Muslims have about 14 years of total education, placing them third behind Hindus and Jews in terms of levels of educational attainment among religious populations outside of Christians. In 2016, the Pew Research Center found that roughly 39 percent of U.S. Muslims held at least a bachelor's degree from a four-year university.

Muslim women in the United States also are one of the most educated minority religious populations in the country. U.S. Muslim women hold more college or postgraduate degrees than Muslim men, and they are more likely to work in professional fields than women from most other minority religious populations (Yan 2015). Because of their higher levels of educational attainment, U.S. Muslims are more likely to be employed in higher-paying occupations. In comparison to the wider U.S. population, U.S. Muslims are as likely to report household incomes of $100,000 or more. Furthermore, at least 45 percent of U.S. Muslims report making at least $30,000 per year, a share that is approximately 36 percent higher than the rest of the U.S. population.

U.S. Muslims are also integrating into the political culture of the U.S. by adopting mainstream ideologies, political party identifications, and policy positions held by longer-settled U.S. citizens (Wilson and Nowrasteh 2015). The Council on American-Islamic Relations (CAIR) found in 2016 that more than one million U.S. Muslims were registered to vote in the 2016 elections, an all-time high number (Farivar 2016). Experts on the political integration of U.S. Muslims attribute this number to an increase in voter turnout activism at the local, state, and national levels.

The Institute for Social Policy and Understanding (ISPU) issued its annual report in May 2019, which revealed that U.S. Muslims overwhelmingly voted in favor of Democratic candidates. Three-quarters of U.S. Muslims (76 percent) cast their ballots for Democrats, a trend mirrored among U.S. Jews (69 percent) (Mogahed and Mahmood 2019). Nonetheless, the ISPU poll also revealed that only 73 percent of U.S. Muslim citizens are registered to vote. The voter registration gap is most pronounced among young U.S. Muslims between the ages of 18 and 29 years old, only 63 percent of whom report being registered to vote compared to 85 percent of their peers in the overall U.S. population (Mogahed and Mahmood 2019).

Polls also show, however, that U.S. Muslim politicians and candidates for political office are more likely to face backlash from U.S. voters on the grounds of objections toward the Islamic faith. According to Gallup, 40 percent of U.S. citizens in 2015 said that they would not support a "qualified" Muslim for president (Saad 2015). An earlier Pew Research Center poll from 2015 found similar results in that only 38 percent of U.S. citizens said that they would vote for a qualified Muslim candidate for president (Keeter and Kohut 2005).

One often hears talk of "Muslims *in* America" or "Islam *in* the United States." But as scholar Amir Hussain suggests in *Muslims and the Making of America,* this "brings up an image of two mutually exclusive realities" (Hussain 2016, 116). He continued, "Swapping the word *in* with *and* makes all the difference, because people are able to see the reality of their interconnectedness" (Hussain 2016, 116).

See also: Civil Rights; Freedom of Religion; Freedom of Speech; LGBTQ; Pluralism; Social Justice Activism; U.S. Founding Fathers

Further Reading

Considine, Craig. 2018. *Muslims in America: Examining the Facts.* Santa Barbara, CA: ABC-CLIO.

Farivar, Masood. 2016. "More Than 1 Million US Muslims Now Registered to Vote." VOANews.com, November 2, 2016. Retrieved from https://www.voanews .com/usa/us-politics/more-1-million-us-muslims-now-registered-vote.

Hussain, Amir. 2016. *Muslims and the Making of America.* Waco, TX: Baylor University Press.

Keeter, Scott, and Andrew Kohut. 2005. "American Public Opinion about Muslims in the U.S. and Abroad." In *Muslims in the United States: Identity, Influence, Innovation.* Washington, DC: Woodrow Wilson International Center for Scholars.

Mogahed, Dalia, and Azka Mahmood. 2019. "American Muslim Poll 2019: Predicting and Preventing Islamophobia." Washington, DC: Institute for Social Policy and Understanding. Last modified May 1, 2019. Retrieved from https://www.ispu.org/american-muslim-poll-2019-predicting-and-preventing -islamophobia/?fbclid=IwAR2BcRoFuUXJlJunv0Qvo-sX3D03CAlop W1CYoT_fH_zCVdx3hUvmJMFXK4.

Pew Research Center. 2017. "2. Identity, assimilation and community." Washington, DC: Pew Research Center. Last modified July 26, 2017. Retrieved from http:// www.pewforum.org/2017/07/26/identity-assimilation-and-community/.

Saad, Lydia. 2015. "Support for Nontraditional Candidates Varies by Religion." Gallup.com. Last modified June 24, 2015. Retrieved from https://news.gallup .com/poll/183791/support-nontraditional-candidates-varies-religion.aspx.

Wilson, Sam, and Alex Nowrasteh. 2015. "The Political Assimilation of Immigrants and Their Descendants." Washington, DC: CATO Institute. Last modified February 24, 2015. Retrieved from https://www.cato.org/publications/economic -development-bulletin/political-assimilation-immigrants-their-descendants.

Yan, Holly. 2015. "The Truth about Muslims in America." CNN.com, December 9, 2015. Retrieved from https://www.cnn.com/2015/12/08/us/muslims-in-america -shattering-misperception/index.html.

Islamophobia

Islamophobia is the commonly used term to summarize fear of, hostility toward, hatred of, and discrimination or prejudice against Muslims. Islamophobia is associated with other frequently referenced terms like anti-Islam, anti-Muslim, and anti-Muslim racism. Scholars believe that the origins of Islamophobia, as a sociological concept, is traced back to Edward Said, author of *Orientalism* (1978), a book that criticized Western civilization's patronizing depiction of "Islamic civilization" and the "Arab world." While Said did not specifically use the term "Islamophobia" in his book, he nevertheless had concluded that Westerners generally perceived Muslims and Arabs as inferior people who were prone to using violence as a means to dominate the world.

The term Islamophobia had been definitively used by the Runnymede Trust, a think tank and registered charity based in the United Kingdom. In their 1997 report "Islamophobia: A Challenge for Us All," the Trust welcomed several of the leading scholars of the Islamic faith to elaborate on the dynamics of the unfounded fear, closed-mindedness, and hatred of Muslims. The Runnymede Trust offered the following eight components to define Islamophobia:

1) Islam is seen as a monolithic bloc, static and unresponsive to change;
2) Islam is seen as separate and Other. It does not have values in common with other cultures, is not affected by them, and does not influence them;
3) Islam is seen as inferior to the West. It is barbaric, irrational, primitive, and sexist;
4) Islam is seen as violent, aggressive, threatening, supportive of terrorism, and engaged in a clash of civilizations;
5) Islam is seen as a political ideology and is used to acquire political or military advantage;
6) Criticism of the West by Muslims is rejected out of hand;
7) Hostility toward Islam is used to justify discriminatory practices toward Muslims and the exclusion of Muslims from mainstream society;
8) Anti-Muslim hostility is seen as natural or normal.

Since the publication of "Islamophobia: A Challenge for Us All," scholars have had to refine the eight components of Islamophobia.

The Islamophobia industry, as Nathan Lean popularized in his book *The Islamophobia Industry: How the Right Manufactures Fear of Muslims,* is a term that is used by experts to describe the right-wing network of bloggers, pundits, religious leaders, and politicians who work to convince U.S. citizens and residents that Muslims are the enemy of Western civilization (Lean 2012). This lucrative and influential network had access to at least $205 million in total earnings between 2008 and 2013 after having been funded by at least seven charitable foundations. The Council on American-Islamic Relations found that the inner core groups of the Islamophobia industry had access to at least $119,662,719 in total revenue between 2008 and 2011.

Despite the rhetoric coming out of the Islamophobia industry, the facts speak for themselves as they pertain to the lived experiences of U.S. Muslims. Anti-Muslim discrimination is widespread and increasing in the United States. According to the results of a far-reaching 2017 survey by the Pew Research Center, U.S. Muslims said that they faced a lot of discrimination—the share of U.S. Muslims polled who have experienced discriminatory treatment is trending upward, with at least 48 percent of respondents saying they were subjected to at least one discriminatory incident based on religion in 2016, compared with 40 percent a decade before (Pew Research Center 2017).

Islamophobia also can lead to job discrimination—in the hiring process as well as the workplace environment—for U.S. Muslims (Considine 2018, 147–52). Muslim physicians and clinicians across the United States reported in a 2014 national survey that they "experience[d] religious discrimination at work," particularly those for whom their Muslim identity is most pronounced and important (Padela et al. 2016, 149).

The problem of bullying, especially among Muslim youth, is an area of growing concern for Muslim parents, teachers, school administrators, and community members. Muslims in the United States are nearly twice as likely to report bullying among their school-age children as U.S. Jews (42 percent versus 23 percent), and four times as likely as the general public (10 percent) (Mogahed and Chouhoud 2017, 4). In 2012, the California chapter of the Council on American-Islamic Relations (CAIR-CA) issued the first statewide survey on U.S. Muslim youth experiences in school. The survey, which polled 471 U.S. Muslim students attending public school between the ages of 11 and 18, found the majority of school-related cases reported to CAIR involved teacher discrimination. More than 10 percent of students reported physical bullying such as slapping, kicking, or punching, and female respondents who observed *hijab* reported being bullied at least once because of this. Furthermore, and perhaps most importantly, 50 percent of the Muslim youth polled by CAIR reported being subjected to mean comments and rumors about them because of their Islamic faith (Council on American-Islamic Relations 2012, 2–3).

Various forms of bullying and other forms of discrimination also result in mental health challenges for Muslim youth as well as Muslim adults living in the United States. In a study on discrimination and psychological distress among U.S. Muslims, Goleen Samari found that Islamophobia negatively influences health by disrupting several systems, including the individual (stress reactivity and identity concealment), the interpersonal (social relationships and socialization processes), and the structural (institutional policies and media coverage) (Samari 2016).

According to Khaled A. Beydoun, law professor and critical race theorist, the concept of "dialectical Islamophobia" is useful in discussions on the relationship between government policy and anti-Muslim prejudice and discrimination. Beydoun defined "dialectical Islamophobia" as a form of government action that "legitimizes misconceptions, misrepresentations, and stereotypes of Islam," which in turn "communicates damaging ideas through state-sponsored policy, programming, or rhetoric" (Beydoun 2018). The result of these governmental policies is private violence against Muslims and those who are perceived to be Muslims.

See also: Clash of Civilizations; *Dhimmi*; Hate Crimes; *Jihad*; *Jizya*; Muslim Travel Ban and Immigration Policies; *Sharia*; *Taqiyya*

Further Reading

Allen, Chris. 2010. *Islamophobia*. Farnham, UK: Ashgate.

Beydoun, Khaled A. 2018. *American Islamophobia: Understanding the Roots and Rise of Fear*. Oakland: University of California Press.

Bleich, Erik. 2011. "What Is Islamophobia and How Much Is There? Theorizing and Measuring an Emerging Comparative Concept." *American Behavioral Scientist* 20: 1–20.

Chandrasekhar, Charu A. 2003. "Flying while Brown: Federal Civil Rights Remedies to Post-9/11 Airline Racial Profiling of South Asians." *Asian American Legal Journal* 10: 21552.

Considine, Craig. 2018. *Muslims in America: Examining the Facts*. Santa Barbara, CA: ABC-CLIO.

Council on American-Islamic Relations. 2012. "Growing in Faith: California Muslim Youth Experiences with Bullying, Harassment & Religious Accommodation in Schools." Santa Clara, Sacramento, Anaheim, and San Diego, CA: CAIR. Retrieved from https://ca.cair.com/sfba/wp-content/uploads/sites/10/2018/04/GrowingInFaith.pdf?x93160.

Lean, Nathan. 2012. *The Islamophobia Industry: How the Right Manufactures Fear of Muslims*. London: Pluto Press.

Mogahed, Dalia, and Youssef Chouhoud. 2017. *American Muslim Poll 2017: Full Report*. Washington, DC: Institute for Social Policy and Understanding. Retrieved from https://www.ispu.org/american-muslim-poll-2017/.

Padela, Aasim I., Huda Adam, Maha Ahmad, Zahra Hosseinian, and Farr Curlin. 2016. "Religious identity and workplace discrimination: A national survey of American Muslim physicians." *AJOB Empirical Bioethics* 7, no. 3: 149–59.

Pew Research Center. 2017. "U.S. Muslims Concerned about Their Place in Society, but Continue to Believe in the American Dream." Washington, DC: Pew Research Center. Last modified July 26, 2017. Retrieved from http://www.pewforum.org/2017/07/26/findings-from-pew-research-centers-2017-survey-of-us-muslims/.

Runnymede Trust. 1997. "Islamophobia: A Challenge for Us All." TheRunnymede Trust.org. Retrieved from http://www.runnymedetrust.org/uploads/publications/pdfs/islamophobia.pdf.

Said, Edward. 1978. *Orientalism*. New York: Pantheon Books.

Samari, Goleen. 2016. "Islamophobia and Public Health in the United States." *American Journal of Public Health* 106, no. 11: 1920–25.

J

Jesus and Mary

Jesus, or *Isa,* as he is known in Arabic, is recognized and embraced as one of the most significant prophets and messengers of God according to the Qur'an. The Qur'an defines Jesus by several phrases including the *Ru Min Allah,* the Arabic phrase for "Spirit of God"; *Mushia Bi'l Baraka,* or "the Messiah—someone blessed by God"; *Kalimah Min Allah,* or "Word from/ of God"; and *Rasul,* or "Prophet/Messenger of God." A Muslim cannot be a Muslim in a strict sense if a person does not accept Jesus as a prophet of God.

The Qur'an explains that Jesus was born of the Virgin Mary (Qur'an 19:20–21), destined to "speak to the people in cradle and in maturity" (Qur'an 3:46), and is "high honored in this world and the next one" (Qur'an 3:45). Jesus is mentioned 25 times in the Qur'an, compared to only four mentions of Muhammad. Just as with other prophets, Muslims typically say, "*as-salamu 'alaikum,*" the Arabic term for "peace be upon him," every time they refer to Jesus. Like Christians, Muslims believe that Jesus will return on the Day of Judgment to annihilate *ad-dajjal,* or the anti-Christ. Muhammad, the prophet of Islam, spoke highly about the life and legacy of Jesus: "Whoever loves Jesus and me receives a double blessing."

While Jesus is revered as a prophet and messenger of God's word by Muslims worldwide, there are important distinctions regarding Jesus's divinity in the Christian and Islamic traditions. Firstly, Muslims do not worship Jesus as Christians do. Jesus is considered to be the "Son of God" by most Christians around the world, but Muslims refer to him as simply a "prophet" or even more simply as a human being. The Qur'an recognizes the miracles that Jesus performed in his life, but the Qur'an does not ascribe these miracles to his divinity. The Qur'an also appears to deny the popular Christian belief that Jesus was crucified and resurrected. Instead, the Qur'an claims that God took Jesus up into heaven by Himself. For Christians, Jesus died for the sins of humankind and ascended into heaven.

The Qur'an (4:157–58), on the other hand, reveals that Jesus did not die and had not been crucified: "They did not kill him, nor did they crucify him, but it only seemed to them [as if it had been so]. And those who differ in this matter are in doubt concerning it. They have no definite knowledge about it, but only follow mere conjecture. But they certainly did not kill him. God raised him towards Himself. God is almighty and wise." While Jesus is revered as *Rasul Allah,* or the "Messenger of God," in the Qur'an, *Surah Maryam* rejects that idea that Jesus is the son of God. Jesus's affiliation to Mary, his mother, is meant to honor him and to demonstrate his exalted status in the Qur'an.

Mary herself also is honored in the Qur'an because of who she was on her own. Mary, or *Maryam* in Arabic, is the only woman in the Qur'an to have an entire *surah,* or chapter, of the Qur'an named after her, thus making her the only female figure to hold such an esteemed position. Surah 19 in the Qur'an, named *Maryam,* has 98 verses and begins with the miraculous birth of Jesus, her son, as well as the birth of their cousin, John the Baptist. Mary is mentioned more times—34, to be exact—in the Qur'an than in the New Testament. According to the Qur'an, God had chosen Mary: "The angels said, 'Mary, God has selected you over [all] women of your time'" (Qur'an 3:42). Mary is described in the Qur'an as the most sanctified woman holding the most exalted spiritual position among women. As noted in the Study Qur'an, "other female figures are identified only by their relation to others, such as the wife of Adam and the mother of Moses, or by their title, such as the Queen of Sheba."

The 19th chapter of the Qur'an recognizes the foundational miracle of Christianity—the Virgin Birth—by explaining that the Angel Gabriel visited Mary, who asked how she could bear a son if no man had ever touched her. The Qur'an (19:16–22) affirmed the New Testament's view of Mary's miraculous pregnancy:

Recount in the Book how Mary withdrew from her people to an eastern place and kept herself in seclusion from them. We sent her Our angel, who presented himself to her as a full-grown human being. When she saw him, she said, "I seek refuge in the compassionate God from you;

[do not come near] if you fear the Lord." "I am only the messenger of your Lord," he replied. "I shall bestow upon you the gift of a son endowed with purity." She said, "How can I have a son when no man has touched me; and neither have I been unchaste?" [The angel] replied, "So shall it be; your Lord says, 'This is easy for me; and We shall make him a sign to people and a blessing, from Us.' This has been decreed." So she conceived him and withdrew with him to a distant place.

U.S. Muslims honor Jesus and Mary by dedicating their *masjids* in their name. The Northshore Masjid Isa Ibn Maryam (the "mosque of Jesus and Mary") is located in the Cloverleaf neighborhood in Houston, Texas. Another *masjid* in the Houston area is named the Maryam Islamic Center, which was founded in Sugar Land in 2003.

For U.S. Muslims and Muslims worldwide, there are few figures quite as important as Jesus, hence why some Muslims in the United States celebrate the holiday of Christmas, the annual festival day commemorating the birth of Jesus, though it should be made clear that the majority of Muslims in the United States do not (Ali-Karamali 2015). U.S. Muslims may celebrate the birth of Jesus for a number of reasons, among them having love for Jesus and an interest in partaking in the festive holiday spirit.

See also: Abrahamic Tradition

Further Reading

Akyol, Mustafa. 2017. *The Islamic Jesus: How the King of the Jews Became a Prophet of the Muslims*. New York: St. Martin's Press.

Al-Jerrahi, Muzaffer Ozak. 1991. *Blessed Virgin Mary*. Westport, CT: Pir Publications.

Ali-Karamali, Sumbul. 2015. "Merry Christmas from My Muslim Family to Yours— Whatever Your Religion (Or Not)." The Huff Post, December 16, 2015. Retrieved from https://www.huffingtonpost.com/sumbul-alikaramali/merry-christmas-from -my-muslim-family_b_8814068.html?ncid=engmodushpmg00000003&fbclid =IwAR0hFRvgKxhTjZYWG_kFZtvWTcyjCD67kqngXQIBWvRxNjYV8JWm Kfnaek0.

Khalidi, Tarif. 2001. *The Muslim Jesus: Sayings and Stories in Islamic Literature*. London: Harvard University Press.

Parrinder, Geoffrey. 2013. *Jesus in the Qur'an: Makers of the Muslim World*. London: Oneworld Publications.

Siddiqui, Mona. 2014. *Christians, Muslims, and Jesus*. New Haven, CT: Yale University Press.

Jihad

Jihad is an Arabic word and Islamic concept that is frequently associated with "violence" and "terrorism" in the United States and around the world. A closer examination of the term, however, presents a different picture. The word *jihad* literally means "striving" or putting forward effort to overcome a struggle, whether it be a struggle with the ego, the body, or a larger societal conflict like inequality, corruption, or war. This form of struggle or *jihad* may also more broadly relate to the challenge of following the Five Pillars of Islam as well as the teachings of the Prophet Muhammad.

Jihad does not mean "holy war." In fact, the Islamic tradition does not have any notion of "holy war" in the literal sense. The actual word for "war" in Arabic is *qital,* not *jihad.* The Qur'an and *ahadith* also use the Arabic word *harb* to denote war. With that said, the Qur'an is clear that war is permitted, but strictly for defensive purposes: "Permission to fight is granted to those who are attacked, because they have been wronged— God indeed has the power to help them—they are those who have been driven out of their homes injustly, only because they said, 'Our Lord is God'" (Qur'an 22:39–40). Making war with communities or nations who offer peace to Muslims also is forbidden: "He does not forbid you to deal kindly and justly with anyone who has not fought you on account of your faith or driven you out of your homes: God loves the just" (Qur'an 60:8).

Muslims are permitted to physically defend the right to practice their faith, but they must engage in "just war." Declaring a "just war" in an Islamic context must be guided by specific rules of engagement that require the protection of life. The Prophet Muhammad outlined ten rules that of engagement when fighting is permitted:

> O people! I charged you with ten rules; learn them well . . . for your guidance in the battlefield! Do not commit treachery, or deviate from the right path. You must not mutilate dead bodies. Neither kill a child, nor a woman, nor an aged man. Bring no harm to the trees, nor burn them with fire, especially those which are fruitful. Slay not any of the enemy's flock, save for your food. You are likely to pass by people who have devoted their lives to monastic services; leave them alone.

The Prophet Muhammad referred to warfare as the "lesser *jihad*" (*jihad-e-ashgar*). The "lesser *jihad*" allows the use of physical violence or war, but only to prevent the enemies of Muslims from impinging on their homeland or human right to practice their religion freely. On the other hand, the Prophet Muhammad referred to a higher form of struggle— *jihad-a-akbar,* or "the greater *jihad*"—as the personal struggle to improve one's self by cleansing the heart, mind, and body of harmful urges, ideas, and desires, such as arguing with others, being angry, or focusing too much on wealth and greed. The greater *jihad* is mentioned in a *hadith* that explains a party of the Prophet Muhammad's companions as they returned from a military expedition. Muhammad addressed his companions by saying, "Now we are returning from a lesser *jihad* to a greater *jihad.*" When the companions asked him the meaning of the greater *jihad,* Muhammad responded clearly: "The *jihad* of an individual against his inner self."

Activists, think tanks, and politicians have erroneously argued that *jihad* training camps exist on U.S. soil. In a campaign rally in 2015, Republican presidential candidate Donald Trump said that he was "going to look at [*jihad* camps]" after a rally attendee said that President Barack Obama was a Muslim and that "[The United States has] training camps, growing, they [Muslims] want to kill us" (Bump 2015). The conspiracy theory surrounding the existence of *jihad* camps on U.S. soil centers around the Jamaat Ul-Fuqra, a Muslim group that conspiracy theorists say conducts terrorist training activities across the country. The Jamaat Ul-Fuqra is known for its "headquarters" in Islamberg, a hamlet within the town of Tompkins, New York, that is populated predominantly by African American Muslims. Islamberg is located on 70 acres of land in the western Catskill Mountains and has been the home to approximately 200 African Americans for the last several decades. The claim that Islamberg serves as the breeding ground of a *jihad* camp has been disproven by journalists, law enforcement officials, and the U.S. intelligence community (Considine 2018, 91–95). Local Sheriff Deputy Craig Dumont, for example, called the accusations against the Jamaat Ul-Fuqra "perplexing," and added, "We just don't find any of that to be valid. . . . There are no active threats."

Nonetheless, in January 2019, four men were arrested after the Federal Bureau of Investigation (FBI) found that they were plotting to attack the residents of Islamberg with homemade bombs and an arsenal of assault weapons. Three of the four individuals were charged with three counts of first-degree criminal possession of a deadly weapon and one count of fourth-degree conspiracy to carry out an act of terrorism. A few years earlier, in 2014, a federal grand jury returned a one-count indictment charging a Tennessee minister and former candidate for the House of Representatives,

Robert Doggart, "with soliciting another person to violate federal civil rights laws by burning down a mosque in Islamberg" (U.S. Department of Justice 2015). An official news release of the New York chapter of the Council on American-Islamic Relations (CAIR), the United States's leading civil rights and advocacy organization for legal matters pertaining to the experiences of U.S. Muslims, called on federal law enforcement authorities to bring charges against three men and a teenager who planned to attack the Islamberg Muslim community.

U.S. Muslims and anti-Muslim activists clashed in 2013 over the public use of the word *jihad*. The *New York Times* referred to the clash as an "advertising war" that pitted CAIR against the American Freedom Defense Initiative (AFDI), a hate group run by Pamela Geller, whom the Southern Poverty Law Center calls "the anti-Muslim movement's most visible and flamboyant figurehead" (Southern Poverty Law Center n.d.). The CAIR-Chicago chapter promoted nonviolent meanings of the word—"to struggle"—on buses. Supporters were determined to reclaim the definition with the ad campaign called My *Jihad* (Yaccino and Teng 2013). The AFDI responded by mimicking the My *Jihad* ads. The group featured photos and quotations from figures like Osama bin Laden and groups like Hamas, the Palestinian organization in the occupied territory of Gaza that the U.S. government declared a "terrorist organization." "Killing Jews is worship that draws us closer to *Allah*," says one ad, attributing the quotation to a Hamas television station. The ad ended with the statement: "That's his *jihad*. What's yours?" (Yaccino and Teng 2013).

Ahmed Rehab, the founder of the My *Jihad* campaign and former executive director of CAIR-Chicago, explained the meaning of the public advertisements: "It is also about pushing for an intelligent and informed understanding of Islam and its concepts and practices in the media, the educational circles and the public." Most of all, Rehab continued, the campaign is about "giving voice to our views, our practices, and simply put, our reality, a reality that is too big to be left out of the conversation" (*Huffington Post* 2012).

See also: Clash of Civilizations; Countering Violent Extremism (CVE); The Prophet Muhammad

Further Reading

Ahmad, Bashir. 2017. *The Life & Character of the Seal of the Prophets: Volume III*. Surrey, UK: Islam International Publications.

Bump, Philip. 2015. "Donald Trump and the 'terrorist training camps' conspiracy theory, explained." WashingtonPost.com, September 18, 2016. Retrieved from https://www.washingtonpost.com/news/the-fix/wp/2015/09/18/donald-trump -and-the-terrorist-training-camps-conspiracy-theory-explained/?utm_term =.c55f86d52c73.

Considine, Craig. 2018. *Muslims in America: Examining the Facts*. Santa Barbara, CA: ABC-CLIO.

El Fadl, Khaled A. 2002. *The Place of Tolerance in Islam*. Boston: Beacon Press.

Esack, Farid. 2002. *Qur'an, Liberation and Pluralism: An Islamic Perspective of Interreligious Solidarity against Oppression*. Oxford, UK: Oneworld.

Huffington Post. 2012. "'My Jihad' Bus Ads Debut in Chicago." HuffingtonPost .com, December 14, 2012. Retrieved from https://www.huffpost.com/entry/my -jihad-bus-ads-debut-in_n_2303222.

Khan, Wahiduddin Khan. 2008. *The True Jihad. The Concepts of Peace, Tolerance and Non-Violence in Islam*. New Delhi: Goodword Books.

Lumbard, Joseph E. 2008. *Submission: Faith & Beauty*. Berkeley, CA: Zaytuna Institute.

Southern Poverty Law Center. n.d. "Pamela Geller." Montgomery, AL: SPLC. Retrieved from https://www.splcenter.org/fighting-hate/extremist-files/individ ual/pamela-geller.

U.S. Department of Justice. 2015. "Chattanooga, Tennessee, Man Charged with Solicitation to Burn Down a Mosque in Islamberg, New York." Washington, DC: U.S. Department of Justice. Last modified July 7, 2015. Retrieved from https:// www.justice.gov/opa/pr/chattanooga-tennessee-man-charged-solicitation-burn -down-mosque-islamberg-new-york.

Yaccino, Steven, and Poh Si Teng. 2013. "Using Billboards to Stake Claim Over 'Jihad.'" NYTimes.com, March 6, 2013. Retrieved from https://www.nytimes .com/2013/03/07/us/ad-campaigns-fight-it-out-over-meaning-of-jihad.html.

Jizya

The term *jizya* is similar to Islamic concepts such as *sharia, jihad,* and *dhimmi* in the sense that these terms are often misunderstood and used by anti-Muslim polemicists to further demonize Muslims in the United States. *Jizya* is translated from Arabic to mean a special "tax" imposed on religious minority populations by an "Islamic state." This kind of tax is a yearly tax that guarantees groups like Jews and Christians several things like physical safety, protection of families and property, exemption from serving in the military, and fighting in war. Anti-Islam critics use the *jizya* as a means to denigrate U.S. Muslims and paint the population as a "fifth column" or enemy group trying to destroy the United States from within. Hate-group leader Pamela Geller, for example, said in December 2014 that President Barack Obama's defense of the civil rights of U.S. Muslims amounted to the imposition of the *jizya* (Tashman 2014). Geller also accused the U.S. Department of Justice of morphing into the "de-facto legal arm of many of these Muslim Brotherhood groups in the [United States]."

Some Muslim groups share the same understanding of the *jizya* as Geller. Daesh, commonly referred to as the Islamic State of Iraq and Syria (ISIS), claimed that it recognized Christian communities under their territorial control as long as Christians paid the *jizya*. According to *Dabiq*, Daesh's propaganda magazine, Christians are to be referred to as "pagans" rather than "People of the Book." *Dabiq* also stated that Muslims are commanded to "break crosses," oppress priests, and destroy churches in its realm. In late August 2016, Christian leaders from the Middle East traveled to Italy in an effort to raise awareness of the plight of Christians under Daesh rule. In meetings with politicians from Western countries, the Christian leaders described Daesh's alleged use of the *jizya* as "propaganda to add theological legitimacy to the group by linking it to the practices of historical caliphates, when, in fact, it is merely just another desperate attempt to fund their cult" (De Pulford 2016).

The implementation of the *jizya* is guided by the *sharia* as outlined in Islamic holy texts. The *jizya* is mentioned in the Qur'an (9:29), which reads as follows: "Fight those from among the People of the Book who believe neither in God, nor in the Last Day, nor hold as unlawful what God and His Messenger have declared to be unlawful, nor follow the true religion, until they pay the tax willingly and agree to submit." According to critics, Qur'an 9:29 is a badge of dishonor and embarrassment for the *kafir* or the "non-believers," and punishes non-Muslims who are not willing to convert to the Islamic faith. Other critics argue that this verse calls on Muslims to physically fight Jews, Christians, and religious minority populations wherever they find them.

The historical and political context of Qur'an 9:29 sheds further light on the necessity of such a verse. At the time of the verse's revelation the Prophet Muhammad was engaged in a conflict with the Ghassanids, an Arab Christian state of the Byzantine Empire. Sharhabeel Ibn Amir Al-Ghassani, the governor of Al-Balqa and close ally to the emperor of the Byzantine Empire, had assassinated Al-Hartih Ibn Umair Al-Azdi, a companion who was sent by the Prophet Muhammad to deliver a letter to the ruler of Busra.

The *jizya* proclaimed in Qur'an 9:29 is, therefore, a distinct response to aggression by a powerful Christian figure of the Byzantine Empire.

The Prophet Muhammad made it clear in his diplomatic endeavors with Christians that the *jizya* is not to be enforced if Christians are unable to afford the tax. These diplomatic endeavors are recorded in a series of covenants with various Christian communities and nations of his time. In the Covenant with the Christians of Mount Sinai, Persia, and Najran, Muhammad made it clear that Muslims are not to exact from Christians more money than they are able to pay. Rather, the Prophet commanded Muslims to "adjust matters with their consent, without force or violence." Even if the *jizya* was collected, it was to be used by Muslim leaders for the betterment of the "public good" (Considine 2016, 10). The Covenant with the Christians of Persia and the Covenant with the Christians of Najran record nearly identical passages in relation to enforcing the *jizya*. Furthermore, Muslim leaders who followed the Prophet Muhammad also waived the *jizya* contract. Suraqah Ibn 'Amir waived it for the Armenians, and so did Habib Ibn Maslaman Al-Fihri when he waived the *jizya* contract from the people of Antakya. The *jizya* was also waived by Abu 'Ubayida ibn al Jarrah from the people of a city that is located in Al-Jarajemah, located on the Turkish-Syria border.

See also: Abrahamic Tradition; *Dhimmi*

Further Reading

Abdel Haleem, M.A.S. 2012. "The *jizya* Verse (Q. 9:29): Tax Enforcement on Non-Muslims in the First Muslim State." *Journal of Qur'anic Studies* 14, no. 2: 72–89.

Considine, Craig. 2016. "Religious Pluralism and Civic Rights in a 'Muslim Nation': An Analysis of Prophet Muhammad's Covenants with Christians." *Religions* 7, no. 15: 1–21.

De Pulford, Luke. 2016. "Islamic State's 'Jizya tax' for Christians is pure propaganda." Blogs.Spectator.co.uk, September 5, 2016. Retrieved from https://blogs.spectator.co.uk/2016/09/islamic-states-jizya-tax-christians-pure-propaganda/.

El Fadel, Khaled Abou. 2002. *The Place of Tolerance in Islam.* Boston: Beacon Press.

Oxford Dictionary of Islam. n.d. "Jizya." Oxford, UK: Oxford University. Retrieved from http://www.oxfordislamicstudies.com/article/opr/t125/e1206.

Tashman, Brian. 2014. "Geller: Obama Imposing Islamic Jizya Tax on Non-Muslim Americans." RightWingWatch.org, December 15, 2014. Retrieved from http://www.rightwingwatch.org/post/geller-obama-imposing-islamic-jizya-tax-on-non-muslim-americans/.

L

Latin American Muslims

Like African Americans in the early and middle 1900s, Latin people are rediscovering their own historical and cultural ties to "Islamic civilization." Latin Americans are the fastest growing segment of the overall U.S. Muslim population as of 2019. By embracing Islam, as author Hisham Aidi noted on Al Jazeera, Latin people are reclaiming the history of "Muslim Spain," popularly referred to as Al-Andalus, stripped from them by slavery and imperialism (Aidi 2016). For more than 800 years during the Middle Ages, Muslims ruled Spain and made the Iberian Peninsula one of the most advanced civilizations of the time. The civilization that developed over this period is one that saw Jews, Christians, and Muslims flourishing side by side, tolerating one another, borrowing from one another's cultures and religions, and meshing together art, architecture, and political concepts to create a productive and positive society. Today, more than 4,000 words in the Spanish language are said to have roots in the Arabic language, and Latin Muslims value the extended family and Islamic traditions like offering hospitality to strangers.

In one of the first ever, large-scale studies on Latin Muslims throughout the United States, scholar Gastón Espinosa surveyed 560 Latin Muslims. While Espinosa cautions that the survey results should not be generalized to the entire U.S. Latin Muslim population, he did find that Latin Muslims on U.S. soil are developing a complex, combinative, and variegated form of "Latino Islamidad" (Latin Islamic identity), which is shaped by the high percentage of recent converts, an Islamic *tahwid* (the Arabic term for "oneness") centered spirituality, the history of "Islamic Spain," the concept of reversion, and the promotion of racial equality and charity (Espinosa, Morales, and Galvan 2017, 43). The survey also found that "the belief in monotheism, desire for a more direct experience of God, the concept of reversion back to their pre-Catholic Hispanic identity, and connection to a Muslim friend play major roles in conversion" processes. Moreover, the survey found that "marriage plays a statistically smaller role and that prison does not play a significant role in the way in which most Latin Muslims are first introduced to Islam" (Espinosa, Morales, and Galvan 2017, 43).

American Muslims trace their population's roots to the 1920s. Early converts to the Islamic faith were primarily found in African American–majority Muslim communities in urban environments, though there were some others who entered the faith through ties to Muslim immigrants (Bowen 2013). One of the earliest references to Latin Muslims in the United States came in a 1929 issue of the Moorish Science Temple's bimonthly periodical, the *Moorish Guide*. Juanita Richardson-Bey is listed as the managing editor and the secretary-treasurer of the Young People's Moorish League (Bowen 2010, 400). The U.S. Ahmadiyya periodical, *The Moslem Sunrise,* also documents several early Latin American converts to the Islamic faith. Thirteen people with "Latino/a-type names" (seven females and six males to be specific) living in the United States are listed among the new converts named between 1921 and 1924, with the earliest-listed person having converted sometime during 1920 (Bowen 2010, 402). The most notable of these converts were "Mr. and Mrs. Alberto" from Tampa Bay, Florida, who were praised in multiple issues for their zealous proselytizing efforts (Bowen 2010, 402). Another literary reference to Latin American Muslims occurs in Puerto Rican poet Piri Thomas's memoir *Down These Mean Streets* (1967), a book about growing up in Spanish Harlem, New York City, in the 1930s and 1940s (Aidi 2016).

Scholars have found that Latin Americans have converted to Islam in U.S. prisons and continue to convert in prisons across the country. While there are no precise figures to pinpoint exactly how many Latino/as have converted to Islam, there are numerous historical and contemporary examples to document. Piri Thomas, the Harlem-born son of Puerto Rican and Cuban parents, converted in prison around the early 1950s after becoming involved with the Nation of Islam (NOI) at Comstock Prison (Bowen 2010, 405). On the other side of the country in Oakland, California, a 24-year-old Puerto Rican named Benjamin Perez became a member of an NOI mosque (Bowen 2010, 405). More recent stories include Efrain Diaz, a Mexican American and native of Brighton Park, Illinois, who was caught up in gang activity and decided to convert to the Islamic faith in a jail cell while facing drug charges.

The conversion of Latin people to the Islamic faith in prison, however, should not be taken as proof that these conversions happen only behind bars. This is a common stereotype about Latin Muslim conversion. The facts paint a different picture. According to Gastón Espinosa's survey research of Latin Muslims, only 4 percent of Latino/as embrace Islam because of a prison ministry, prisoner reentry, or rehabilitation programs.

One of the earliest Latin Muslim groups to appear in the United States was the Bani Sakr, which Puerto Ricans formed in Newark, New Jersey, in the mid-1970s. Bani Sakr was influenced by the Nation of Islam, the Black Nationalist Movement, and Hajj Hisham Jaber, who led Malcolm X's funeral prayer (Aidi 2016). In 1975, the leadership of the Bani Sakr joined the Islamic Party of North America, a Washington, DC–based organization that expressed the Islamic faith through civic engagement, poverty prevention, and socio-economic justice. An article by Ramon Francisco Ocasio, the co-founder of the Alianza Islámica, noted that Bani Sakr members became part of a pan-Latin group representing Muslims from Brazil, Costa Rica, Panama, and Puerto Rico in 1979.

Also in the 1970s, the Alianza Islámica was created in East Harlem by a small group of Puerto Rican converts. According to the Alianza Islámica website, a group of Puerto Rican teens went on to create the United States's first Spanish-language mosque and Latin-specific Islamic organization (Alianza Islámica Organization n.d.). The Alianza also had an activist mission and provided social services as well as neighborhood security. According to Ibrahim Gonzáles, one of the leaders of Alianza Islámica, some Latin people are attracted to the Islamic faith because "within Islam there [is] every spectrum of people, regardless of class, regardless of race . . . we [are] attracted to that universal principle of human interaction and communion with the divine" (Castillo 2003).

Centro Islámico, an Islamic center in Houston, Texas, is among the first Latin Muslim communities to organize since the creation of Alianza Islámica. The interior of Centro Islámico is decorated with motifs that echo the striped arches of La Mezquita de Córdoba, a 10th-century mosque still standing in southern Spain (Schuessler 2016). IslamInSpanish, the organization that founded Centro Islámico, is an educational nonprofit 501(c)(3) organization that was established out of the need to educate Latin people about the Islamic faith in the Spanish language after the 9/11 attacks (IslamInSpanish n.d.). The founder of IslamInSpanish, Jaime "Mujahid" Fletcher, is a second-generation Colombian American convert. Fletcher embraced the Islamic faith approximately two months before

9/11. He has helped to bring hundreds of people into the fold of Islam. Fletcher, however, is adamant in stressing that IslamInSpanish's mission is not to convert people to the faith. In an interview with Good.is, Fletcher stated, "We're not pushing an agenda to convert people because that's not what we do. We basically educate people [who are interested], especially when they learn that Islam ties back into their roots" (Sager 2017).

César Dominguez is another leader among Latin Muslims in the United States. The Los Angeles–based Mexican American grew up in Tijuana, Mexico, but returned to California as an adult. As of 2019, Dominguez serves as the *imam* of the nonprofit group La Asociación Latino Musulmana de América (LALMA). Dominguez teaches weekly Qur'an and Islamic studies classes in Spanish at the Omar Ibn Al-Khattab Mosque, located in downtown Los Angeles near the University of Southern California (Sager 2017). The LALMA is an organization that was created in 1999 to share more Islamic resources in the Spanish language. The co-founder of LALMA, Marta Felicitas Ramirez de Galedary, is a nurse who also currently works with the Muslim Anti-Racism Collaborative, or Muslim ARC. According to its website, LALMA "promotes a better understanding of Islam to the Spanish speaking community and establishes a forum of spiritual nurturing and social support to Latino Muslims, building bridges among the monotheistic community and advocating for social justice in accordance with Islamic values." In addition to providing resources for people to learn more about Islam, LALMA provides several critical programs including a CPR course, first aid treatment, community safety programs, teen counseling, and interfaith initiatives.

See also: Converts; *Ummah*

Further Reading

Alianza Islámica Organization. n.d. "About: Alianza Islámica: Islam in the Barrio." Alianza Islámica. Retrieved from http://alianzaislamica.org/about.

Aidi, Hisham. 2016. "Latino Muslims are part of US religious landscape." AlJazeera .com, February 3, 2016. Retrieved from https://www.aljazeera.com/indepth/opin ion/2016/02/latino-muslims-part-religious-landscape-160202081705201.html.

Bowen, Patrick D. 2010. "Early U.S. Latina/o-African-American Muslim Connections: Paths to Conversion." *The Muslim World* 100 (October): 390–413.

Bowen, Patrick D. 2013. "U.S. Latina/o Muslims Since 1920: From 'Moors' to 'Latino Muslims.'" *Journal of Religious History* 37, no. 2: 165–84.

Castillo, A. Mario. 2003. "Are There More José Padillas To Come?" HispanicMuslims
.com. Last modified June 11, 2003. Retrieved from http://www.hispanicmuslims
.com/articles/arethere.html.

Espinosa, Gaston, Harold Morales, and Juan Galvan. 2017. "Latino Muslims in the
United States: Reversion, Politics, and Islamidad." *Journal of Race, Ethnicity,
and Religion* 8, no. 1 (June): 1–48.

Galvan, Juan. 2017. *Latino Muslims: Our Journeys to Islam.* CreateSpace Independent Publishing Platform.

IslamInSpanish. n.d. *The Story of IslamInSpanish.* Houston, TX: IslamInSpanish.
Retrieved from https://www.islaminspanish.org/our-story-1/.

Menocal, María Rosa. 2003. *The Ornament of the World: How Muslims, Jews,
and Christians Created a Culture of Tolerance in Medieval Spain.* Columbus,
GA: Back Bay Books.

Morales, Harold D. 2018. *Latino and Muslim in America: Race, Religion, and the
Making of a New Minority.* Oxford, UK: Oxford University Press.

Ocasio, Ramon Francisco. 2016. "Alianza Islamica: The True Story." TheIslamic
Monthly.com, May 14, 2016. Retrieved from https://www.theislamicmonthly
.com/alianza-islamica-the-true-story/.

Sager, Rebekah. 2017. "What It's Like Being Latino Muslim in America." Good
.is, July 31, 2017. Retrieved from https://www.good.is/features/americas-only
-latino-mosque.

Schuessler, Ryan. 2016. "Latino Muslims at country's only Spanish-speaking
mosque: 'Islam changed my life.'" TheGuardian.com, May 9, 2016. Retrieved
from https://www.theguardian.com/world/2016/may/09/latino-muslims-spanish
-mosque-cinco-de-mayo.

LGBTQ

Lesbian, Gay, Bisexual, Transgender, or Queer (LGBTQ) Muslims are on a journey of living out their sexual orientation and gender identity in a way that synthesizes the various layers of their identity, especially their Muslim identity, which is frequently regarded as being inherently against gay lifestyles. Like the U.S. public as a whole, however, U.S. Muslims have become much more accepting of gay people and same-sex relationships, including same-sex marriage, since the early 2000s. Results from a Pew Research Center poll published in 2017 found that 52 percent of U.S. Muslims say gay lifestyles should be accepted by society (Pew Research Center 2017). In contrast, only 34 percent of white evangelical Protestants believed in 2016 that gay lifestyles should be accepted by U.S. citizens. These statistics show that LGBTQ Muslim experiences are shifting in an age when same-sex marriages and gay lifestyles are accepted more and more in the United States. While these shifts tend to be explained by the increasing secularization of U.S. society, it should be properly noted that U.S. Muslims and Muslim communities across the country are giving more attention, energy, and space to the intersection of LGBTQ rights and the Islamic faith.

Urooj Arshad, an LGBTQ Muslim activist and member of the Muslim Alliance for Sexual and Gender Diversity (MASGD), told the *Huffington Post* in 2017 that Muslims' support for the gay community may hinge on a common experience that both groups share—being victims of discrimination (Kuruvilla 2017). MASGD works to support, empower, and connect LGBTQ Muslims, challenge the "root causes of misogyny and xenophobia, increase the acceptance of gender and sexual diversity within Muslim communities, and promote a progressive understanding of Islam that is centered on inclusion, justice, and equality" (Muslim Alliance for Sexual and Gender Diversity n.d.).

Following the Pulse nightclub shooting in Orlando, prominent U.S. Muslim leader Omar Suleiman stood in solidarity with the LGBTQ community. In an interview with *Dallas News,* Suleiman referred to homophobia as "a real problem in this country" and criticized people for targeting LGBTQ people as less than human because they choose to live their lives in a particular way (Di Furio 2016). The Pulse nightclub shooting also brought together Muslim, LGBTQ, and Latin communities. Fifty-nine organizations released a joint statement in 2017 to renew their commitment to honor the victims with action by protecting one another and standing for the United States's ideals of freedom, liberty, and equality under the law for all people (National LGBTQ Task Force 2017). Signees of the pledge included Muslim Advocates, Harvard Islamic Society (and the Anti-Islamophobia Network), Islamic Networks Group (ING), Muslim Legal Fund of America (MLFA), Muslim Public Affairs Council (MPAC), and Muslims for Progressive Values (MPV).

Several LGBTQ-friendly mosques have recently appeared on U.S. soil. National Public Radio ran a profile in April 2018 on Masjid Al-Rabia in Chicago (National Public Radio 2018). Congregants at Masjid Al-Rabia are a mix of LGBTQ Muslims, straight Muslims, converts, and people born into the faith. The founder of the mosque, Mahdia Lynn, is said to be motivated by an interpretation of the Qur'an that challenges traditional

Islamic understandings of sex between the same gender as sin (National Public Radio 2018). The Light of Reform Mosque in Washington, DC, also was founded in 2011 to be a safe space for LGBTQ values and practices that other U.S. mosques may eschew (Khan and Waheed 2013).

Daayiee Abdullah, an African American convert to the Islamic faith, is the *imam,* or Muslim religious leader, of the Light of Reform Mosque. He is one of the few publicly gay *imams* in the world. Imam Abdullah provides services that are unique for an *imam* of a U.S. Muslim community, like marrying same-sex couples (Khan and Waheed 2013). In an interview with the *Times of India,* Abdullah noted that the Qur'an does not say anything on the impermissibility of gay lifestyles (Singh 2016). He also pointed to the Wahhabi and Salafist interpretations of Islam as the reasons for the backlash against gay lifestyles among Muslims.

Recognizing these progressive developments toward fuller acceptance of LGBTQ people within U.S. Muslim communities does not mean that people should overlook the very real challenges still faced by LGBTQ Muslims. Many LGBTQ Muslims have shared their difficult experiences in "coming out," or revealing their sexuality to their communities. Several U.S. Muslim organizations are making the deliberate effort to actively provide resources to LGBTQ Muslims to deal with these kinds of challenges. The website of Muslims for Progressive Values (MPV) provides videos of lectures, organizations, guides, books, and other pieces of scholarship to help LGBTQ Muslims navigate their everyday lives and relations with family members and peers. A resource guide by the Muslim Youth Leadership Council was also created in 2018 to encourage young LGBTQ Muslims to not only share their experiences, but to ensure that they also have accurate and age-appropriate information about sexuality and sexual health.

A great deal of attention has been given in recent years on the rights granted to LGBTQ people in the Islamic tradition, specifically as outlined in the Qur'an and *ahadith.* At the height of its power in 2014 and 2015, for example, Daesh—the group popularly referred to as the Islamic State of Iraq and Syria (ISIS)—gained worldwide notoriety for executing LGBTQ Muslims in front of hundreds of watchers. Daesh's brutal condemnation of gay lifestyles is on the extreme end of the Muslim world's approach to gay lifestyles, but other Muslim-majority countries also engage in oppressive measures toward LGBTQ Muslims. Extreme prejudice against LGBTQ Muslims, both in the social and legal spheres, exists around the "Muslim world" including in the countries of Afghanistan, Iran, Saudi Arabia, Somalia, and Yemen, among others.

The justification for persecuting and even outlawing gay lifestyles along Islamic lines is rooted in conservative interpretations of Islamic texts. The biblical story of Sodom and Gomorrah is at the heart of the Islamic view on gay lifestyles. Islamic theological justification for rejecting gay lifestyles also appears in the Qur'anic story of Lut ("Lot" in Judeo-Christian scripture) (Minwalla et al. 2005). God sends "two angels to Lut, who offers them shelter, [and] the neighboring people surround his house and demand that he release the visitors so that they 'might know them,' suggesting gang rape of men" (De La Huerta 1999). The subsequent destruction of Lut's people "has traditionally been interpreted as a condemnation of their sexual practices" (Jamal 2001).

Traditionalist Muslim contexts tend to assume that Islam condemns gay lifestyles, same-sex relationships, and transsexualism. Tariq Ramadan, a professor of Islamic studies at Oxford University, has insisted for more than 20 years that "homosexuality is forbidden in Islam," but he adds that "we must avoid condemning or rejecting individuals" (Ramadan 2009). Similarly, influential scholar Yusuf Al-Qaradawi defines gay lifestyles as a "sexual perversion" and a "major sin" (Al-Qaradwi 1999, 169). Despite these claims that the Islamic faith condemns gay lifestyles, a number of scholars have found that reinterpretation of Qur'anic verses and contextualization of the *ahadith* may lead to empowering forms of Islam (Cervantes-Altamirano 2013, 83). According to scholar Mustafa Akyol, the hostility of many Muslims toward gay lifestyles actually has little basis in the Qur'an (Akyol 2015).

See also: Civil Rights

Further Reading

Akyol, Mustafa. 2015. "What Does Islam Say about Being Gay?" NYTimes.com, July 28, 2015. Retrieved from https://www.nytimes.com/2015/07/29/opinion /mustafa-akyol-what-does-islam-say-about-being-gay.html.

Al-Qaradawi, Yusuf. 1999. *The Lawful and the Prohibited in Islam*. Indianapolis: American Trust Publications.

Cervantes-Altamirano, Erendira. 2013. "Islamic Feminism and the Challenges of Gender, Sexuality and LGBTQ Rights in Contemporary Islam." *The International Journal of Religion and Spirituality in Society* 2: 76–85.

De La Huerta, Christian. 1999. *Coming Out Spiritually: The Next Step*. New York: Putnam.

Di Furio, Dom. 2016. "Q&A: Islamic scholar Omar Suleiman on the Quran and homosexuality." *Dallas News,* June 2016. Retrieved from https://www.dallas

news.com/opinion/commentary/2016/06/16/qa-islamic-scholar-omar-sulei
man-on-the-quran-and-homosexuality.

Jamal, Amreen. 2001. "The Story of Lot and the *Qur'an*'s Perceptions of the Morality of Same-Sex Sexuality." *Journal of Homosexuality* 41: 1–88.

Khan, Azmit, and Amina Waheed. 2013. "Meet America's first openly gay imam." AlJazeera.com, December 20, 2013. Retrieved from http://america.aljazeera .com/watch/shows/america-tonight/america-tonight-blog/2013/12/20/meet -america-s-firstopenlygayimam.html.

Kuruvilla, Carol. 2017. "American Muslims Are Now More Accepting of Homosexuality Than White Evangelicals." HuffingtonPost.com, August 1, 2017. Retrieved from https://www.huffingtonpost.com/entry/american-muslims -are-now-more-accepting-of-homosexuality-than-white-evangelicals_us_597f3 d8de4b02a4ebb76ea3d.

Minwalla, Omar, B. R. Simon Rosser, Jamie Feldman, and Christine Varga. 2005. "Identity Experience among Progressive Gay Muslims in North America: A Qualitative Study within Al-Fatiha." *Culture, Health & Sexuality* 7, no. 2: 113–28.

Muslim Alliance for Sexual and Gender Diversity. n.d. "About MASGD." Muslim Alliance.org. Retrieved from http://www.muslimalliance.org/aboutmasgd.

National LGBTQ Task Force. 2017. "Pulse Shooting Day of Remembrance Brings Together LGBTQ, Muslim, and Latinx Communities." Washington, DC: The Task Force. Retrieved from http://www.thetaskforce.org/pulse-shooting-day-of -remembrance-brings-together-lgbtq-muslim-and-latinx-communities/.

National Public Radio. 2018. "A Mosque for LGBTQ Muslims." NPR.org, April 15, 2018. Retrieved from https://www.npr.org/2018/04/15/602605271 /a-mosque-for-lgbtq-muslims.

Pew Research Center. 2017. "Like Americans overall, Muslims now more accepting of homosexuality." Washington, DC: Pew Research Center. Last modified July 25, 2017. Retrieved from http://www.pewforum.org/2017/07/26/political -and-social-views/pf_2017-06-26_muslimamericans-04new-06/.

Ramadan, Tariq. 2009. "Islam and Homosexuality." TariqRamadan.com. Last modified May 29, 2009. Retrieved from https://tariqramadan.com/english /islam-and-homosexuality/.

Singh, Aaarti Tikoo. 2016. "There are 8 openly gay imams in the world: Daayiee Abdullah." TimesofIndia.com, June 15, 2016. Retrieved from https:// timesofindia.indiatimes.com/world/us/There-are-8-openly-gay-imams-in-the -world-Daayiee-Abdullah/articleshow/52754600.cms.

M

Media Coverage and the Entertainment Industry

Recent research shows that representations of Muslims in Western media coverage are often associated with conflict and violence, mostly notably "terrorism." Since the 9/11 attacks, Western media coverage reveals a pattern of coverage that focuses on Muslims, Arabs, and the Islamic faith as the main "terrorist threats" to the United States. Domestic terrorist acts committed by white supremacists, on the other hand, are cast as a minor threat that occurs in isolated incidents by "lone wolves" or "troubled individuals."

Overall, the Western media coverage of Muslims is negative in tone. Scholars from the Shoreinstein Center at Harvard University found that there was not a single month between April 1, 2015, and March 31, 2017, when television news stories showed Muslims as positive protagonists (Stone 2017, 4). In more than 40 percent of those months, "negative stories outnumbered positive stories by four-to-one or more. When the coverage is broken down by news outlets, Fox New's coverage was the most negative" (Stone 2017, 4). Further research carried out by scholars at the University of Alabama found that terrorist acts committed by Muslim extremists received 357 percent more media coverage in the United States than those committed by "non-Muslims" in the United States (Kearns, Betus, and Lemieux 2018). Data from the Global Terrorism Database reveal that terrorist acts committed by "non-Muslims" (or by people whose religion was unknown) received an average of 15 headlines, while terrorist acts committed by Muslim extremists received 105 headlines between 2006 and 2015.

Negative media representations of Muslims as violent terrorists and enemies of the United States is not a new phenomenon that merely popped up after the 9/11 attacks. In his article "The Othering of Muslims:

Discourses of Radicalization in the *New York Times*, 1969–2014," scholar Derek Silva analyzed 607 articles from the *New York Times,* one of the United States's leading newspapers. Silva's research revealed that "discourses evoked in the so-called era of 'Islamic radicalization' are not all that new and have been deployed by the news [outlets] as a symbolic marker for various conflicts since at least the 1960s" (Silva 2017, 156). He added that the *New York Times* historically deployed "several backgrounding strategies to contribute to conceptual distinctions or 'symbolic boundaries' that work to construct notions of 'us' and 'them' through reference to radicalization" (Bail 2008).

Negative media representations of Muslims in the United States and abroad also influence public policies that single out Muslims as threats to U.S. society. Exposure to media coverage portraying Muslims as "terrorists" is positively associated with support for military action in Muslim-majority countries around the world (Saleem et al. 2017, 841). Exposing U.S. citizens to negative Muslim media footage also increases perceptions of Muslims as "aggressive" and increases support for civil rights crackdowns on U.S. Muslims (Saleem et al. 2017, 841).

Fox News is frequently cited as a leading anti-Muslim news station in the United States. Following Fox News's host Jeannine Pirro's comments in March 2019 on Representative Ilhan Omar and the false claim that "Islamic doctrine" is "antithetical to the United States Constitution," *Huffington Post* journalist Rowaida Abdelaziz documented the historic types of Islamophobia on Fox News in an article titled "These Are the Types of Islamophobia Fox News Is OK With." As Abdelaziz noted, Pirro advocated in a 2016 segment on Fox News for mosques to be surveilled and supported Newt Gingrich's call to "test every person here who is of a Muslim background, and if they believe in [the] *sharia,* they should be deported." In 2015, in the aftermath of the *Charlie Hebdo* attack, Pirro's show promoted anti-Muslim conspiracies, at which point Fox News was forced to issue four corrections in a single day of coverage of Muslims (Abdelaziz 2019). Before publishing her article on the *Huffington Post,* Abdelaziz interviewed Rebecca Lenn, the director of external affairs for Media Matters, a news watchdog organization that exposes far-right conspiracy theories of U.S. Muslims and the Islamic faith at large. Lenn told Abdelaziz that anti-Muslim narratives on Fox News are "definitely not isolated to [Pirro's] show. That's a given. Fox News has definitely been a leading driver of the anti-Muslim fervor in the media landscape for a long time. There is no doubt." Abdelaziz highlights many other recent cases of

Islamophobia on Fox News including "Fox & Friends" co-host Brian Kilmeade's claiming in 2010 that "all terrorists are Muslims" and Jesse Watters's stating on "The O'Reilly Factor" in 2017, "You have to admit, there is a Muslim problem in the world."

News coverage is not the only source of media that contributes to the fostering of anti-Muslim sentiment in the United States. Hollywood movies, as scholar Jack Shaheen revealed in his book *Reel Bad Arabs: How Hollywood Vilifies a People,* construct Arabs and Muslims as murderers, rapists, religious fanatics, oil-rich men, and abusers of women. Shaheen's book sheds light on his research on over 1,200 Hollywood movies, of which approximately 932 depicted Arabs and Muslims in the aforementioned stereotypical manner. Only 12 films analyzed by Shaheen had a positive depiction of these populations.

Artist and scholar Maytha Alhassen echoed similar findings in her report "Haqq & Hollywood: Illuminating 100 Years of Muslim Tropes and How to Transform Them." She too concluded that Hollywood movies misrepresent Muslims to U.S. audiences through the prism of Orientalism, anti-blackness, anti-Muslim, patriarchy, and imperialism (Alhassen 2018, 7). In doing so, Alhassen continues, the entertainment industry at large has "never reflected the diversity, richness, and humanity of Muslim communities." Alhassen recommends that philanthropists and the entertainment industry make "substantial, ongoing investments in all stages of the pipeline for Muslim creatives, starting at points of entry and continuing through a long-term career trajectory" (Alhassen 2018, 42).

Several Hollywood movies in the post-9/11 era are singled out for typecasting Muslims in the role of terrorists. Movies like *Argo* (2012) and *American Sniper* (2014) are cases in point. Directed by Hollywood star Ben Affleck, *Argo* covers the Iran hostage crisis of 1979 by showing the Central Intelligence Agency's maneuvers to free six U.S. citizens from the hands of Iranian mobs, most of whom are depicted as brown, bearded men. *American Sniper,* on the other hand, reveals the story of Chris Kyle, a U.S. Navy SEAL played by Hollywood star Bradley Cooper. Critics of *American Sniper* said that the film glorified the Iraq War and heroized Kyle despite the fact that he referred to Muslims as "savages" in his autobiography. The American-Arab Anti-Discrimination Committee (ADC) said that the release of *American Sniper* led to an increase in threats against U.S. Muslims.

Television shows like *Homeland* and *24* are also criticized by critics for presenting a sinister and suspicious image of both Muslims and the

Islamic faith as a whole. The archvillain of season one of *Homeland* is virtually a stand-in for Osama bin Laden, the alleged perpetrator of the 9/11 attacks, who is a member of Al-Qaeda that is plotting an act of terrorism against the United States. Abu Nazir, the name of the villain, is seen in the beginning of season two meeting with the leader of Hezbollah, a Palestinian-Lebanese group designated by the U.S. government as a "terrorist organization." One episode of *24* focuses on a friendly and seemingly "mainstream" Turkish Muslim family that is secretly acting as an enabler of "terrorist sleeper cells." In one scene the father prepares his son for a terrorist event by telling him, "What we will accomplish today will change the world. We are fortunate that our family has been chosen to do this." In selecting these words, the producers of *24* exacerbate the stereotype and peddle the accusation that Muslims are commanded to sacrifice themselves for a "holy war" against Westerners.

Muslim actors and characters of Arab and North African descent are also ignored in the casting of television shows or stereotyped as tyrants and terrorists. A study sponsored by the Middle Eastern and North Africa Arts Advocacy Coalition examined 242 scripted prime-time series on broadcast, cable, and streaming during the 2015–2016 season and found that "between 90 percent and 97 percent had no characters of North African ethnicity. When those characters do appear, 78 percent are tyrants or trained terrorists, agents, or soldiers" with foreign accents (Yuen et al. 2018).

Breaking into the Hollywood movie industry remains a difficult task for U.S. Muslims. Part of the reason is due to the fact that less than 1 percent of U.S. Muslims pursue careers as directors, producers, actors, and screenwriters (Nisar n.d.). The low figure of 1 percent may be due to the fact that many U.S. Muslims are first-generation who often seek more lucrative careers in the fields of medicine, engineering, or academia. The Muslim Public Affairs Council (MPAC), a national U.S. Muslim advocacy and public policy organization headquartered in Los Angeles, has responded to this reality by creating its own Hollywood Bureau, which focuses on building relationships between Muslims and Hollywood movie industry professionals, consulting on film and television projects, and holding networking events to create opportunities for Muslims in Hollywood (Obeidi 2014).

President Barack Obama also raised the need for more Muslim characters in Hollywood movies and television shows that transcend the stereotypical roles. During his first and only visit to a U.S. mosque as president, he noted, "Our television shows should have some Muslim characters that are unrelated to national security." President Obama continued, "There was a time when there were no Black people on television. And you can tell good stories while still representing the reality of our communities."

See also: Clash of Civilizations; Islamophobia

Further Reading

Abdelaziz, Rowaida. 2019. "These Are the Types of Islamophobia Fox News Is OK With." *Huffington Post,* March 12, 2019. Retrieved from https://www.huffpost.com/entry/fox-news-islamophobia_n_5c8811ebe4b038892f482d12.

Alhassen, Maytha. 2018. "Haqq & Hollywood: Illuminating 100 years of Muslim Tropes and How to Transform Them." PopCollab.org. Retrieved from http://popcollab.org/wp-content/uploads/2018/10/HaqqAndHollywood_Report.pdf.

Bail, Christopher. 2008. "The Configuration of Symbolic Boundaries against Immigrants in Europe." *American Sociological Review* 73, no. 1: 37–59.

Feeney, Nolan. 2016. "Obama Thinks TV Needs More Muslim Characters." TIME.com, February 3, 2016. Retrieved from http://time.com/4206620/obama-muslims-television/.

Kearns, Erin M., Allison Betus, and Anthony Lemieux. 2017. "Why Do Some Terrorist Attacks Receive More Media Attention Than Others." Social Science Research Network. Retrieved from https://papers.ssrn.com/sol3/papers.cfm?abstract_id=2928138.

Kearns, Erin, Allison Betus, and Anthony Lemieux. 2018. "Why Do Some Terrorist Attacks Receive More Media Attention Than Others?" *Justice Quarterly*. Retrieved from https://papers.ssrn.com/sol3/papers.cfm?abstract_id=2928138.

Nisar, Hasher. n.d. *Muslims Speak: An Action Project Proposal for Humanity in Action.* New York: HumanityinAction.org. Retrieved from: http://www.humanityinaction.org/fi les/743-ActionPlan-HasherNisar.pdf.

Obeidi, Suhad. 2014. "Changing the Narrative of Muslims in Hollywood." HollywoodJournal.com, February 17, 2014. Retrieved from http://hollywoodjournal.com/industry-impressions/changing-the-narrativeof-muslims-in-hollywood/20140217/.

Powell, Kimberly A. 2011. "Framing Islam: An Analysis of U.S. Media Coverage of Terrorism Since 9/11." *Communication Studies* 62, no. 1 (January 31): 90–112.

Saleem, Muniba, Sara Prot, Craig A. Anderson, and A. F. Lemieux. 2017. "Exposure to Muslims in Media and Support for Public Policies Harming Muslims." *Communication Research* 44, no. 6: 841–69.

Shaheen, Jack. 2009. *Reel Bad Arabs: How Hollywood Vilifies a People*. Brooklyn, NY: Olive Branch Press.

Silva, Derek M. D. 2017. "The Othering of Muslims: Discourses of Radicalization in the *New York Times*, 1969–2014." *Sociological Forum* 32, no. 1 (March): 138–61.

Stone, Meighan. 2017. *Snake and Stranger: Media Coverage of Muslims and Refugee Policy*. ShoreinsteinCenter.org. Last modified Spring 2017. Retrieved from https://shorensteincenter.org/wp-content/uploads/2017/06/Media-Coverage-Muslims-Meighan-Stone.pdf?x78124.

Yuen, Nancy Yang, Christina B. Chin, Meera E. Deo, Faustina M. DuCros, Jenny Jong-Hwa Lee, and Noriko Milman. 2018. "Terrorists & Tyrants: Middle Eastern and North African (MENA) Actors in Prime Time & Streaming Television." Los Angeles: MENA Arts Advocacy Coalition. Retrieved from https://www.menaartsadvocacy.com/.

Mosques and Organizations

The term mosque, the English word for *masjid* or *jami,* literally means "a place for self-prostration." In the social context a mosque is treated as a place formally designated for the saying of Islamic prayers. A mosque is typically a house or building that hosts a collection of prayergoers in which Muslims worship God according to Islamic scripture. Any open prayer area, however, also is recognized as serving the purposes of mosques.

Historically, mosques have served as much more than prayer spaces—they have been used as spaces wherein Muslims and their visitors can study the Islamic faith, discuss current affairs, and host meals and fundraisers and other social gatherings that serve a constructive purpose for the betterment of the community in which the mosque is located. Mosques are typically run by an *imam,* an Arabic word meaning "leader" or "prayer leader." *Imams* typically lead Islamic prayer services, but also serve as community leaders who provide religious, spiritual, and educational guidance to Muslims.

After the *shahada,* or the testimony of the Islamic faith, the most important of the Five Pillars of Islam is *salah* or *salat,* the Arabic terms for "prayer." All Muslims who have reached puberty are obligated to pray five times a day—sunrise (*salah al-fajr*), noon (*salah al-zuhr*), midday (*salah al-'asr*), sunset (*salah al-maghrib*), and evening *(salah al-'isha)* (Lumbard

2008, 44). Islamic prayers begin with the *wudu'*, or ablution, that is, the washing of the face, hands, arms, and feet. The ablution is said to wash away the dross of the world and reestablish harmony between the body, soul, and spirit (Lumbard 2008, 44). Following the ablution, Muslims arrange themselves in orderly rows behind a single prayer leader, the *imam*, and engage in prayer. Arranging themselves in orderly rows teaches Muslims the lesson of unity and equality. During prayers, Muslims perform a series of movements that go with the prayer itself. Muslims briefly kneel and touch their foreheads to the ground as a sign of *islam*, the Arabic term that literally translates to "submission" to the will of God.

Fridays are typically the largest prayer gathering in any given week for Muslims. Friday is called *Yawm Al-Juma'ah* in Arabic, meaning the "Day of Assembly." As the Pluralism Project of Harvard University notes, the Friday prayer is exactly like the ritual prayers, or *salat*, performed during the rest of the week, except that on Friday the *imam* (prayer leader) or special guest delivers a *khutba*, the Arabic word meaning "sermon." The *khutba* at any given mosque is designed to empower and motivate Muslims to live a better life in accordance with God's law, the *sharia*. The *khutba* also tends to avoid topics, especially political issues, that could divide the community.

Far from being merely religious spaces for prayer, mosques also serve as important cultural, civic, and social institutions for U.S. Muslims. Mosques on U.S. soil serve as spaces for social gatherings, community and political involvement, community resources (i.e., legal, financial, social, and cultural), social services, and education (Nguyen 2017, 96). Many mosques in the United States provide full-time and weekend Islamic schools, Islamic study classes, *khatirah* (short lectures), Arabic classes, sisters' (women only) activities or programs, Qur'an memorization classes, youth activities or programs, classes for recently converted Muslims, fitness and martial arts classes, and sports teams (Bagby, Perl, and Froehle 2001).

In recognition of the diversity within the U.S. Muslim population, many mosques in the United States work to bring together various peoples for the purpose of dissolving racial and cultural barriers, as well as sectarian divisions. Ramadan, the Islamic holy month, is a period in which Muslims of various backgrounds as well as people of varied faiths congregate in mosques. Ramadan refers to the ninth month of the Islamic lunar calendar and represents the starting date of the Prophet Muhammad's emigration, or *hijra*, from Mecca to Medina in 622 CE. Once a year, Muslims are required to fast, or *sawm* in Arabic. Fasting is the fourth pillar of Islam that requires abstention from food, drink, sexual activity, lying, insulting, and impure thoughts or actions from dawn to sunset for all adult Muslims whose health permits.

The Arabic term *iftar* refers to the fast-breaking meal during the month of Ramadan. Every mosque in the United States, if mosque resources permit, hosts an *iftar* for Muslims and frequently people of other faiths. An *iftar* is a time of expressing gratitude for God's creation, but also an awareness of human beings' dependence on God and of human frailty. These measures are not merely an act of penitence, but a method of self-purification, both physically and spiritually. Fasting is often understood as a form of worship that increases peoples' spirituality and elevates people to a higher plane so that they may be closer to God. Observing the fast of Ramadan, however, is typically a greater challenge in the United States than in Muslim-majority countries around the world. Ramadan does not have the social status or recognition of other holidays such as Christmas.

Normally, the first mosque in Islamic history is recognized as the "Quba Mosque," located in a town south of Medina, Saudi Arabia, where the Prophet Muhammad and his companions rested on the *hijra,* or migration, from Mecca to Medina in 622 CE. The second mosque, built out of bricks by Muhammad in the city of Medina, Saudi Arabia, is referred to as Al-Masjid An-Nabawi, which had an open-air building that also served as a community center, religious school, and court. In 628 CE, Muhammad built a *minbar,* or pulpit, in the mosque so that he was raised above the crowds. In 634 CE Muhammad declared that prayer be directed toward Mecca instead of Jerusalem. In 706 CE Caliph Al-Walid created a new mosque on the site that contained the tomb of Muhammad.

The "Prophet's Mosque" in Medina, as it is known today, also is the site of one of the first instances of Christian and Muslim interaction. When a prominent Christian delegation came from Najran in southern Saudi Arabia to engage in diplomacy and theological discussions over the nature of God, the Prophet Muhammad invited the Najran Christians to perform their Christian prayers inside the mosque. Today, the "Prophet's Mosque" is one of the three holiest sites of the Islamic tradition, alongside the Kaaba and Al-Masjid Al-Haram in Mecca, Saudi Arabia, and the Al-Aqsa mosque in Jerusalem.

The first mosque in the history of the United States is said to be "the Mother Mosque of America" in Cedar Rapids, Iowa. The Mother Mosque was built by Arab Muslim immigrants from Jordan, Lebanon, Palestine, and Syria. These immigrants were largely classified as "Turks," as Muslims were in the 19th and early 20th centuries. By the mid-1920s, the Arab Muslim community of Cedar Rapids is said to have incorporated dozens of shops and grocery stores. By 1925, an Arab American Muslim group known as the "Rose of Fraternity Lodge" decided to rent out a building to serve as a place of worship. Years later, in 1934, the Cedar Rapids community was financially stable enough to open its doors to the Mother Mosque. One of the prominent Arab American Muslim families of Cedar Rapids, the Aossey family, contributed significant funds to create the first Muslim National Cemetery in Cedar Rapids around 1948.

U.S. Muslim communities and leaders are accused by anti-Islam activists of running "radical mosques." New York Representative Peter King in the House of Representatives claimed in January 2011 on Fox News that U.S. mosques were "infected" by "radical jihadi sentiment" and that more than 80 percent of U.S. mosques were controlled by "radical *imams*." The Council on American-Islamic Relations estimated that there are at least 2,106 mosques in the United States, meaning that, according to Representative King's projection, there exist over 1,600 "radical mosques" on U.S. soil. Such claims stand in stark contrast to research carried out by CAIR's "Mosque Study," which sampled more than 500 mosques and *imams*. The overwhelming majority of U.S. mosques were found to be "mainstream" (Bagby, Perl, and Froehle 2001). In 2012, CAIR, the Islamic Society of North America, and the Islamic Circle of America found similar data after asking hundreds of mosque leaders about the nature of "radicalization" within their communities. The survey found that 87 percent of mosque leaders agreed with the statement that "radicalization" was not increasing among young U.S. Muslims.

Empirical evidence gathered by the Institute for Social Policy and Understanding (ISPU), a research organization based in Washington, DC, found that U.S. Muslims "who regularly attend mosques are more likely to be civically engaged" and that Muslims who attend mosques regularly are more likely than others to "work with their neighbors to solve community problems" (Institute for Social Policy and Understanding 2016, 2). Similarly, scholar Amaney Jamal examined the patterns of U.S. Muslim political behavior and their levels of mosque participation and concluded that mosques "take on the multifaceted role of mobilization vehicle and school of civic participation" (Jamal 2005, 521). Jamal also discovered that mosques promote and foster a sense of group consciousness particularly for Arab Muslims and African American Muslims.

The Women's Mosque of America was opened in Los Angeles in 2015. Founded by M. Hasna Maznavi, a filmmaker and comedy writer who has long been involved with Muslim communities in the city, the Women's Mosque is said to be the first women's only mosque in the United States (Hussain 2016, 90). The Friday prayers are held in the Pico Union Project, which was built in 1909 as the home of Sinai Temple, a building that symbolizes interfaith cooperation between Jews and Muslims (Hussain 2016, 90).

Islamic Organizations

The Council on American-Islamic Relations (CAIR) is regarded by many as the leading civil rights advocacy group in the United States. CAIR's vision is to be a leading advocate for social justice and mutual understanding between people of various racial and religious populations in the country. The core principles of CAIR are listed on the organization's official website. These principles include, but are by no means limited to, supporting "free enterprise, freedom of religion, and freedom of expression; protecting the civil rights of all Americans, regardless of faith; [supporting] domestic policies that promote civil rights, diversity, and freedom of religion; [and opposing] domestic policies that limit civil rights, permit racial, ethnic, or religious profiling, infringe on due process, or that prevent Muslims and others from participating fully in American civic life" (Council on American-Islamic Relations n.d.). CAIR also has an active government affairs department that conducts and organizes lobbying efforts on issues related to Islam and Muslims (Council on American-Islamic Relations n.d.). Despite its efforts to promote civil rights and defend the rights of U.S. citizens, CAIR has been erroneously accused of being an Islamic organization that justifies, promotes, and exacerbates terrorism. A 2014 article in the *National Review* questioned, "Is CAIR a Terror Group?" and claimed that the group is directly connected to Hamas, a Palestinian organization officially classified as a "terrorist organization" by the U.S. government (Pipes 2014).

The Islamic Society of North American (ISNA) is another large Islamic organization based on U.S. soil. The ISNA regularly engages in interfaith dialogue initiatives in order to "connect Muslims and people of other faiths with one another in order to build mutual respect and understanding" (Islamic Society of North American n.d.). In 2010, the ISNA helped to launch the Shoulder-to-Shoulder Campaign, an interfaith movement of

28 national religious organizations that works to end anti-Muslim senti-ment by strengthening the voice of freedom and peace across religious communities (Shoulder-to-Shoulder n.d.).

The Muslim Public Affairs Council (MPAC) is an organization dedi-cated to strengthening the political profile of U.S. Muslims. As part of its mission to protect the civil rights of U.S. Muslims and to encourage pluralism in the United States, MPAC works in coalition with a wide variety of interfaith partners—spanning nearly a dozen faiths—to en-hance interreligious understanding and freedom for all Americans (Muslim Public Affairs Council n.d.). Furthermore, the Islamic Circle of North America (ICNA) was formed in 1968 as an organization initially focused on educating its members about Islam. Since then, the ICNA has transformed into a multicultural, inclusive, and diverse organization working toward community building and establishing a place for Islam in the United States (Islamic Circle of North America n.d.a). The ICNA operates under the principle that "all people are created equal" and that promoting justice through human development with all Americans can lead to a healthy and productive society (Islamic Circle of North America n.d.b).

See also: Integration; Pluralism; *Ummah*

Further Reading

Bagby, Ihsan, Paul M. Perl, and Bryan T. Froehle. 2001. "The Mosque in Amer-ica: A National Portrait—A Report from the Mosque Study Project." Washington, DC: Council on American-Islamic Relations. Last modified April 26, 2001. Retrieved from http://icnl.com/files/Masjid_Study_Project_2000 _Report.pdf.

Council on American-Islamic Relations. n.d. "About Us." Washington, DC: Council on American-Islamic Relations. Retrieved from https://www.cair.com /about_us.

Hussain, Amir. 2016. *Muslims and the Making of America.* Waco, TX: Baylor University Press.

Institute for Social Policy and Understanding. 2016. "ISPU American Muslim Poll Key Findings." Washington, DC: ISPU. Retrieved from https://www.ispu .org/wp-content/uploads/2016/08/ampkeyfindings-2.pdf.

Islamic Circle of North America. n.d.a. "About ICNA." New York: Islamic Circle of North America. Retrieved from http://www.icna.org/about-icna.

Islamic Circle of North America. n.d.b. "Social Services." New York: Islamic Circle of North America. Retrieved from http://www.icna.org/social-services/.

Islamic Society of North America. n.d.. "Interfaith Dialogue." Plainfield, IL: Islamic Society of North America. Retrieved from http://www.isna.net/inter faith-relations/.

Jamal, Amaney. 2005. "The Political Participation and Engagement of Muslim Americans: Mosque Involvement and Group Consciousness." *American Politics Research* 33, no. 4: 521–44.

Kortmann, Matthias, and Kerstin Rosenow-Williams. 2013. *Islamic Organizations in Europe and the USA: A Multidisciplinary Perspective*. Basingstoke, UK: Palgrave Macmillan.

Lumbard, Joseph E. 2008. *Submission: Faith & Beauty*. Berkeley, CA: Zaytuna Institute.

Muslim Public Affairs Council. n.d. "Religious Freedom." Los Angeles: Muslim Public Affairs Council. Retrieved from https://www.mpac.org/issues/religious -freedom.php.

National Park Service. n.d. "Iowa: The Mother Mosque of America." Washington, DC: National Park Service. Retrieved from https://www.nps.gov/articles /mothermosque.htm.

Nguyen, Ann W. 2017. "Mosque-Based Social Support and Collective and Personal Self-Esteem among Young Muslim American Adults." *Race and Social Problems* 9, no. 2: 95–101.

Pipes, Daniel. 2014. "Is CAIR a Terror Group?" NationalReview.com, November 28, 2014. Retrieved from https://www.nationalreview.com/2014/11/cair-terror -group-daniel-pipes/.

Shoulder-to-Shoulder. n.d. "About." ShouldertoShoulderCampaign.org. Retrieved from http://www.shouldertoshouldercampaign.org/about/.

The Muslim Brotherhood

The Muslim Brotherhood was founded in Egypt in 1928 by Hassan Al-Banna, an Islamic scholar. He envisioned a universal Islamic system that could be actualized by engaging societies through outreach (*daw'ah*) and charity (*zakat*). Some experts argue that the ideology of the Brotherhood is focused mainly on reforming the existing political and social systems in the *ummah* while other critics claim that the organization is motivated by "Islamic supremacy" to overtake Western democracies.

Today, the Brotherhood has chapters in dozens of countries that are nominally coordinated by a transnational network helmed by the "Supreme Guide" in Egypt. The Brotherhood has inspired political and social movements in countries such as Jordan, Indonesia, Morocco, and Turkey. It is difficult to assess the strength of the ties between the Brotherhood's command in Egypt and the various branches around the world, because the Brotherhood is relatively secretive. The organization has operated underground for many years as a result of systematic oppression in Egypt. However, even in Egypt, the Brotherhood has been unable to maintain a strong presence. The Brotherhood's command has been recently split, with its previous generations either in prison, exiled, or dead. The Brotherhood also no longer has a robust internal organization, vast financial resources, or even a clearly defined ideology.

The idea of designating the Muslim Brotherhood as a "terrorist organization" has been kicking around the United States for years. This is part of a larger movement for a kind of "civilizational battle" between Western countries and Muslim-majority countries worldwide. Organizations such as the Center for Security Policy (CSP), which the Southern Poverty Law Center describes as "notoriously Islamophobic," have suggested that the Brotherhood is engaged in violent *jihad* and intends to destroy the United States with the support of cells that the Brotherhood already has on U.S. soil.

To stop the alleged threat of the Brotherhood, Republican Senator Ted Cruz of Texas introduced a bill in January 2017 to legally classify the group as a Foreign Terrorist Organization (FTO). This bill was Cruz's second attempt to add the Brotherhood to the United States's list of foreign terrorist organizations. In November 2015, he sponsored a similar document for review by the Senate Foreign Relations Committee, which was approved by the House Judiciary Committee in February 2016. The first bill required the Secretary of State to report to the U.S. Congress on "whether the Muslim Brotherhood meets the criteria for designation as a [FTO]" and, if not, would include "a detailed justification as to which criteria have not been met."

Scholars have played a crucial role in pushing back on the politicization of the "terrorist organization" designation of the Brotherhood. According to Shadi Hamid, a senior fellow at the Brookings Institute, there is "quite literally not a single American expert on the Muslim Brotherhood who supports the designation" (Hamid 2017). John Esposito, a professor of Islamic studies at Georgetown University, claims that designating the Brotherhood as an FTO sends the signal to Muslims worldwide that the U.S. government welcomes autocracy, but not democratization. Speaking to the U.S. House Judiciary Committee in 2016, Esposito pointed out that for more than 30 years, the Brotherhood has "been a force for democratization and stability in the Middle East" (The Bridge Initiative 2017).

Civil rights lawyers, such as professor Arjun Singhi Sethi, have blamed anti-Islam activists and organizations for fueling the conspiracy theories about the Brotherhood. Writing for the *Washington Post,* Sethi noted that the Islamophobia industry's treatment of the Brotherhood is like the "Red Scare" of the 1950s, which Sethi claims "saw the chimerical specter of worldwide communism everywhere" (Sethi 2017). Sethi also singled out Frank Gaffney, the founder and president of the Center for Security Policy, for peddling the "civilizational *jihad*" conspiracy. Gaffney claims that three of the largest U.S. Muslim organizations—the Islamic Society of North America (ISNA), the Council on American-Islamic Relations (CAIR), and the North American Islamic Trust (NAIT)—are affiliates of the Brotherhood. There is no evidence to support Gaffney's claim, apart from an obscure memo dated to 1991. The memo, written by a leader of the Brotherhood, outlined a plan to eliminate and destroy the United States from within. The memo has since been used by individuals and organizations who spread anti-Islam misinformation, rhetoric, and propaganda. Further, the memo has been called a "fantasy" by the Southern Poverty Law Center (Southern Poverty Law Center n.d.). The Bridge Initiative, an anti-Islamophobia organization based at Georgetown University, ran the memo's key phrase—civilizational *jihad*—through arabiCorpus, a linguistics analytical tool that searches through a database containing over 30 million words from Arab literature and Islamic texts, spanning back to 2012. The key phrase was mentioned only once in the entire arabiCorpus collection (The Bridge Initiative 2016).

Designating the Brotherhood as a "terrorist organization" raises further issues. One is that the organization "is not in a meaningful sense a single organization at all (McCants and Wittes 2017). The Brotherhood is "simply too diffuse and diverse to characterize and it certainly cannot be said as a whole to engage in terrorism that threatens the United States" (McCants and Wittes 2017). A second reason is that the U.S. government would invoke dangerously broad and expansive material-support-of-terrorism laws that focus predominantly on U.S. Muslims. If the Muslim Brotherhood is designated a "terrorist organization," U.S. Muslims could be criminally prosecuted for providing support, services, resources, expert advice, or assistance to the Brotherhood without any evidence that U.S. Muslims support terrorist activity (Sethi 2017).

To be fair, elements of the Brotherhood have engaged in terrorist activity and other forms of political violence. During the 1970s and 1980s, the Brotherhood helped to fight an insurgency against the Syrian government. The Brotherhood in Palestine occasionally used violent tactics against the Israeli state. Notwithstanding, scholars have noted that while the Brotherhood might turn a blind eye to violence, the organization does not orchestrate or officially call for violence at an international level (Trager and Shalabi 2015). Even during the Arab Spring, a series of democratic revolutions across the Middle East, the Brotherhood publicly articulated an ideology of nonviolence and democratic participation in Egypt and beyond.

The scholarly opinion about the Brotherhood stands in stark contrast to the conspiracy theories peddled by the Islamophobia industry. The Brotherhood is not trying to topple the U.S. government, nor is the group a "terrorist organization." There are several key issues at play here: one is that experts have questioned whether the Brotherhood is even an organization, and the second is that being a "terrorist organization" involves the indiscriminate killing of civilians, something no expert argues the Brotherhood is doing on U.S. soil or anywhere in the world. There also is no evidence that the Brotherhood is waging a "civilizational *jihad*" to topple the U.S. government. The reality is that the Brotherhood does not even have a known presence on U.S. soil, and most U.S. Muslims know very little about the organization. It would quite simply be unconstitutional for the U.S. government to slap the "terrorist organization" designation on a group for purely ideological grounds.

See also: Foreign Policies

Further Reading

Bridge Initiative, The. 2016. "'Civilizational Jihad': Debunking the Conspiracy Theory." Washington, DC: The Bridge Initiative. Last modified February 2, 2016. Retrieved from http://bridge.georgetown.edu/civilization-jihad-debunking-the-conspiracy-theory/.

Bridge Initiative, The. 2017. "Ted Cruz's Muslim Brotherhood Terrorist Bill." Washington, DC: The Bridge Initiative. Last modified January 18, 2017. Retrieved from http://bridge.georgetown.edu/ted-cruzs-muslim-brotherhood-terrorist-bill/.

Hamid, Shadi. 2017. "The Muslim Brotherhood and the Question of Terrorism." TheAtlantic.com, February 12, 2017. Retrieved from https://www.theatlantic.com/international/archive/2017/02/muslim-brotherhood-designation/516390/.

Hirschkind, Charles. 2010. "What Is Political Islam?" In *Political Islam: A Critical Reader.* Edited by Frederic Volpi. London: Routledge.

McCants, William, and Benjamin Wittes. 2017. "Should the Muslim Brotherhood be designated a terrorist organization?" Washington, DC: The Brookings Institution. Last modified January 30, 2017. Retrieved from https://www .brookings.edu/blog/markaz/2017/01/30/should-the-muslim-brotherhood-be -designated-a-terrorist-organization/.

Sethi, Arjun Singh. 2017. "Calling the Muslim Brotherhood a terrorist group would hurt all American Muslims." WashingtonPost.com, February 8, 2017. Retrieved from https://www.washingtonpost.com/posteverything/wp /2017/02/08/calling-the-muslim-brotherhood-a-terrorist-group-would-hurt -all-american-muslims/?noredirect=on&utm_term=.05cad32d813d.

Southern Poverty Law Center. n.d. "Extremists." Montgomery, AL: SPLC. Re-trieved from https://www.splcenter.org/fighting-hate/extremist-files/individual /frank-gaffney-jrThe.

Trager, Eric, and Marina Shalabi. 2015. "Egypt's Muslim Brotherhood Gets a Facelift." ForeignAffairs.com, May 20, 2015. Retrieved from https://www .foreignaffairs.com/articles/egypt/2015-05-20/egypts-muslim-brotherhood -gets-facelift.

Muslim Travel Ban and Immigration Policies

The "Muslim Travel Ban" is the colloquial name for Donald Trump's im-migration policy that emerged in late 2015, when Trump, then the Repub-lican presidential candidate, held a press conference in which he called for "a total and complete shutdown of Muslims entering the United States until our country's representatives can figure out what is going on." After the speech, an ABC News/*Washington Post* survey found that only 36 percent of U.S. citizens believed that Trump's proposal "was the right thing to do."

Upon taking office in January 2017, President Trump turned his atten-tion to officially adopting the "Muslim travel ban" as policy. The first ban, officially known as Executive Order 13769, titled "Protecting the Nation from Foreign Terrorist Entry into the United States," barred foreign na-tionals from seven predominantly Muslim countries around the world from entering the United States for a total of 90 days. The countries listed in the order were Iran, Iraq, Libya, Somalia, Sudan, Syria, and Yemen. Executive Order 13769 also indefinitely suspended the entry of all Syrian refugees and further prohibited all additional refugees from entering the United States for 120 days. According to the official text, Executive Order 13769 aimed to "protect the American people from terrorist attacks by foreign nationals admitted to the United States." The order also stated, "Numerous foreign-born individuals have been convicted or implicated in terrorism related crimes since September 11, 2011. The United States must be vigilant during the visa-assurance process to ensure that those approved for admission do not intend to harm Americans and that they have no ties to terrorism."

Approximately one week after the signing of Executive Order 13769 in January 2017, Federal District Court Judge James Robart in Seattle, Washington, issued a nationwide restraining order that blocked the travel ban from being implemented. On February 9 the U.S. Court of Appeals for the 9th Circuit, based in San Francisco, California, also refused to reinstate the ban, ruling that there was insufficient proof that Muslims from the seven predominantly Muslim countries listed in the order posed a national security threat to the United States.

Indeed, study after study has proven that Muslims from the seven predominantly Muslim countries listed in Executive Order 13769 posed little, if any, security threat to U.S. national security (Considine 2018, 123–27). The CATO Institute, a conservative think tank based in Washington, DC, found that Muslim immigrants and refugees from the seven countries listed killed zero people in terrorist attacks on U.S. soil between 1975 and 2015 (Nowrasteh 2017). The CATO report, titled "Little National Security Benefit to Trump's Executive Order on Immigration," added that between 1975 and 2015, "the annual chance of being murdered by somebody other than a foreign-born terrorist was 252.9 times greater than the chance of dying in a terrorist attack committed by a foreign-born terrorist" (Nowrasteh 2017).

In any case, President Trump issued Executive Order 13780, a revised travel ban, on March 6, 2017, that targeted only six countries and exempted visa- and green card–holders. Yet as was the case with Executive Order 13769, a federal district judge, Derrick Watson of Hawaii, issued a nationwide halt to the revised ban. Similarly, a day after Watson's ruling, Federal District Judge Theodore Chuang of Maryland blocked part of the revised ban that applied to people traveling to the United States from the six predominantly Muslim countries. Judge Watson's ruling was then upheld by the U.S. Court of Appeals for the 4th Circuit in Richmond, Virginia, on the basis of unconstitutional religious discrimination against Muslims.

Not least of all, President Trump issued Presidential Proclamation 9645, essentially a third executive order, which Judge Watson of Hawaii blocked yet again in October 2017 on the grounds that it "suffers from precisely the same maladies as its predecessor" and "plainly discriminates based on nationality." Judge Chuang of Maryland echoed Judge Watson's ruling by referring to Trump's third executive order as one that violated the freedom of religion clearly outlined in the First Amendment of the U.S. Constitution.

Finally, on June 26, 2018, the U.S. Supreme Court reversed the ruling of the 9th Circuit Court of Appeals in a 5–4 ruling, thereby handing a major victory to the Trump administration. The ban applied to all people from Iran, Libya, Somalia, Syria, and Yemen. It also placed limits on the entry of people from North Korea and Venezuela. Justice Sonia Sotomayor of the U.S. Supreme Court issued a scathing rebuttal of the high court's decision to uphold Trump's ban on Muslims traveling to the United States. Justice Sotomayor pointed out that the policy, which originated in anti-Muslim animus, "masquerades behind a façade of national-security concerns." She also noted that the ruling was unreasonable because it was "ignoring the facts" and "turning a blind eye to the pain and suffering the Proclamation inflicts upon countless families and individuals, many of whom are United States citizens" (Sotomayor 2018, 9).

It is also worth noting that fighters of Daesh, also referred to as the Islamic State of Iraq and Syria (ISIS), took to social media platforms to hail the initial Executive Order 13769 as the "blessed ban," saying it proves to their followers and Muslims worldwide that the U.S. government—as well as U.S. citizens—really do hate Muslims (McKernan 2017; Perez 2017). In addition, U.S. intelligence agencies referred to the idea of a "Muslim travel ban" as a strategic mistake because it played into the vision and goals of Daesh. Robert Richer, a 35-year CIA veteran and former chief of the agency's Near East division, told the *Washington Post* that the ban was a mistake. He stated: "[Trump's proposed ban on Muslims is] a win for jihadists and other anti-U.S. forces" because "it fuels the belief out there that Americans are anti-Islam. Otherwise, it accomplishes nothing."

While many U.S. citizens were surprised by Trump's targeting of potential Muslim immigrants, there is nothing really "new" about the Muslim travel ban. The U.S. government, in fact, has a long history of implementing immigration policies that have blocked or restricted the immigration of Muslims to U.S. soil (Considine 2018, 13). The Naturalization Act of 1790 set the precedent that made it virtually impossible for "non-White"

Muslims worldwide to become U.S. citizens. The act read, "Any alien, being a free white person, may be admitted to become a citizen of the United States, or any of them" (Naturalization Act 1790), thus excluding Muslims of African and Asian descent.

In the 20th century, the 64th U.S. Congress enacted a sweeping immigration law called the Immigration Act of 1917, also known as the Asiatic Barred Zone of 1917. This law defined the barred zone as including areas like the Middle East, the South Asian subcontinent, and East Asia, a combination of countries that effectively banned the majority of the world's Muslims from immigrating to the United States. The Asiatic Barred Zone was driven by a turn toward nativism in the United States and by groups like the Immigration Restriction League, which had in the late 19th century supported the idea of literacy tests to incoming immigrants. The official text of the Asiatic Barred Zone also included a list of people who were deemed to be undesirable including "political radicals," "idiots," "illiterates," "persons with constitutional psychopathic inferiority," and "polygamists."

The first immigration law to create numerical quotas for immigrants based on nationality was the Emergency Quota Act of 1921. This act severely limited the ability of the U.S. Muslim population to grow by means of new immigration (Considine 2018, 15). The National Origins Act of 1924, also known as the Immigration Act, also severely limited the number of Muslim immigrants allowed entry into the United States. The National Origins Act restricted the number of immigrants to 2 percent of the U.S. native-born white population as determined by their national origins and completely excluded immigrants from Asia (Douglas 2008). Adolf Hitler praised this U.S. immigration policy in his autobiography *Mein Kampf*, writing, "There is currently one state in which one can observe at least weak beginnings of a better conception. This is of course not our exemplary German Republic, but the American Union . . . which categorically refuses the immigration of physically unhealthy elements, and simply excludes the immigration of certain races. In these respects, America already pays obeisance, at least in tentative first steps, of the characteristic völkich [or political ideology] . . . of the [Nazi] state."

The U.S. government's position on immigration changed drastically after the Immigration and Naturalization Act of 1965, also referred to as the Hart-Celler Act. In no uncertain terms, the Act of 1965 read that "no person shall receive any preference or priority or be discriminated against in the issuance of an immigrant visa because of the person's race, sex, nationality, place of birth or place of residence." This act replaced long-standing laws that favored white northern European immigrants by allowing entry into the United States to people from the Middle East, South Asia, and Africa, three continents with large Muslim populations. Following 1965, the U.S. Muslim population increased along with the diversity of the community. Prior to the act, the majority of U.S. Muslims would have identified themselves as African American.

Following the 9/11 attacks, the U.S. government implemented a program called the National Security Entry-Exit Registration System, or NSEERS. This program, which helped the government fine, arrest, and deport Muslims, some of whom resided in the United States legally, was introduced in June 2002 by Attorney General John Ashcroft. The "Special Registration" provision of NSEERS "required all male teen and adult nationals of 25 different countries to allow themselves to be fingerprinted and registered by the federal government or be subject to immediate deportation to their home countries." Khaled A. Beydoun, author of *American Islamophobia: Understanding the Roots and Rise of Fear,* referred to NSEERS as a "clear manifestation of the structural Islamophobic presumption that Muslim identity was correlative with terrorism" (Beydoun 2018, 101). Beydoun explained: "Twenty-four of the twenty-five countries of interest listed in the NSEERS legislation were Muslim-majority nations. . . . [The program] was predominantly concerned with tracking the activity of Muslim immigrants, particularly while they were within the United States, as evidenced by the nations it honed in on and the arrests made after its enactment. Immediately after it went into force, 80,000 men were entered into the NSEERS registry, the vast majority of them Muslims" (Beydoun 2018, 101). While dissolved in 2011, as Beydoun (2016) again noted, NSEERS explicitly reintegrated the Islamophobic baseline that Muslims were presumptive national security threats.

See also: Clash of Civilizations; *Jihad*; Refugees

Further Reading

Agarwal, Kritika. 2017. "Shadows of the Past. South Asian American Digital Archive." Philadelphia, PA: South Asian American Digital Archive. Last modified February 5, 2017. Retrieved from https://www.saada.org/tides/article/shadows-of-the-past.

Beydoun, Khaled A. 2016. "Islamophobia: Toward a Legal Definition and Framework." *Columbia Law Review Online* 116, no. 108. Retrieved from https://papers.ssrn.com/sol3/papers.cfm?abstract_id=2933156.

Beydoun, Khaled A. 2018. *American Islamophobia: Understanding the Roots and Rise of Fear*. Oakland: University of California Press.

Considine, Craig. 2018. *Muslims in America: Examining the Facts*. Santa Barbara, CA: ABC-CLIO.

Douglas, Karen M. 2008. "National Origins System." In *Encyclopedia of Race, Ethnicity, and Society*. Edited by Richard Schaefer. Thousand Oaks, CA: Sage Publications.

McKernan, Bethan. 2017. "ISIS Hails Donald Trump's Muslim Immigration Restrictions as a 'Blessed Ban.'" Independent.co.uk, January 30, 2017. Retrieved from http://www.independent.co.uk/news/world/middle-east/isis-donald-trump-muslim-ban-immigration-iraq-iran-restrictionstravel-islamic-state-us-visa-a7552856.html.

Naturalization Act. 1790. *Naturalization Acts of 1790 and 1795*. mountvernon.org. Retrieved from https://www.mountvernon.org/education/primary-sources-2/article/naturalization-acts-of-1790-and-1795/.

Nowrasteh, Alex. 2017. "Little National Security Benefit to Trump's Executive Order on Immigration." Washington, DC: CATO Institute. Last modified January 25, 2017. Retrieved from https://www.cato.org/blog/little-national-security-benefit-trumps-executive-order-immigration.

Perez, Chris. 2017. "Islamic State Fighters Reportedly Calling Trump Travel Ban the 'Blessed Ban.'" NYPost.com, February 9, 2017. Retrieved from http://nypost.com/2017/02/08/isis-fighters-call-trumpstravel-order-a-blessed-ban/.

Pew Research Center. 2018. "Muslims in America: Immigrants and those born in U.S. see life differently in many ways." Washington, DC: Pew Research Center. Last modified April 17, 2018. Retrieved from http://www.pewforum.org/essay/muslims-in-america-immigrants-and-those-born-in-u-s-see-life-differently-in-many-ways/.

Sotomayor, Sonia. 2018. *Donald J. Trump, President of the United States, Et Al., Petitioners v. Hawaii, Et Al.* 17 U.S. 965. Washington, DC: U.S. Supreme Court. Last modified June 26, 2018. Retrieved from https://www.supremecourt.gov/opinions/17pdf/17-965_h315.pdf.

P

Pluralism

Pluralism is a concept that has been discussed by theologians, philosophers, and politicians of various religious and political orientations for centuries. In recent years the concept of pluralism has been referred to in varied ways including "equality" among religious traditions and religious populations, unity of humanity, and the interaction among people of various religious and spiritual backgrounds. In the context of the Islamic tradition, the Prophet Muhammad's teachings stress submission to Allah, but also embracing religious, ethnic, and racial diversity in any given community.

The Qur'an, the Islamic holy book, does not merely call on Muslims to respect and embrace diversity; rather, it demands that Muslims do so in accordance with God's will. According to the Qur'an, all human beings are acknowledged as equal in the eyes of God: "Mankind! We have created you from a male and female, and made you into peoples and tribes, so that you might come to know each other. The noblest of you in God's sight is the one who fears God most. God is all knowing and all-aware" (Qur'an 49:13). The Qur'an refers to Jews and Christians by using the Arabic term *Ahl al-Kitab*, which translates to "People of the Book." This special designation symbolizes the respect accorded to Jews and Christians in the Qur'an, and also signals the debt that the Islamic tradition owes to prophets such as Abraham, Moses, David, and Jesus, all of whom are recognized as prophets in the Qur'an. The Qur'an (3:64) also uses the phrase "common word" to encourage stronger relations between religious populations: "Say: 'People of the Book, let us come to a word common to us that we shall worship none but God and that we shall associate no partner with Him and that none of us shall take others, besides God, for lords.'"

Pluralism is more than simply "religious equality" or the recognition that all religious traditions contain elements of "truth." According to Diana L. Eck, founder of the Pluralism Project at Harvard University, pluralism (specifically religious pluralism) is a *process* of interreligious human connection and social interaction that is best captured as "the energetic engagement with religious diversity." Pluralism, in this context, is distinguished from "religious tolerance." Scholars like Eck (2006) argue that religious tolerance reproduces stereotypes and social structures that divide communities because tolerance is "stand-offish" and does not require cross-cultural or cross-religious engagement. Pluralism is different from tolerance in the sense that the former actively seeks dialogue, education, and understanding across lines of social, cultural, racial, and religious differences.

The active or energetic process of pluralism encourages people of diverse backgrounds to commit themselves to partnerships and mutual obligations in order to foster social cohesion between populations. Pluralism is further described as "the acknowledgement and acceptance, rather than tolerance, of Otherness and diversity, both within the Self and within the Other" (Esack 2002, xii). "In the context of religion it means the acceptance of diverse ways of responding to the impulse, which may be both innate and socialized, within each human being towards the transcendent" (Esack 2002, xii). Put another way, as scholar Eboo Patel does in his book *Acts of Faith: The Story of an American Muslim, the Struggle for the Soul of a Generation*, "[r]eligious pluralism is neither mere coexistence nor forced consensus . . . [it] is an intentional commitment that is imprinted through action" (Patel 2007, xv).

Roger Williams, a Puritan Christian dissident who arrived in Massachusetts Bay Colony from England in 1631, is considered by some scholars to be the founding father of religious pluralism in the United States. In Massachusetts Bay Colony, which later became the state of Massachusetts, Williams clashed with the more conservative Puritan Christian factions of the colony over the confiscation of Native American land and the denial of freedom of religion at large. Eventually, the General Court of Massachusetts banned Williams from living in the colony, thus forcing him into exile. With the help of the Narragansett tribe, Williams established a new colony named Providence Plantation, which later became the present-day state of Rhode Island. In 1640, Williams and the settlers of the plantation signed the Providence Agreement, whereby religious freedom, civil rights, and separation of religion and state were guaranteed by rule of law. Williams even argued forcefully against coercion: "It is the will and command of God, that (since the coming of his Son the Lord Jesus) a permission of the most Paganish, Jewish, Turkish, or Anti-Christians consciences and worship, be granted to all men in all Nations and Countries" (Williams n.d.).

See also: Abrahamic Tradition; Freedom of Religion; Integration; The Prophet Muhammad; U.S. Founding Fathers

Further Reading

Ahmed, Akbar. 2010. *Journey into America: The Challenge of Islam.* Washington, DC: Brookings.

Considine, Craig. 2016. "Religious Pluralism and Civic Rights in a 'Muslim Nation': An Analysis of Prophet Muhammad's Covenants with Christians." *Religions* 7, no. 15: 1–21.

Eck, Diana L. 2006. "What Is Pluralism?" Pluralism.org. Retrieved from http://pluralism.org/what-is-pluralism/.

Esack, Farid. 2002. *Qur'an, Liberation and Pluralism: An Islamic Perspective of Interreligious Solidarity against Oppression.* Oxford, UK: Oneworld.

Patel, Eboo. 2007. *Acts of Faith: The Story of an American Muslim, the Struggle for the Soul of a Generation.* Boston: Beacon Press.

Safi, Louay M. 2011. "Religious Freedom and Interreligious Relations in Islam: Reflections on *Da'wah* and Qur'anic Ethics." *The Review of Faith & International Affairs* 9, no. 2 (Summer): 11–16.

Williams, Roger. n.d. "A Plea for Religious Liberty." Constitution.org. Retrieved from http://www.constitution.org/bcp/religlib.htm.

Polygamy

One of the many erroneous claims made against U.S. Muslims is that their Islamic faith is patriarchal and oppressive toward women and gives unfair advantages and rights to husbands in relation to their wives. Some critics claim that the Islamic faith approves of polygamy, or the marrying of multiple wives by men. These critics claim that Muslim women are coerced into polygamous relationships and that they are manipulated and abused by their husbands, all justified by the *sharia*, or "Islamic law."

Generally, there are two types of marriages in the Islamic tradition. The first is monogamy, in which one man is married to one woman. The second type of marriage—limited polygamy—is an arrangement in which one man is married to two, three, or at the most four wives. Polygamy is deemed to be permissible in the following Qur'anic verse: "If you fear that you cannot deal fairly with orphan girls, you may marry women of your choice, two or three or four; but if you fear that you might not be able to treat them with equal fairness, then only one—or [from among] those whom you rightfully possess. That is more likely to keep you from committing an injustice" (Qur'an 4:3). Chapter 4, or *Sura An-Nisa* ("The Women"), makes it clear that polygamy is neither mandatory nor encouraged, but merely permitted under certain circumstances.

Sura An-Nisa is said to have been revealed after the Battle of Badr in 624 CE and the Battle of Uhud in 625 CE. The Muslim army at these battles lost a significant number of men and, therefore, left behind widows and orphans. The loss of life in the battles of Badr and Uhud raised the question of how to ensure a sustainable welfare for the family members of the deceased soldiers. In the context of the Qur'an (4:3), Allah permitted polygamy in order to provide emergency welfare to grieving individuals and better manage society at one of the most vulnerable times for the *ummah*, or Muslim nation.

Anti-Islam critics oftentimes argue that the Prophet Muhammad was a womanizer because he had multiple wives at the same time. After his first wife, Khadijah, passed away when he was 50 years old, the Prophet Muhammad is said to have had twelve more wives until he passed away in 632 CE. Scholar Jamal Badawi, however, objects to the claim perpetuated by anti-Islam critics that Muhammad sustained multiple marriages with women at the same time for the sake of his pleasure and needs. In his argument, Badawi states that Islam delves deeper into the problems of individuals and societies and "provides for legitimate and clean solutions that are far more beneficial than would be the case if they were ignored" (Badawi n.d.).

The permissibility of polygamy in the Islamic faith is rooted in the Jewish tradition. According to the Torah, Abraham had three wives, David had many wives, of which eight are named in the Torah, and Solomon had hundreds of wives. The practice of polygamy continued in limited circumstances until German Rabbi Gershom Bin Yehudah issued an edict banning polygamy during his famous Synod of the Takkanot in 1000 CE. Rabbi Gershom banned polygamy to prevent husbands from taking advantage of their wives and to avoid any rivalries or conflicts between wives. While the Torah does not officially outlaw polygamy, the practice of having multiple wives or husbands is virtually nonexistent among the world-wide Jewish population (Silberberg n.d.).

Polygamy within the U.S. Muslim population and Muslim communities nationwide is not a matter that receives significant attention, primarily because so few Muslims actually participate in polygamous relationships or marriages. While there are no official estimates on the number of polygamous relationships within the U.S. Muslim population, experts are confident that the numbers are extremely low and predict that the numbers will recede further in the future. Debra Mubashshir Majeed, a scholar, estimated that less than 1 percent of U.S. Muslims participate in the practice of polygamy—and these practitioners of polygamy are most often African American Muslims or recent immigrants from West Africa. Typically, a man marries one woman under civil law, and then marries one, or multiple women, in religious ceremonies that are not recognized by state law (Hagerty 2008). The majority of polygamous relationships or marriages involve first-generation immigrants from Muslim-majority countries where these sorts of arrangements are more commonplace.

Although polygamy is illegal in the United States and most mosques try to discourage polygamous marriages, some U.S. Muslims in the country have quietly married multiple wives (Hagerty 2008). Prominent U.S. *imam* Siraj Wahhaj was quoted in Paul Barrett's book *American Islam* (2007) as saying that he has performed polygamous unions at his Al-Taqwa mosque in Brooklyn, New York. On the other hand, Tahir Anwar, *imam* of a well-established mosque in San Jose, California, told *Slate* that he would discourage any Muslims seeking a polygamous marriage and would not perform the ceremony: "It is not allowed in the land that we live in, a land to whom we have promised that we will follow all of its laws" (Useem 2007).

The fact of the matter is that the Islamic faith may encourage polygamy under certain circumstances, primarily to protect orphans or widows, but the overwhelming majority of U.S. Muslims, if not practically all, do not condone this practice. Attempts to link U.S. Muslims to the condoning of polygamy is a gross distortion of the contemporary realities and lived experiences of U.S. Muslims.

Further Reading

Alidu, Abdul-Nasser. 2015. "Polygamy in Islam: A Question of Lust or Social Welfare?" Circumspecte.com. Last modified April 8, 2015. Retrieved from

https://circumspecte.com/2015/04/guest-post-by-abdul-nasser-alidu-poly
gamy-in-islam-a-question-of-lust-or-social-welfare/.

Badawi, Jamal. n.d. "Misconception about Islam: All Muslim Men Marry Four
Wives." VeniceInterfaith.org. Retrieved from http://veniceinterfaith.org/announ
cements/125-misconception-about-islam-all-muslim-men-marry-four-wives.

Hagerty, Barbara Bradley. 2008. "Some Muslims in U.S. Quietly Engage in
Polygamy." NPR.org, May 27, 2008. Retrieved from https://www.npr.org
/templates/story/story.php?storyId=90857818.

Silberberg, Naftali. n.d. "Does Jewish Law Forbid Polygamy?" Chabad.org.
Retrieved from https://www.chabad.org/library/article_cdo/aid/558598/jewish
/Does-Jewish-Law-Forbid-Polygamy.htm.

Useem, Andrea. 2007. "What to Expect When You're Expecting a Co-Wife."
Slate.com, July 24, 2007. Retrieved from https://slate.com/human-interest
/2007/07/why-american-muslims-don-t-care-to-legalize-polygamy.html.

The Prophet Muhammad

The Prophet Muhammad is the "messenger" of God who delivered the
Qur'an to the Arabs of modern-day Saudi Arabia in the 7th century. Muhammad is considered by Muslims to be the "Seal of Prophets." Muslims
worldwide proclaim that there can be no prophets after him (Nasr 2000,
23). He was born in 570 CE in Mecca, Saudi Arabia, and died on June 8,
632 CE. His name derives from *hamada*, the Arabic verb meaning "to
praise, to glorify." Throughout his life Muhammad was popularly referred
to as "The Trustworthy One," or *Al-Ameen* in Arabic. His peers saw his
special and exemplary qualities, primarily his consistency and honesty in
interpersonal and business matters. Even one of his Meccan enemies, Abu
Jahl, said that Muhammad never told a lie. The study of the Prophet's life
shows that whenever he had to choose between two courses, he would always opt for the easier one (Sahih Al-Bukhari n.d.).

The Prophet Muhammad's childhood was one of hardship and promise. His father, Abd Allah Bin Al-Muttalib, died before he was born. After
his father's death, Muhammad's mother, Amina Bint Wahb, took the
young Muhammad to Yathrib (also known as Medina), an oasis town a
few hundred miles north of Mecca, to stay with relatives and visit his father's grave for the first time. On the return to Mecca, Amina fell ill and
passed away, later being buried in Abwa, a village on the Mecca-Medina
road. At this point in Muhammad's life, about six years old, he was an

orphan in the care of Hallma, his nurse, who brought him back to Mecca and entrusted him to the care of Muhammad's paternal grandfather, Abdul Al-Muttalib. Some scholars attribute Muhammad's humbling early years as an orphan as one of the reasons why he commanded Muslims to care for the underprivileged members of society.

After his grandfather passed away in 578 CE, Muhammad, then about eight years old, was put in the care of Abu Talib Ibn Abd Al-Muttalib, Muhammad's uncle, and Fatimah Bint Asad, Abu Talib's wife. As a teenager, Muhammad worked as a shepherd and traveled with Abu Talib, who worked as a merchant, on various caravan excursions to prominent trade centers. Later in his life, the 25-year-old Muhammad was asked by Khadija Bint Khuwaylid, a 40-year-old widow and wealthy merchant, for his hand in marriage. Khadija is considered around the world by Muslims to be the "Mother of the Believers" because she is the first person to recognize and accept Muhammad's calling and prophecy.

The *ahadith* collection Sahih Muslim sheds light on the amount of trust and love Muhammad had for Khadija: "God almighty never granted me anyone better in this life than her. She accepted me when people rejected me; she believed in me when people doubted me; she shared her wealth with me when people deprived me; and God granted me children only through her." Together, Muhammad and Khadija are said to have had a total of six children.

In 610 CE, Muhammad retreated to Hira, a mountain cave, and reported being visited by the Angel Gabriel, who gave Muhammad his first revelation from God. Following his life-altering experience on Mount Hira, Muhammad returned home to Khadijah, his wife. Khadijah is said to have accepted the legitimacy of his experiences, thereby becoming the first believer, or Muslim, of Muhammad's prophethood. A Christian man named Waraqa Ibn Nawfal, Khadijah's cousin, is said to have been the second "witness" or "believer" of Muhammad's prophethood. At the age of 43, Muhammad started revealing these revelations in the public sphere, proclaiming that "God is One."

The Prophet Muhammad entered into a series of treaties with Christians during the 7th century. These treaties are popularly referred to as "The Covenants of the Prophet Muhammad with the Christians of his time" (Morrow 2013). The Covenants have been further described as fostering religious pluralism and standing for civic nation building in terms of building a "Muslim nation" (Considine 2016). The Sunnah of the Prophet also shows that he allowed the Christian Arab diplomats of Najran to conduct religious services in his mosque in Medina (Salmi, Majul, and Tanham 1998, 134).

The Prophet Muhammad has been used by critics throughout history as a means to dehumanize Muslims and to portray the value system of the Islamic faith as antithetical to "Western values." François-Marie Arouet, a French Enlightenment writer better known today as Voltaire, wrote a blistering attack on Muhammad in a five-act tragedy play titled *Le Fanatisme, ou Mahomet le Prophète* (1741). After initially staging and becoming a success in Paris and London, Voltaire's play would be performed in 1780 in the United States. The plot of *Mahomet* is a direct assault on Muhammad, who is portrayed as a manipulative religious fanatic. Voltaire described his play as "written in opposition to the founder of a false and barbarous sect." Similar sentiments toward the Prophet Muhammad were expressed by several of the U.S. Founding Fathers. Research by James H. Huston of the Library of Congress revealed that an evangelical Baptist spokesman denounced "'Mahomet' (Muhammad) as a 'hateful' figure who, unlike the meek and gentle Jesus, spread his religion at the point of a sword. A Presbyterian preacher in rural South Carolina dusted off Grotius' 17th century reproach that the 'religion of Mahomet originated in arms, breathes nothing but arms, is propagated by arms" (Hutson 2002).

Modern critics of the Prophet Muhammad continue to misportray him as a barbarous figure. The Reverend Jerry Vines, a Christian preacher and former pastor of what was once the United States's third largest Southern Baptist church, gave a speech at the Pastors Conference of the Southern Baptist Convention in which he called Muhammad "a demon-possessed pedophile who had twelve wives, the last one of which was a nine-year old girl." Bloggers like Robert Spencer, author of *The Truth about Muhammad: Founder of the World's Most Intolerant Religion*, depict Muhammad as someone who condoned pedophilia and forcefully discriminated against religious minority populations like Jews and Christians.

Portrayals of the Prophet Muhammad reached a boiling point in February 2006 after the Danish newspaper *Jyllands-Posten* published a dozen cartoons depicting Muhammad as a terrorist. One cartoon depicted Muhammad with a turban in the shape of a bomb. Another cartoon showed him at the gates of heaven, arms raised, saying to men who seem to be suicide bombers, "Stop, stop, we have run out of virgins" (Brinkley and Fisher 2006). George W. Bush's administration responded to the cartoons by stating, "We find them offensive, and we certainly understand why Muslims would find these images offensive" (Weigel 2012). Leaders of

Muslim-majority countries condemned the publications as heinous and harmful to international relations. Muhammad Sayyid Tantawy, the Grand *imam* of Al-Azhar Mosque and Grand *sheikh* of Al-Azhar University, the leading Sunni center of learning in the world, called for protests. The Upper House of the Pakistani Parliament issued a unanimous resolution condemning the cartoons of the Prophet Muhammad as blasphemous and urged the Danish government to take action against the cartoonists.

More than 200 protesters, some armed, berated the Prophet of Islam outside the Islamic Community Center of Phoenix, Arizona, in May 2015, weeks after two Muslims opened fire at an anti-Islam event in Texas. Some among the protesters, some of whom called Islam "a religion of murderers," waved copies of caricatures of Muhammad drawn at the Phoenix event (Reuters 2015).

Even though these portrayals of the Prophet Muhammad have had a lasting impact on the perception of Muslims and the Islamic faith, it is worth pointing out that the moral virtues held by Muhammad were used as models for social justice in the formative years of the United States. In advocating for the humane treatment of Native Americans persecuted by Christians in 1764, Benjamin Franklin, a prominent U.S. Founding Father, "passionately invoked a story of the Prophet Muhammad rebuking a cruel Muslim for not being merciful in times of conflict" (Muhammad 2013, 4). In his text *A Narrative of the Late Massacres in Lancaster County, of A Number of Indians, Friends of this Province, By Persons Unknown*, Franklin condemned the actions of his fellow Christians, citing the Prophet Muhammad, among others, as historical figures who had been merciful to their enemies. Franklin wrote:

> As for the Turks [i.e., Muslims], it is recorded in the Life of Mahomet, the founder of their religion, that Khaled, one of his captains, having divided a number of prisoners between himself and those that were with him, he commanded the hands of his own prisoners to be tied behind them, and then, in a most cruel and brutal manner, put them to the sword; but he could not prevail on his men to massacre their captives, because in fight they had laid down their arms, submitted, and demanded protection. Mahomet [Prophet Muhammad], when the account was brought to him, applauded the men for their humanity; but said to Khaled, with great indignation, "O Khaled, thou butcher, cease to molest me with thy wickedness. If thou possessedst a heap of gold as large as Mount Obod, and shouldst expend it all in God's cause, thy merit would not efface the guilt incurred by the murder of the meanest of those poor captives" (Franklin 1856, 73–74).

The "Indians," Franklin proclaimed, would had been safer with Muslims than the "Christian white savages" among his coreligionists because "ever since Mahomet's reproof to Khaled, even the cruel Turks never kill prisoners in cold blood."

Moreover, a frieze of the Prophet Muhammad is located in the U.S. Supreme Court, where Muhammad is depicted holding the Qur'an and a sword. The frieze, erected in 1935 by President Franklin D. Roosevelt, was created to honor and celebrate "the great lawgivers of history" and included images of other religious figures like Moses, Solomon, and Confucius (Hussain 2016, 28–29).

See also: Ahadith

Further Reading

Ali, Kecia. 2016. *The Lives of Muhammad*. Cambridge, MA: Harvard University Press.

Armstrong, Karen. 2000. *Islam: A Short History*. New York and Toronto: Modern Library.

Brinkley, Joel, and Ian Fisher. 2006. "U.S. Says It Also Finds Cartoons of Muhammad Offensive." *The New York Times*, February 4, 2006. Retrieved from https://www.nytimes.com/2006/02/04/politics/us-says-it-also-finds-cartoons-of-muhammad-offensive.html.

Considine, Craig. 2016. "Religious Pluralism and Civic Rights in a 'Muslim Nation': An Analysis of Prophet Muhammad's Covenants with Christians." *Religions* 7, no. 15: 1–21.

Franklin, Benjamin. 1856. *The Works of Benjamin Franklin; Containing Several Political and Historical Tracts Not Included in Any Former Edition and Many Letters Official and Private, Not Hitherto Published; with Notes and a Life of the Author*. Edited by Jared Sparks. Boston: Whittemore, Niles, and Hall.

Hazelton, Lesley. 2014. *The First Muslim: The Story of Muhammad*. New York: Riverhead Books.

Hussain, Amir. 2016. *Muslims and the Making of America*. Waco, TX: Baylor University Press.

Hutson, James H. 2002. "The Founding Fathers and Islam: Library Papers Show Early Tolerance for Muslim Faith." Washington, DC: Library of Congress. Last modified May 2002. Retrieved from https://www.loc.gov/loc/lcib/0205/tolerance.html.

Morrow, John Andrew. 2013. *The Covenants of the Prophet Muhammad with the Christians of the World*. Tacoma, WA: Angelico Press/Sophia Perennis.

Muhammad, Precious Rasheeda. 2013. *Muslims and the Making of America*. New York: Muslim Public Affairs Council. Retrieved from https://virtuecenter

.s3.amazonaws.com/files/2013-02-08-10/Muslims-and-the-Making-of -America.pdf.

Nasr, Seyyed Hossein. 2000. *Ideals and Realities of Islam*. Chicago: ABC International Group, Inc.

Reuters. 2015. "Protesters berate Muhammad during anti-Islam protest at Phoenix mosque." *The Guardian*, May 30, 2015. Retrieved from https://www.theguardian .com/us-news/2015/may/30/protestors-berate-prophet-muhammad-at-anti -islam-protest-at-phoenix-mosque.

Safi, Omid. 2010. *Memories of Muhammad: Why the Prophet Matters*. New York: HarperOne.

Sahih Al-Bukhari. n.d. "Virtues and Merits of the Prophet (pbuh) and his Companions." Sunnah.com, accessed July 26, 2019. Retrieved from https:// sunnah.com/bukhari/61/69.

Salmi, Ralph H., Cesar Adib Majul, and George K. Tanham. *Islam and Conflict Resolution: Theories and Practices*. Lanham, New York, and Oxford: University Press of America.

Weigel, David. 2012. "Bush Administration on 2006 Danish Cartoons: 'We Certainly Understand Why Muslims Would Find These Images Offensive.'" Slate.com, September 12, 2012. Retrieved from http://www.slate.com/blogs /weigel/2012/09/12/bush_administration_on_2006_danish_cartoons_we _certainly_understand_why_muslims_would_find_these_images_offensive _.html.

Q

Qur'an

The Qur'an, the Islamic holy scripture, is sacred to over one billion Muslims worldwide. The term *qur'an* is said to be non-Arabic in origin, but related to the ancient Syriac word meaning "recitation" (Al-Jerrahi 1991, v). According to Farid Esack, author of *The Qur'an, Liberation and Pluralism: An Islamic Perspective of Interreligious Solidarity Against Oppression*, the majority of Arabic scholars hold the view that the word *qur'an* is derived from the Arabic root *qara'a*, which means "he read," or an adjective from *qarana*, "he gathered or collected" (Esack 2002, 52). In the Qur'an itself, *qur'an* is employed in the sense of "reading" (17:93), "recital" (75:18), and a "collection" (75:17) (Esack 2002, 52).

Muslims worldwide consider the Qur'an to be the literal word of God and God's final message to humanity as given to the Prophet Muhammad, the final messenger of God and the "Seal of the Prophets." The Qur'an is said to have been delivered to Muhammad by the Archangel Gabriel in 610 CE while Muhammad had retreated to Hira, a cave located on Jabal An-Nour, a mountain near Mecca, Saudi Arabia. Scholars say that he retreated to Hira, as he often did, to contemplate his concern with Arab society's prevailing social order of ignorance over divine guidance, an order that Muslims worldwide popularly refer to as *jahiliyyah*, the Arabic term that means "ignorance," but that is generally associated with social ills like oppression of women, wealth inequality, and racism.

The Qur'an was revealed by God to Muhammad over the span of approximately 22 years. The Qu'ran consists of 114 chapters and 6,000 verses. Muhammad started sharing God's revelations when he was 40 years old after Gabriel visited him in Hira. Scholars tend to claim that Muhammad shared the revelations with a scribe who copied down the words and revelations into a single collection. After the Prophet

Muhammad's death in 632 CE, the revelations were joined together to form a single text known today as the Qur'an.

The Islamic holy text is regarded by Muslims as a confirmation and continuation of the Jewish Torah (Old Testament) and Christian Gospels (New Testament). The Qur'an, therefore, is a sacred book that reiterates the revelations given to the *Ahl al-Kitab*, the Arabic term meaning the "People of the Book." In this context, the pluralist nature of the term *Ahl al-Kitab* contends that Jews, Christians, and Muslims are fundamentally part and parcel of the same monotheistic tradition that started with the revelations received by Abraham. Scholar Joseph E. Lumbard explained that the "People of the Book" are admired for their piety and promised salvation as mandated through God, though he added that the Qur'an criticizes parts of Jewish and Christian populations for engaging in practices of polytheism and altering the scripture of God's own words for their own self-serving purposes (Lumbard 2008, 28).

The Qur'an has come under further scrutiny in part because of media attention given to anti-Islam activists in the United States and beyond. In September 2010, a fringe evangelical pastor, Reverend Terry Jones of the Dove World Outreach Center, hosted "International Burn a *Qur'an* Day" on his church property in Gainesville, Florida. Reverend Jones issued a series of tweets and appeared on mainstream news channels, saying that Islam is "of the devil" and "fascist." The Council on American-Islamic Relations (CAIR), a leading advocate for civil rights on U.S. soil, called on U.S. Muslims to respond to the church's planned protest by hosting educational "Share the *Qur'an iftar*" (the Arabic term for "breaking the fast") gatherings during Ramadan, the Islamic holy month. The CAIR National Communications Director Ibrahim Hooper issued an official response statement stating that CAIR's research reveals that U.S. citizens are able to better connect with Muslims and anti-Muslim bias decreases through accurate information about the Islamic faith and Muslim lived experiences. Although Reverend Jones decided to call off "International Burn the *Qur'an* Day," the effects of his action reverberated throughout the United States and the world.

The Qur'an also has been incorporated into acts of civic engagement in U.S. history. Upon taking his individual ceremonial oath to serve Minnesota's 5th Congressional District in the U.S. House of Representatives, Keith Ellison requested to take the oath on Thomas Jefferson's personal copy of George Sale's 1734 translation of the Qur'an, commonly called the "Alcoran of Mohammed" (Library of Congress 2007). For Ellison, using Jefferson's Qur'an to be sworn into Congress "demonstrates that from the very beginning of our country, we had people who were visionary, who were religiously tolerant, who believed that knowledge and wisdom could be gleaned from any number of sources, including the *Qur'an*." Ellison's ceremonial act of religious freedom was met by opposition from anti-Islam critics in the United States. Dennis Prager, a nationally syndicated conservative radio talk show host, wrote an article on Townhall stating that Ellison "should not be allowed [to take his oath of office on the Qur'an])—not because of any American hostility to the Koran but because the act undermines American civilization" (Prager 2006). Similarly, Republican Representative Virgil Goode of Virginia wrote a letter to his constituents, warning that without immigration overhaul there will be many more Muslims elected to office demanding the use of the Qur'an (CNN 2006). The letter added that "when I raise my hand to take the oath on Swearing in Day, I will have the Bible in my other hand. I do not subscribe to using the *Qur'an* in any way."

CAIR asked Goode to apologize: "Goode's Islamophobic remarks send a message of intolerance that is unworthy of anyone elected to public office. There can be no reasonable defense for such bigotry" (Hoar 2006). In the cases of Prager and Goode, U.S. Muslims were represented as a fifth column intent on undermining and eventually replacing U.S. democracy and "Western civilization" with *sharia* and "civilizational *jihad*," as the Southern Poverty Law Center (n.d.) notes.

See also: Ahadith; The Prophet Muhammad

Further Reading

Council on American-Islamic Relations. 2018. "Respond to 'Burn a Koran Day' with Educational Iftar." Washington, DC: CAIR. Last modified July 28, 2018. Retrieved from https://pa.cair.com/actionalert/burn-koran-response/.

Esack, Farid. 2002. *Qur'an, Liberation and Pluralism: An Islamic Perspective of Interreligious Solidarity against Oppression.* Oxford, UK: Oneworld.

Hoar, Jennifer. 2006. "Rep. Goode: No Apology For Muslim Letter." CBSNews.com, December 20, 2006. Retrieved from https://www.cbsnews.com/news/rep-goode-no-apology-for-muslim-letter/.

Al-Jerrahi, Muzaffer Ozak. 1991. *Blessed Virgin Mary.* Westport, CT: Pir Publications.

Library of Congress. 2007. "Thomas Jefferson's Copy of the Koran to Be Used in Congressional Swearing-in Ceremony." Washington, DC: Library of Congress. Last modified January 3, 2007. Retrieved from https://www.loc.gov

/item/prn-07-001/use-of-thomas-jeffersons-koran-for-congressional-swearing-in-ceremony/2007-01-03/.

Lumbard, Joseph E. 2008. *Submission: Faith & Beauty*. Berkeley, CA: Zaytuna Institute.

Prager, Dennis. 2006. "America, Not Keith Ellison, decides what book a congressman takes his oath on." Townhall.com. Last modified November 28, 2006. Retrieved from https://townhall.com/Columnists/dennisprager/2006/11/28/america,-not-keith-ellison,-decides-what-book-a-congressman-takes-his-oath-on-n792991.

Rashid, Qasim. 2017. "Anyone who says the Quran advocates terrorism obviously hasn't read its lessons on violence." Independent.co.uk, April 10, 2017. Retrieved from https://www.independent.co.uk/voices/islam-muslim-terrorism-islamist-extremism-quran-teaching-violence-meaning-prophet-muhammed-a7676246.html.

Siddiqui, Mona. 2008. *How to Read the Qur'an (How to Read)*. New York: W. W. Norton & Company.

Southern Poverty Law Center. n.d. "Anti-Muslim." Birmingham, AL: SPLC. Retrieved from https://www.splcenter.org/fighting-hate/extremist-files/ideology/anti-muslim.

Wills, Gary. 2017. *What the Qur'an Meant: And Why It Matters*. New York: Viking Press.

R

Racialization

The term *racialization* is a sociological concept that captures a process during which certain physical features associated with a population are attached to an individual's "race." This process of racialization is increasingly important in understanding the lived experiences of U.S. Muslims because "Muslim identity" is oftentimes stereotyped with physical features like Arab identity, brown skin, and beards. Scholars who use the term *racialization* in the context of Muslims do so in order to connect prejudice and discrimination of Muslims to racism against Muslims, or anti-Muslim racism. Racism may be defined as the attribution of social significance and meaning to particular patterns of difference, which—along with real or supposed other characteristics—are linked to people based on descent (Miles 1993, 2350). Nasar Meer, a scholar of the intersection of race and Islamophobia, has insisted that Islamophobia should be understood as anti-Muslim racism instead of merely discrimination against the Islamic faith. He claimed that discussions of Islamophobia "need to be able to grasp the ways in which discrimination against Muslim minorities picks out people on the basis of supposedly discernible characteristics" (Meer 2017).

According to scholar Neil Gotanda, the "Muslim terrorist" in popular U.S. culture is not new, but within an established tradition of racializing Muslims throughout U.S. history. Gotanda pointed out three dimensions of the racialization of Islam: "raced body, racial category, and ascribed subordination." The raced body is "the 'brown' body of immigrants and descendants of immigrants from North Africa, the Middle East, and Central and Southern Asia" (Gotanda 2011, 184). He continued by discussing how "Muslim" as a racial category has acquired meaning beyond religion and now also describes a racial category: those whose ancestry traces to countries where the Muslim population is significant (Gotanda 2011, 184). Linked to that category are the stereotypes of "terrorist," "spy," or "saboteur"—understandings within the traditions of characterizing Asian Americans as permanent, unassimilable foreigners (Gotanda 2011, 184).

An academic study by Saher Selod also examined the racialization of U.S. Muslims. Through qualitative in-depth interviews, she found that when U.S. Muslims were identified as Muslims rather than some other identity, they were treated as if they were a potential threat to U.S. cultural values and national security (Selod 2014, 77). The process of racialization occurred when the participants of Selod's study experienced "de-Americanization" whereby their privileges associated with citizenship, such as being viewed as a valued member of society, were denied to them (Selod 2014, 77).

Hate crimes against Muslims also are blamed on the racialization of the Islamic faith whereby race and religion are fused to create a stereotypical depiction of Muslims as bearded, dark-skinned, and turban-wearing (Considine 2017). Muslims as well as Sikhs and Hindus have been victims of Islamophobic incidents at a growing rate. For example, in April 2019, Isaiah Joel Peoples intentionally drove his car into a group of pedestrians in Sunnyvale, California, whom he believed were Muslims. Another case, Balbir Singh Sodhi, a U.S. Sikh and gas station owner in Mesa, Arizona, was murdered in a hate crime days after the 9/11 attacks. Sodhi was a practicing Sikh who wore a beard and turban in accordance with his religious obligations. His murderer, Frank Silva Roque, mistook Singh for an Arab Muslim, according to the testimony of Roque.

These cases suggest that Islamophobia does not belong in the realm of "rational" criticism of the Islamic faith or simply discrimination against Muslims; it is often discrimination against people who look different from the majority white population in the United States.

See also: African American Muslims; Arab American Muslims; Asian American Muslims; European American Muslims; Hate Crimes; Islamophobia; Latin American Muslims; Turkish American Muslims; *Ummah*

Further Reading

Considine, Craig. 2017. "The Racialization of Islam in the United States: Islamophobia, Hate Crimes, and 'Flying while Brown.'" *Religions* 8, no. 9: 165–84.

Gotanda, Neil. 2011. "The Racialization of Islam in American Law." *The Annals of the American Academy of Political and Social Science* 637 (September): 184–95.

Joshi, Khyati Y. 2006. "The Racialization of Hinduism, Islam, and Sikhism in the United States." *Equity & Excellence in Education* 39, no. 3 (November 23): 211–26.

Meer, Nasar. 2017. "Returning to Islamophobia as the Racialization of Islam and Muslims." TheMaydan.com. Last modified December 6, 2017. Retrieved from https://www.themaydan.com/2017/12/returning-islamophobia-racialization -islam-muslims/.

Miles, Robert. 1993. *Racism after 'Race Relations.'* London and New York: Routledge.

Selod, Saher. 2014. "Citizenship Denied: The Racialization of Muslim American Men and Women post-9/11." *Critical Sociology* 41, no. 1 (April 1): 77–95.

Selod, Saher. 2018. *Forever Suspect: Racialized Surveillance of Muslim Americans in the War on Terror.* New Brunswick, NJ: Rutgers University Press.

Refugees

Refugees from Muslim-majority countries around the world became the center of U.S. politics on December 7, 2015, when Republican presidential candidate Donald Trump called for "a total and complete shutdown of Muslims entering the United States." Popularly referred to as the "Muslim travel ban," Trump's proposed policy was widely considered to be both "anti-refugee" and "anti-Muslim." In January 2017, President Donald Trump signed Executive Order 13769 titled "Protecting the Nation from Foreign Terrorist Entry into the United States" that suspended the resettlement of Syrian refugees on U.S. soil.

Trump's "travel ban" is drastically impacting the Muslim refugee population in the United States. According to the Pew Research Center, the number of Muslim refugees admitted to the United States in the first half of fiscal year 2018 had "dropped from the previous year more than any other religious group, falling to nearly 1,800 compared with the roughly 22,900 admitted in all of fiscal 2017" (Connor and Krogstad 2018). This is the lowest yearly total of Muslim admissions into the country since 2002, the year after the 9/11 attacks. President Trump's capping of refugee admissions at 45,000 people in fiscal 2018 is the lowest since the U.S.

Congress created the current refugee program in 1980 (Connor and Krogstad 2018). Today, no Muslim-majority countries are represented among the top five nationalities of refugees admitted in 2018, a startling number considering the amount of violence and warfare carried out in many Muslim-majority countries around the world. Similarly, as noted by the U.S. Department of State, the number of Muslim refugees admitted to the United States dropped 91 percent from 2016 to 2018.

Regardless of the significant decrease in Muslim refugee admittance, Muslim refugees do not pose a threat to U.S. national security (Considine 2018, 123–27). Yet despite these facts, fewer and fewer U.S. citizens believe that the United States has a responsibility to accept Muslim refugees. According to the Pew Research Center, more than half of U.S. citizens—51 percent—"believe the United States should welcome immigrants fleeing violence and persecution in their home countries" (Hartig 2018).

Depicting Muslim refugees as serious and direct national security threats inevitably impacts how U.S. citizens perceive U.S. Muslims and Muslim refugees living in the United States. For example, three right-wing militiamen from rural Kansas were found guilty in April 2018 in a plot to slaughter Muslim refugees living in an apartment complex, home to many Somali Muslims. The three men—Patrick Stein, Gavin Wright, and Curtis Allen—were found guilty on charges of weapons of mass destruction and conspiracy against civil rights (Reilly and Mathias 2018). The men were enthusiastic supporters of Donald Trump, who made the vilification of refugees a key element of his political platform during the presidential campaign of 2016 (Reilly and Mathias 2018). The Trump administration's vilification of refugees stands in contrast to the Islamic teaching of welcoming the vulnerable and persecuted people into communities and nations. The embrace of refugees in the Islamic tradition is captured by the Qur'an (4:100): "Whoever emigrates for the cause of God will find many places of refuge in the land and plentiful provision. Those who leave home for the cause of God and His Messenger, but is then overtaken by death, shall be recompensated by God. God is most forgiving and ever-merciful."

The Prophet Muhammad and the early Muslim community were welcoming of refugees because they, too, were once refugees. Facing persecution from the Qur'aysh, a polytheistic tribe that ruled Mecca, the first Muslim community was told by the Prophet Muhammad to seek refuge in the Christian Kingdom of Aksum, formerly referred to as Abyssinia and located in the present-day countries Ethiopia and Eritrea. An early account of Muhammad's commandment is related in a *hadith:* "When [Muhammad] saw the affliction of his companions . . . he said to them: 'If you were to go to Abyssinia (it would be better for you), for the king will not tolerate injustice and it is a friendly country.'" The Negus or King of Aksum, Ashama Ibn Abjar, granted the Muslim refugees asylum in 615 CE. On one occasion, when listening to the Muslims share verses of the Qur'an in his royal palace, King Ibn Abjar is said to have picked up a stick and said, "I swear, the difference between what we believe about Jesus, the Son of Mary, and what you have said is not greater than the width of this twig."

Islamic Relief USA, a nonprofit 501(c)(3) humanitarian agency and member of the Islamic Relief Worldwide group of organizations, has worked to provide humanitarian aid for refugees since its founding around 1993 (Islamic Relief USA n.d.a). In the United States, Islamic Relief USA supports programs that provide shelter and helps refugees integrate and find jobs. One such program, called the Refugee Assistance Program (RAP), started in North Carolina in 2017. The RAP was built to focus on refugees who have the most difficulty settling because of medical conditions, psychological trauma, and low English proficiency (Islamic Relief USA n.d.b).

See also: Islamophobia; Muslim Travel Ban and Immigration Policies

Further Reading

Bier, David. 2018. "Trump Cut Muslim Refugees 91%, Immigrants 30%, Visitors by 18%." Washington, DC: CATO Institute. Last modified December 7, 2018. Retrieved from https://www.cato.org/blog/trump-cut-muslim-refugees-91-immigrants-30-visitors-18.

Connor, Phillip, and Jens Manuel Krogstad. 2018. "The number of refugees admitted to the U.S. has fallen, especially among Muslims." Washington, DC: Pew Research Center. Last modified May 3, 2018. Retrieved from http://www.pewresearch.org/fact-tank/2018/05/03/the-number-of-refugees-admitted-to-the-u-s-has-fallen-especially-among-muslims/.

Considine, Craig. 2018. *Muslims in America: Examining the Facts*. Santa Barbara, CA: ABC-CLIO.

Hartig, Hannah. 2018. "Republicans turn more negative toward refugees as number admitted to U.S. plummets." Washington, DC: Pew Research Center. Last modified May 24, 2018. Retrieved from http://www.pewresearch.org/fact-tank/2018/05/24/republicans-turn-more-negative-toward-refugees-as-number-admitted-to-u-s-plummets/.

Islamic Relief USA. n.d.a. "Aid for Refugees." Alexandria, VA: Islamic Relief USA. Retrieved from http://irusa.org/refugee-crisis/.

Islamic Relief USA. n.d.b. "United States Refugee Assistance." Alexandria, VA: Islamic Relief USA. Retrieved from http://irusa.org/united-states-refugee-assistance/.

Reilly, Ryan J., and Christopher Mathias. 2018. "Right-Wing Extremists Guilty in Terror Plot against Muslim Refugees." HuffingtonPost.com, April 18, 2018. Retrieved from https://www.huffingtonpost.com/entry/trump-muslim-militia-terror-plot-kansas_us_5ad78882e4b029ebe0207801.

Watt, W. Montgomery. 1961. *Muhammad: Prophet and Statesman*. Oxford, UK: Oxford University Press.

S

Sharia

The word *sharia* is one of the more misunderstood terms in the context of U.S. Muslims. The *sharia*, generally referred to as "Islamic law," is often viewed through the prism of oppression toward non-Muslims, the persecution of gay people, honor killings, female genital mutilation, and child brides. This framing of the *sharia*, however, is deeply misguided and wrongly associates Muslims with "un-American" lifestyles, religious beliefs, and worldviews.

The literal meaning of *sharia* is "the road to the watering hole," otherwise known as the clear, right, or straight path to be followed by Muslims (Esposito 1998, 78). This makes the *sharia* the collection of principles that regulate a Muslim's life, because it comprises laws by which Muslims are to live their lives, as well as laws to help govern society (Zafar 2014, 61). The *sharia* has been further described as "a system of divine laws that trump any moral considerations or ethical values that are not fully codified in the law" (El Fadel 2002, 4). Under the *sharia*, God is "manifested through a set of determinate legal commands that specify the right way to act in virtually all circumstances" (El Fadel 2002, 4). When Muslims refrain from drinking alcohol or eating pork, that is the *sharia*. When Muslims greet each other with *asalamalaikum*, or "peace be upon you," that too is the *sharia*.

U.S. Muslims follow aspects of the *sharia* in their everyday lives, including in their daily prayers, marriage agreements, alimony, wills, custody, community property, and commercial transactions across state borders. Corey Saylor of the Council on American-Islamic Relations said that the *sharia* teaches "marital fidelity, generous charity, and a thirst for knowledge" in addition to the daily guidelines of "praying, fasting, giving charity, helping the needy, feeding the hungry, and caring for the environment."

Family law is a particularly important aspect of the *sharia*. One of the basic concepts underlying Muslim marriage and divorce—a *mahr*, or dowry—is an important part of an Islamic marriage contract under the *sharia*. The *mahr*, "which may include money, property, valuables, or stock, is paid by the husband and is held in trust for the wife, who receives it upon divorce or the husband's death. It is intended to serve as a form of insurance so that, should a wife no longer be able to rely on her husband for financial support, she is able to support herself" (Fallon 2013, 159–60).

Like the Islamic faith itself, the *sharia* is not a monolith. Treating the *sharia* as a monolith denies the existence of the various schools, or *madhabs* in Arabic, of the *sharia*. These schools range from the mainstream Hanafi school to the more conservative Hanbali school. Different schools of the *sharia* understand the content of this law differently (El Fadel 2002, 4). For Sunni Islam, four major schools predominate: the Hanafi, Hanbali, Maliki, and Shafi (Esposito 1998, 84–85). Today, they are dominant in different parts of the Muslim world—the Hanafi in the Middle East and South Asia; the Maliki in North, Central, and West Africa; the Shafi in East Africa, southern Arabia, and Southeast Asia; and the Hanbali in Saudi Arabia (Esposito 1998, 85). The most important *madhab* of the Shi'a tradition is the Jafari, named for Jafar Al-Sadiq, the sixth *imam* (Esposito 1998, 85). The Jafari school of thought and jurisprudence recognizes four sources of Islamic law: the Qur'an, the *Sunnah* (including the traditions reported by the Prophet and the *imams*), consensus (which must include the Prophet's or an infallible *imam*'s opinion to establish its validity), and human reason (*Oxford Dictionary of Islam* n.d.c). Other schools of the *sharia* are rooted in Ahmadiyya as well as Sufism. Anti-Islam activists who treat the *sharia* as a totalitarian and monolithic system overlook the diversity of the *sharia* and the ways in which these schools are compatible with the U.S. Constitution.

After the passing of the Prophet Muhammad in 632 CE, a significant amount of reasoning entered into the development of the *sharia*. The exertion in the formation of one's individual judgment of the *sharia* is called *ijtihad*, a term derived from the Arabic verb *ijtahada*, which means "to exert oneself" (Salmi, Majul, and Tanham 1998, 53). The *Oxford Dictionary of Islam* refers to *ijtihad* as the Sunni legal term meaning "independent reasoning" (*Oxford Dictionary of Islam* n.d.). *Ijtihad* is utilized by Sunni scholars when the Qur'an and *Sunnah* are silent or may be unclear on particular issues relating to the *sharia*. According to scholar Muqtedar Khan, there are two conceptions of *ijtihad*. One is a very narrow, legalistic notion of it as a process of juristic reasoning employed to determine the permissibility of an action when the Qur'an and *Sunnah* are silent or when earlier scholars had not ruled on the matter (Khan 2006). The second view, often espoused by nonjurists and particularly by those who advocate for "Islamic modernism" or "Islamic liberalism," is that *ijtihad* is about freedom of thought, rational thinking, and the quest for truth by using science, rationalism, and critical thinking (Khan 2006).

Further, Islamic jurisprudence, or *fiqh*, requires extensive knowledge of the sources from which one derives the edicts of the *sharia* and the ability to derive them and apply them (Lumbard 2008, 58). In order to explain the *sharia*, the jurisprudent (*faqih*) must have comprehensive knowledge of the Arabic language, the Qur'an, and the sciences of determining the authenticity of the *ahadith* (Lumbard 2008, 58).

Muslims who specialize in the *sharia* are referred to as *mufti*, an Arabic word referring to experts who are qualified to deliver a religious interpretation or legal brief in an Islamic context (Considine 2017, 186). These opinions are generally based on precedent and compiled in legal reference manuals (*Oxford Dictionary of Islam* n.d.b). *Muftis* are known for issuing *fatwa*, which Sheikh Muhammad Hisham Kabbani of the Islamic Supreme Council of America defines as "an Islamic legal pronouncement, issued by an expert in religious law (*mufti*), pertaining to a specific issue, usually at the request of an individual or judge to resolve an issue where Islamic jurisprudence (*fiqh*) is unclear." Some U.S. citizens are under the impression that to issue a *fatwa* is to target a victim and offer a monetary reward for murdering that person. The word *fatwa*, as historian Bernard Lewis (1998, 109) rightly noted, has acquired a common international usage that is wholly negative. *Fatwa*, Lewis again notes, is a technical term in Islamic jurisprudence for a legal opinion or ruling on a point of view.

Anti-Islam critics and protesters oftentimes turn to the *sharia* to explain their argument that "Western civilization" and "Islamic civilization" are fundamentally incompatible entities. For instance, protesters demonstrated across the country in June 2017 for an event titled "March Against Sharia." The nationwide protest, organized by the anti-Islam activist group ACT for America, took place in at least 20 cities across the United States. The Southern Poverty Law Center (SPLC), a leading civil rights organization in the United States, had previously described ACT for America as an "anti-Muslim hate group." The "March Against Sharia" was met by counter-protesters. In Austin, Texas, U.S. Muslims and those people and organizations seeking to ally themselves with the Muslim population organized at the Texas Capitol building. Mohamed-Umer Esmail, an Austin *imam*, referred to the "March Against Sharia" as stoking "irrational fearmongering" of the Islamic faith and U.S. Muslims.

Politicians across the country have recently introduced anti-*sharia* legislation at the state and national levels (Considine 2018, 97–102). According to scholar Asma Uddin, author of *When Islam Is Not a Religion: Inside America's Fight for Religious Freedom*, there are three categories of anti-*sharia* laws in the United States. The first category encompasses legislative bills that "single out" the *sharia* as a specific legal doctrine that encourages anti-American sentiments. The second category of bills includes the *sharia* among a handful of other religion-based laws that should be banned from being practiced in the United States. The third category presents bills that effectively deny U.S. courts the ability to even rule on the *sharia*-related matters. In total, at least 120 anti-*sharia* bills have been introduced in 42 states since 2010 (Southern Poverty Law Center 2017).

Despite claims made by groups like ACT for America, the consideration of the *sharia* in the U.S. legal system is not a sign of "creeping *sharia*." U.S. courts have long considered the *sharia* in "everything from the recognition of foreign divorces and custody decrees to the validity of marriages, the enforcement of money judgments and the awarding of damages in commercial disputes and negligence matters" (Awad 2012). Banning the *sharia* would violate First and Fourteenth Amendment–based U.S. Supreme Court rulings that together bar discriminating on the basis of religion, favoring one religion over another by the government, and restricting freedom of expression and belief. The *sharia* bans thus "violate the voluntary but long-standing principle of comity, which encourages courts to defer to foreign laws where such laws do not prejudice the power or rights of the U.S. government or its citizens" (Fallon 2013, 155).

U.S. Muslims also have been accused of preferring to be governed by the *sharia* rather than the U.S. Constitution. According to a September 2012 poll carried out by the Public Religion Research Institute, the number of U.S. citizens who feel that Muslims are working to subvert the Constitution rose from 23 percent in February 2012 to 30 percent in September 2012, during the height of the anti-*sharia* movement (Saylor 2014). In July 2016, the Center for Security Policy (CSP), a neoconservative think tank, alleged that their survey of 6,000 U.S. Muslims showed "ominous levels of support" for the "Islamic supremacist doctrine" of the *sharia*. The CSP poll was then used by Republican presidential candidate Donald Trump in December 2015 to justify his proposal to temporarily ban all Muslims from entering the United States (Carroll and Jacobson 2015). Critics of the CSP found that the methodology of the survey was profoundly flawed and should not be taken seriously (Lean and Denari 2016). The non-probability-based, opt-in nature of the online survey cannot be generalized to the wider U.S. population. The CSP survey represents the views of the 600 U.S. Muslims polled rather than the overall population across the United States.

Public opinion polls, in reality, show that U.S. Muslims tend to regard the *sharia* as a personal and religious obligation governing the practice of the Islamic faith and not as some legal system to be implemented at the national level over the U.S. Constitution (Considine 2018, 104–8). Approximately 55 percent of U.S. Muslims oppose using the *sharia* as even a single source of many for the laws of the United States (Institute for Social Policy and Understanding 2016).

It is also worth noting that the *sharia* is similar to the Jewish and Christians traditions in that Jews and Christians are also encouraged to follow certain norms and practices in their everyday lives. Jewish law is referred to by the Hebrew term *halakha*. The *halakha* "designates both the system of Jewish law and also the concept of a single rule of law. The *halakha* comprises the entire subject matter of Jewish law, including public, private, and ritual law" (Stone 1993). Many Orthodox Jews use rabbinical courts to obtain religious divorces, resolve business conflicts, and settle other disputes with fellow Jews (Pew Research Center 2013). According to Marshal Breger, professor of law, there are many obvious parallels between the *halakha* and the *sharia*. Both purport to instruct Jews and Muslims on "how to attend to every aspect of one's life, [from] one's getting up and one's going out, to one's sexual practice and one's business practices" (Breger 2012). Breger added that "the vast majority of Muslims, especially those living in [Western countries, view] the *sharia* no differently from the way Jews view the *halakha:* as an overarching guide to ordering one's life" (Breger 2012). In the context of Catholicism, canon law is a code of ecclesiastical laws governing the Catholic Church. *Canon* is the Greek word for rule, norm, standard, or measure. The Roman Catholic Church alone "has nearly 200 diocesan tribunals that handle a variety of cases, including an estimated 15,000 to 20,000 marriage annulments each year" (Pew Research Center 2013).

See also: Ahadith; Qur'an

Further Reading

An-Nai'm, Abdullahi Ahmed. n.d. "Sharia Law—A Literary Zikr Project." MPVUSA.org. Retrieved from http://www.mpvusa.org/sharia-law.

Awad, Abed. 2012. "The True Story of Sharia in American Courts." TheNation .com, June 14, 2012. Retrieved from https://www.thenation.com/article/true -story-sharia-american-courts/.

Breger, Marshall. 2012. "Why Jews Can't Criticize Sharia Law." MomentMag .com, January 5, 2012. Retrieved from https://momentmag.com/why-jews -cant-criticize-sharia-law-2/.

Carroll, Lauren, and Louis Jacobson. 2015. "Trump Cites Shaky Survey in Call to Ban Muslims from Entering US." Politifact.com. Last modified December 9, 2015. Retrieved from http://www.politifact.com/truth-o-meter/statements/2015 /dec/09/donald-trump/trump-cites-shaky-survey-call-ban-muslims-entering/.

Center for Security Policy. 2015. "Poll of U.S. Muslims Reveals Ominous Levels of Support for Islamic Supremacists' Doctrine of Shariah, Jihad." Washington, DC: Center for Security Policy. Last modified June 23, 2015. Retrieved from https://www.centerforsecuritypolicy.org/2015/06/23/nationwidepoll-of-us -muslims-shows-thousands-support-shariah-jihad/.

Considine, Craig. 2018. *Muslims in America: Examining the Facts*. Santa Barbara, CA: ABC-CLIO.

El Fadel, Abou. 2002. *The Place of Tolerance in Islam*. Boston: Beacon Press.

Esposito, John. 1998. *Islam: The Straight Path*. Oxford, UK: Oxford University Press.

Fallon, Sarah M. 2013. "Justice for All: American Muslims, Sharia Law, and Maintaining Comity within American Jurisprudence." *Boston College International and Comparative Law Review* 36, no. 153: 153–82.

Institute for Social Policy and Understanding. 2016. "ISPU American Muslim Poll Key Findings." Washington, DC: ISPU. Retrieved from https://www.ispu .org/wp-content/uploads/2016/08/ampkeyfindings-2.pdf.

Kabbani, Muhammad Hisham. n.d. "What is a Fatwa?" IslamicSupremeCouncil. org. Retrieved from http://www.islamicsupremecouncil.org/understanding -islam/legal-rulings/44-what-is-a-fatwa.html.

Khan, Muqtedar. 2006. "Two Theories of Ijtihad." Washington, DC: Brookings Institution. Last modified March 21, 2006. Retrieved from https://www.brookings .edu/opinions/two-theories-of-ijtihad/.

Lean, Nathan, and Jordan Denari. 2016. "Here's Why You Shouldn't Trust the Latest Poll on American Muslims." HuffingtonPost.com, July 7, 2016. Retrieved from https://www.huffingtonpost.com/nathan-lean/heres-why-you -shouldnt-trust-the-latest-poll-on-american-muslims_b_7688204.html.

Lewis, Bernard. 1998. *The Multiple Identities of the Middle East*. New York: Schocken Books.

Lumbard, Joseph E. 2008. *Submission: Faith & Beauty*. Berkeley, CA: Zaytuna Institute.

Oxford Dictionary of Islam. (n.d.a. "Ijtihad." Oxford, UK: Oxford Islamic Studies. Retrieved from http://www.oxfordislamicstudies.com/article/opr/t125/e990.

Oxford Dictionary of Islam. (n.d.c. "Jafari: Shii Legal Thought and Jurisprudence." Oxford, UK: Oxford Islamic Studies. Retrieved from http://www.oxfordislamic studies.com/article/opr/t125/e1153.

Pew Research Center. 2013. "Applying God's Law: Religious Courts and Mediation in the U.S." Washington, DC: Pew Research Center. Last modified April 8, 2013. Retrieved from http://www.pewforum.org/2013/04/08/applying -gods-law-religious-courts-and-mediation-in-the-us/.

Quraishi-Landes, Asifa. 2016. "5 Myths about Sharia Law Debunked by a Law Professor." DallasNews.com, July 2016. Retrieved from https://www .dallasnews.com/opinion/commentary/2016/07/19/asifaquraishi-landes-5 -myths-shariah-law.

Salmi, Ralph H., Cesar Adib Majul, and George K. Tanham. *Islam and Conflict Resolution: Theories and Practices*. Lanham, MD, New York, and Oxford, UK: University Press of America.

Saylor, Cory. 2014. "The U.S. Islamophobia Network: Its Funding and Impact." *Islamophobia Studies Journal* 2, no. 1 (Spring): 99–118.

Southern Poverty Law Center. 2017. "Anti-Sharia Law Bills in the United States." Montgomery, AL: Southern Poverty Law Center. Last modified August 8, 2017. Retrieved from https://www.splcenter.org/hatewatch/2017/08/08/anti -sharia-law-bills-united-states.

Stone, Suzanne Last. 1993. "In Pursuit of the Counter-Text: The Turn to the Jewish Legal Model in Contemporary American Legal Theory." *Harvard Law Review* 106, no. 4 (February): 813–94.

Uddin, Asma T. 2019. *When Islam Is Not a Religion: Inside America's Fight for Religious Freedom*. New York: Pegasus Books.

Zafar, Harris. 2014. *Demystifying Islam: Tackling the Tough Questions*. Lanham, MD: Rowman & Littlefield.

Shi'ism

Shi'ism, also known as Shi'a Islam, is practiced by Shi'a Muslims, who believe that the Prophet Muhammad's religious leadership, spirituality, authority, and divine guidance were passed on to his descendants, beginning with his son-in-law and cousin, Ali Ibn Abi Talib, his daughter, Fatimah, and their sons, Hasan and Hussein (*Oxford Dictionary of Islam* n.d.). The word *shi'i* means "one who is a partisan" or "supporter" in Arabic. The largest concentration of Shi'a Muslims in the world today is found in the countries of Iran and Iraq. Today, roughly 10 to 15 percent of the Muslim global population is Shi'a and the rest Sunni.

On a theological level, Shi'as and Sunnis show virtually no differences—both populations believe in the same God, the Prophet Muhammad, and the Qur'an, follow the Five Pillars of the Islamic faith, and adhere to broad values associated with the Islamic tradition. The differences between Shi'as and Sunnis are based largely on political matters that date back to the death of the Prophet Muhammad in 632 CE. Shi'as generally believe that the Prophet Muhammad's son-in-law, Ali, was designated as the *caliph,* or rightful political successor as head of the *ummah,* by Muhammad himself. Ali eventually became the *caliph,* but only after several of the Prophet Muhammad's companions—Abu Bakr Al-Siddiq, Umar Ibn Al-Khattab, and Uthman Ibn Affan. Ali also is the father of Hussein, the prominent Shi'a leader who would be martyred at Karbala, in modern-day Iraq, a seminal event in Shi'a history and marked by massive pilgrimages to Karbala today (Ahmed 2007, 44).

The Prophet Muhammad's daughter, Fatimah, was the wife of Ali and the mother of Hassan and Hussein, from whom are descended the Sayyids, the "holy lineage" in the *ummah.* The family of Fatimah is particularly revered in the Shi'a tradition. Shi'a leadership is vested in the *imam,* who, though not a prophet, "is the divinely inspired, sinless, infallible, religio-political leader of the community" (Esposito 1998, 43). Shia *imams* "must be a direct descendant of the Prophet Muhammad and Ali, the first imam" (Esposito 1998, 43).

Like the Islamic tradition itself, Shi'ism is not a monolith. The primary sect of Shi'ism is Twelve-Imam. Also referred to as Ithna Asharis, the "Twelvers" or "Imamis" are the largest group of Shi'as in both number and influence. Twelver Muslims believe in the twelve *imams,* beginning with Ali, the Prophet Muhammad's son-in-law, and ending with Muhammad Al-Mahdi, who, Twelvers claim, "went into occultation and is expected to return at the end of time as [a] messianic *imam* to restore justice and equity on earth" (*Oxford Dictionary of Islam* n.d.). Al-Mahdi is referred to as the *Imam Al-Muntazar,* the expected or awaited *imam.*

Following Twelve-Imam Shi'ism, the Seven-Imam Shi'ism, or Ismailism, and Five-Imam Shi'ism, or Zaydism, are influential sects of

Shi'ism. Ismailis are named after Ismail, the seventh *imam*, who founded the Fatimid Empire. Zaydism is named after Zayd Ibn Ali, the grandson of Hussein, the son of Ali. Zaydism emerged in the 8th century as a doctrine that emphasized rationalism rather than textual literalism. In light of its emphasis on rational thinking, Zaydism is comparable to the Hanafi *madhab*, or school of the *sharia*, in Sunnism.

The Shi'a population in the United States is a minority population within the overall U.S. Muslim population. According to scholars, there are approximately 800,000 Shi'as living in the country. A significant number—estimated to be 30,000—of Shi'as live in the Detroit, Michigan, area, which is often called the "heart of Shi'ism" in the United States. Most of these Shi'as derive from Lebanese and Iraqi descent. An academic study by Liyakat Takim pointed out several challenges that U.S. Shi'as encounter as they navigate their way in the U.S. socio-political climate. These include "the construction of ethnic borders within the community, political engagement, the community's attempts at acculturation in the post-9/11 era and its engagement in academic discourse" (Takim 2018, 73).

One of the largest mosques in the United States—the Islamic Center of America (ICA)—is a Shi'a mosque that opened in 2005. The ICA is recognized as the largest mosque in North America and the oldest Shi'a mosque in the United States. The largest umbrella organization of Shi'a Muslims on U.S. soil is the North American Shia Ithna-Ashermi Muslim Communities (NASIMCO) (Ul-Huda 2006, 6). NASIMCO produces standardized books for religious schools through the Islamic Education Board and publishes resources on Shi'a history and theology. Another important Shi'a institution—the Imam Al-Khoei Foundation in New York—has a full-time accredited school from kindergarten through 12th grade and conducts Shi'a religious rituals in Urdu, Persian, Arabic, and English (Ul-Huda 2006, 6).

Fatima Masselmany is one of the most documented Shi'a Muslims in U.S. history. In 1912, Fatima departed from her home in Beirut, Lebanon, bound for Marseilles, France. She ended up boarding the *Titanic* as a third-class passenger in Cherbourg, France. Fatima survived the *Titanic*'s sinking, but her two male cousins—Mustafa Nasr Alma and Yusuf Ahmad Waznah—passed away. After being treated for hypothermia in New York City, Fatima again departed for Michigan City, Indiana, where she had additional family members. In Michigan City, she married Mohammad Mustafa Ajamy, and the couple eventually moved to Dearborn, Michigan, in the early 1950s. Fatima died in February 1971 and is buried in Roseland Cemetery, Oak Park, Michigan, with her brother Hassan (*Encyclopedia Titanica* n.d.).

See also: Ahmadiyya; Sufism; Sunnism; *Ummah*; Wahhabism

Further Reading

Ahmed, Akbar. 2007. *Journey into Islam: The Crisis of Globalization*. Washington, DC: Brookings Institute.

Esposito, John. 1998. *Islam: The Straight Path*. Oxford, UK: Oxford University Press.

Hazelton, Lesley. 2009. *After the Prophet: The Epic Story of the Shia-Sunni Split in Islam*. New York: Anchor Books.

Nanji, Azim. n.d. "Ismailism." London, UK: The Institute of Ismaili Studies. Retrieved from https://iis.ac.uk/ismailism.

Oxford Dictionary of Islam. n.d. "Shii Islam." Oxford, UK: Oxford Islamic Studies Online. Retrieved from http://www.oxfordislamicstudies.com/article/opr/t125/e2189.

Takim, Liyakat. 2018. "Shi'ism in the American Diaspora: Challenges and Opportunities." *Journal of Muslim Minority Affairs* 38, no. 1: 73–86.

Ul-Huda, Qamar. 2006. "The Diversity of Muslims in the United States: Special Report." Washington, DC: United States Institute of Peace. Last modified February 2006. Retrieved from https://www.usip.org/sites/default/files/sr159.pdf.

Slavery

The first Muslims in U.S. history were slaves from West Africa who were brought to the Western hemisphere during the transatlantic slave trade starting in the 16th century and ending in the 19th century. Approximately 10 to 15 million West Africans in total were brought from the modern-day African countries of Angola, Benin, Cameroon, Democratic Republic of the Congo, Gabon, The Gambia, Ghana, Guinea, Ivory Coast, Liberia, Mozambique, Nigeria, Senegal, and Togo. According to Gwendolyn Midlo Hall, author of *Slavery and African Ethnicities in the Americas*, there were West Africans from approximately 45 distinct ethnic groups that were brought to the Western hemisphere. The ten most prominent ethnic groups according to Hall were (with their modern-day country affiliation): the BaKongo of the Democratic Republic of the Congo and Angola; the

Mandé of Guinea; the Gbe of Togo, Ghana, and Benin; the Akan of Ghana and Ivory Coast; the Wolof of Senegal and The Gambia; the Igbo of Nigeria; the Mbunduo of Angola; the Yoruba of Nigeria; and the Chamba of Cameroon. Most scholars of U.S. Muslim history estimate that approximately 20 percent of the African slaves brought to modern U.S. soil were Muslim. Scholars have estimated that the number of African Muslim slaves transported to the "New World" could have been as low as 10 percent or as high as 40 percent of the entire West African slave population.

Upon their arrival in the so-called "New World," many West African Muslim slaves sold into the U.S. slave plantation system were forced to convert to Christianity or be severely beaten—or even killed—by their Christian slaveowners. Scholars, however, believe that some West African Muslim slaves converted in name only and maintained their Islamic faith despite the threat of violence from Christian slaveowners. Descendants of West African Muslim slaves living on Sapelo Island, Georgia, for example, believe that their ancestors were "Christian by day, Muslim by night." Cornelia Walker Bailey, the direct descendant of West African Muslims, mentioned her family history of ancestors blending together elements of Christianity and Islam to form what is popularly referred to as Geechee culture. Bailey traced her ancestry back to an African Muslim named Bilali, who worked as the head slave manager on the Sapelo plantation owned by Thomas Spalding.

Sapelo Island is recognized by scholars as a doorway to the West African Muslim experiences during the transatlantic slave trade. One of the West African Muslims—Bilali Muhammad—is the focus of contemporary scholarship on the history of U.S. Muslims. Born into the Fulbe people in modern-day Guinea around 1770, Bilali was enslaved in his early 30s, brought to the Bahamas around 1801, and eventually sold to Thomas Spalding, a plantation owner and Georgia politician. On Sapelo Island, Bilali held the prominent position of "head driver" of over 400 slaves. As such, Bilali was sometimes left in charge of Sapelo Island for months on end when Spalding was traveling. According to the Lowcountry Digital History Initiative at the College of Charleston in South Carolina, Spalding also entrusted Bilali as the leader of a local militia of enslaved West Africans during the War of 1812. Pages from Bilali's manuscript also note that Bilali himself called other enslaved people on Sapelo Island as "Christian dogs," which is evidence that even slave populations were not immune to ethnic and religious conflict. In the 1820s, Bilali hand-wrote a 13-page text in Arabic that is currently held in the Hargrett Rare Book and Manuscript Library at the University of Georgia.

Several Muslim slaves who were born in West Africa became public figures during the 19th century. Abdul-Rahman Ibrahim, popularly known today as "the Moorish Prince," was born in the city of Timbuktu, of modern-day Mali. Ibrahim, as one newspaper at the time noted, had read the Bible and understood basic Christian principles, but he also criticized U.S. Christians on the grounds that Christians do not follow the teachings of Jesus. According to a pamphlet titled "A Statement with Regard to the Moorish Prince, Abduhl Rahhahman," written by Thomas H. Gallaudet, Ibrahim was sold into slavery after he was taken captive by the "Hebohs," a rival tribe of his community. Having survived the arduous voyage across the Atlantic Ocean, Ibrahim was sold to Colonel Thomas Foster, who owned a slave plantation in Natchez, Mississippi. In the summer of 1829, as noted by the "Documenting the American South" project at the University of North Carolina at Chapel Hill, Ibrahim returned to his birthplace of Timbuktu after having obtained his freedom from President John Quincy Adams.

African slaves also were the focus of *United States v. Amistad* (1841), a historic case in which the U.S. Supreme Court ruled in favor of African slaves, some of whom were Muslim, who were deemed free under the U.S. Constitution. The case stemmed from the capturing and later rebellion of 53 slaves on board the *Amistad* slave ship, which originally boarded in Havana, Cuba, and later docked in New London, Connecticut, on August 26, 1839. The Africans on board the *Amistad* were imprisoned pending an investigation. After the case made its way through the U.S. court system, the U.S. Supreme Court began hearing the case on February 22, 1841. The African slaves were represented by U.S. Representative John Quincy Adams of Massachusetts, who previously had served as the sixth president of the United States. On March 9, 1841, the U.S. Supreme Court ruled that the Africans were entitled to the human right of freedom.

Critics of the Islamic faith, along with groups such as Daesh, often claim that slavery and the owning of slaves is permissible according to the teachings of the Prophet Muhammad and the principles outlined in the Qur'an and *ahadith*. Recently, Daesh, otherwise known as the Islamic State of Iraq and Syria (ISIS), reinvigorated the centuries old claim that slavery is permitted in the Islamic faith. *Dabiq*, the English-language propaganda magazine of Daesh, published a headline titled "Spoils of War" that referenced the thousands of Yazidi women that the group forced into sex slavery (*The Economist* 2015). *Dabiq* contains additional arguments that enslaving disbelievers is "a firmly established aspect of the Sharia that if one were to deny or mock, he would be . . . thereby apostazizing [*sic*] from Islam" (Zucchino 2014).

During the height of Daesh's rise across the Middle East, more than 100 Muslims scholars and leaders from around the world released an open letter addressed to Abu Bakr Al-Baghdadi, the Daesh leader (Oakford 2014). The document, which was issued in English and Arabic on the website "Letter to Baghdadi," noted that slavery is explicitly forbidden in Islam (Letter to Baghdadi 2014). The letter noted, "No scholar of Islam disputes that one of Islam's aims is to abolish slavery," and that Muslims over the centuries "have been united in the prohibition and criminalization of slavery." Further, the "Letter to Baghdadi" proclaims that the Daesh leader had violated the Islamic teachings of dignity and justice. The letter was translated into 10 languages and signed by more than 120 supporters, from the Grand *Mufti* of Egypt to a professor of Islamic studies at the College of the Holy Cross in Massachusetts (Feldman 2015).

One of the Prophet Muhammad's most trusted companions—Bilal Ibn Rabah—was himself a slave from the modern-day country of Ethiopia. Bilal had been tortured by Ummayah, his owner, for following Muhammad, at which point the Prophet ordered Abu Bakr, another close companion, to purchase Bilal's freedom. Years later, Bilal had risen to a prestigious position within the early Muslim community—that of the *muezzin*, or the person who calls the Muslim faithful to their daily prayers.

Nevertheless, the Qur'an does not abolish the institution of slavery or explicitly condemn it. As in the days of the Hebrew Bible, "slavery was an integral part of the economic system at the time the *Qur'an* was revealed; abolition of slavery would have required an overhaul of the entire socioeconomic system" (Sonn 2004, 16). Therefore, instead of abolishing slavery outright, virtually all jurists of the *sharia* agree that the Qur'an established an ideal model that society should struggle (*jihad*) to achieve. Although slavery was permitted in the Qur'an, it is now banned in Muslim-majority countries. Not a single "Islamic state" or "Muslim-majority government" anywhere in the world practices it.

See also: African American Muslims

Further Reading

Ahari, Muhammad A., al-, Selim Aga, Omar Ibn Said, Abu Bakr Sadiq, Job Ben Sulaiman, and Nicholas Said. 2006. *Five Classic Muslim Slave Narratives*. Chicago: Magribine Press.

Ali, Kecia. 2010. *Marriage and Slavery in Early Islam*. Cambridge, MA: Harvard University Press.

Brown, Jonathan. 2019. *Slavery and Islam*. London: Oneworld Publications.

Documenting the American South. n.d. "From African Prince to Mississippi Slave: Abdul Rahman Ibrahima." Chapel Hill: University of North Carolina at Chapel Hill.

Feldman, Emily. 2015. "How Muslim Groups, Scholars Have Been Fighting ISIS." NBCSanDiego.com, December 9, 2015. Retrieved from https://www.nbcsandiego.com/news/national-international/Muslim-Scholars-Groups-Against-ISIS-Speal-Out-361309791.html?amp=y.

Hall, Gwendolyn Midlo. 2007. *Slavery and African Ethnicities in the Americas: Restoring the Links*. Chapel Hill: University of North Carolina Press.

"Letter to Baghdadi." 2014. LettertoBaghdadi.com. Retrieved from http://letterto baghdadi.com/arabic2.php.

Lowcountry Digital History Initiative. n.d. "Salih Bilali and Bilali Muhammad." Charleston, SC: College of Charleston. Retrieved from http://ldhi.library.cofc .edu/exhibits/show/african-muslims-in-the-south/five-african-muslims /salih-bilali-bilali-mohammed.

Sonn, Tamarra. 2004. *A Brief History of Islam*. Hoboken, NJ: Wiley-Blackwell.

Zucchino, David. 2014. "Islamic State publication seeks to justify slavery and sexual abuse." LATimes.com, October 13, 2014. Retrieved from https://www .latimes.com/world/middleeast/la-fg-islamists-sexual-slaves-20141013-story .html.

Social Justice Activism

The concept of "social justice" is receiving significant attention in U.S. public discourse because of the real and perceived inequalities and injustices in U.S. society. Broadly speaking, the term social justice is defined as a collective process by which individuals, communities, and organizations work with other communities to create a more equitable and just society in terms of access to wealth, opportunities, and privileges in the United States. Social justice in the Islamic context can be linked to *zakat*, the obligatory charitable offering made by Muslims, and *sadaqah*, the voluntary offerings made by Muslims to charities or charitable callings.

Service to humanity, or what is often referred to as social justice activism, is one of the primary teachings of the Islamic faith. Wahiduddin Khan, the author of *Principles of Islam*, states that the Islamic faith inculcates the spirit of love and respect for all human beings (Khan 2004, 136). Therefore, a believer of the Islamic faith is one who possesses the urge or desire to come to the assistance of others without seeking anything in return (Khan 2004, 139). The idea of a common humanity is thus central to Islamic teachings. By knowing God as *rahman* (beneficent) and *rahim* (merciful)—the two most frequently repeated of Allah's 99 names in the Islamic tradition—Muslims know they must embrace even those who may not belong to their community, religion, or nation (Ahmed 2003, 10).

Social activism in the Islamic tradition also is very much based on *da'wah*, an Arabic term that describes a process in which Muslims "invite" people to the Islamic faith in order to raise awareness of God's commandments. *Da'wah* also may be described as a peaceful calling of human beings to the Islamic faith through outreach and education. The *Oxford Dictionary of Islam* outlines four modern trends in *da'wah:* political orientation, interiorization, institutional organization, and social welfare concerns. According to Islamic scholars Hamza Yusuf and Zaid Shakir of the Zaytuna Institute, Muslims are required to create an active outreach, or *da'wah* program, to produce positive results in the United States. Yusuf and Shakir called on U.S. Muslims to "reach out to the non-Muslim community through teaching, doing community work, and feeding others." Similarly, scholar Farid Esack noted in his book *Qur'an, Liberation and Pluralism: An Islamic Perspective of Interreligious Solidarity against Oppression* that the Qur'an (4:3 and 33:5) is specific about areas of social life wherein Muslims should work to counter inequalities, such as taking care of orphans and adopting needy children.

The concept of social justice also is inherently linked to the notion of social solidarity, a sociological term popularized in *The Muqaddimah*, a book authored by Arab scholar Ibn Khaldun in 1377. Khaldun introduced the term *asabiyya*, a word that derives from the Arabic root *asab*, which means "to bind." *Asabiyya* has been defined by an assortment of terms including social cohesion, group consciousness, and group loyalty. His theorization of *asabiyya*, among other notable contributions to the "science of culture," has given him the honorary title of "the father of sociology."

Today, notable U.S. Muslim leaders follow in the footsteps of Ibn Khaldun in working to foster social cohesion and social solidarity across religious and racial divides. Linda Sarsour, the head of the Arab-American Association of New York, is an internationally recognized activist who is taking up a wide range of issues pertaining to Black Lives Matter, LGBTQ rights, women's rights, and the Deferred Action for Childhood Arrivals (DACA), an immigration policy that protects people from deportation. Her work in New York City and Ferguson, Missouri, and elsewhere on U.S. soil has brought her closer to African American activists who are fighting stop and frisk, biased policing, and mass incarceration (Mitter 2015). In March 2018, Sarsour participated in an act of civil disobedience in front of the office of Speaker of the House of Representatives Paul Ryan to demand that he hear concerns about the DACA program (Al Jazeera 2018). Sarsour also helped found the Muslim Democratic Club of New York and launched a web-organizing tool called MPower Change to bring blacks, communities of color, LGBTQ persons, immigrants, and refugees political gravitas (Gharib 2016).

See also: Civil Rights; Integration

Further Reading

Ahmed, Akbar. 2003. *Islam Under Siege: Living Dangerously in a Post-Honor World*. Cambridge, UK: Polity.

Al Jazeera. 2015. "Linda Sarsour's rising profile reflects new generation of Muslim activists." AlJazeera.com, May 9, 2015. Retrieved from http://america.aljazeera .com/articles/2015/5/9/linda-sarsours-rising-profile-reflects-new-generation -of-muslim-activists.html.

Al Jazeera. 2018. "Linda Sarsour arrested at Paul Ryan's office." AlJazeera.com, March 6, 2018. Retrieved from https://www.aljazeera.com/news/2018/03 /linda-sarsour-arrested-paul-ryan-office-180306103336945.html.

Esack, Farid. 2002. *Qur'an, Liberation and Pluralism: An Islamic Perspective of Interreligious Solidarity against Oppression*. Oxford, UK: Oneworld.

Gharib, Ali. 2016. "Muslim, American, & Intersectional: The Activism of Linda Sarsour." New York: American Civil Liberties Union. Last modified August 22, 2016. Retrieved from https://www.aclu.org/blog/immigrants-rights/muslim -american-intersectional-activism-linda-sarsour.

Khan, Wahiduddin. 2004. *Principles of Islam*. New Delhi, India: Goodword Books.

Mitter, Siddhartha. 2015. "Linda Sarsour's rising profile reflects new generation of Muslim activists." AlJazeera.com, May 9, 2015. Retrieved from http:// america.aljazeera.com/articles/2015/5/9/linda-sarsours-rising-profile-reflects -new-generation-of-muslim-activists.html.

Oxford Dictionary of Islam. n.d.a. "Asabiyyah." Oxford Islamic Studies Online. Retrieved from http://www.oxfordislamicstudies.com/article/opr/t125/e202.

Oxford Dictionary of Islam. n.d.b. "Dawah." Oxford Islamic Studies Online. Retrieved from http://www.oxfordislamicstudies.com/article/opr/t125/e511.

Sufism

Sufism, or *tasawwuf* in the Arabic language, is popularly referred to as "Islamic mysticism." A Sufi Muslim, or someone who believes in and practices Islamic mysticism, is someone who may be said to connect to and search for God by turning to love, peace, and knowledge while simultaneously shunning materialism, war, as well as the desires of the ego. Sufi Muslims are said to dedicate themselves to strengthening humanity, enhancing spirituality, embracing the Other, and promoting egalitarianism. Scholars believe that the term "sufi" derives from the Arabic word *suf*, or wool. A "sufi" in the early years of Islam appears to have been someone who "wears wool." Reynold A. Nicholson, widely recognized as one of the 20th century's leading scholars on Sufism, claimed that the term *sufi* stems from an Arabic root that conveys the notion of "purity," which would make *sufi* mean "one who is pure in heart."

One of the more notable Sufi practices is *dhikr*, an Arabic term meaning "remembrance" or "recollection." *Dhikr* is a form of Sufi devotion and practice of constantly repeating and reciting the name of God and God's attributes in a rhythmic motion. *Dhikr* is generally divided into two branches: recollection with the tongue (*dhikr jali*) and recollection in the heart (*dhikr kafi*) (Geels 1996, 229). *Dhikr jali* is often accompanied with a musical instrument. *Dhikr*, or spiritual concerts, arose in the earliest centuries of Islam as Muslims worked to find effective ways to inspire piety through stories about the Prophet Muhammad.

Various Sufi orders like the Mawlawi, Naqshibandi, and Qadiri are to be found in the present-day United States. The Naqshabandi is one of the largest and most widespread Sufi orders in the *ummah*, or global Muslim population. The Naqshabandi-Haqqani, a leading transnational Sufi movement, is led by the Turkish Cypriot Sheikh Muhammad Nazim Adil Al-Haqqani. Al-Haqqani's student, Sheikh Hisham Kabbani, is credited for bringing the Naqshibandi order to the United States around the late 1980s and early 1990s. The Naqshibandi-Haqqani Sufi Order is the official organization of this Sufi branch. The Naqshibandi-Haqqani aims to spread Sufi teachings like universal brotherhood, humanity, and interfaith harmony.

One of the earliest appearances of Sufism in the United States dates back to the migration of Albanian Muslims in the first part of the 20th century and to South Asian Sufis, such as Hazrat Inayat Khan and Bawa Muhyiddin. Rexheb Beqiri, an Albanian-born Sufi who immigrated to the United States in the 20th century, founded a *tekke*, a large Bektashi Sufi meeting house, in Taylor, Michigan, in 1954. The Bektashi Sufi order is headquartered in Tirana, Albania. Beqiri, better known by his religious name Baba Rexheb, published his voluminous *Islamic Mysticism and Bektashism* in 1970. The Albanian Islamic Center in Harper Woods, Michigan, was established in 1963.

Jalal Ad-Din Muhammad Rumi, better known simply as Rumi, was a 13th-century Sufi poet whose poems have been widely published across the world. Today, Rumi is said to be the best-selling poet in the United States. Organizations across the United States have also dedicated their business to Rumi. The Rumi Forum in Washington, DC, was founded in 1999 to foster interfaith and intercultural dialogue as well as democracy, freedom of speech, pluralism, and social justice.

Sufism shares similar practices to mystical religious traditions in Judaism and Christianity. While the Jewish and Islamic traditions are very much based on "law" rather than inward experiences of God, the scholar of Jewish mysticism Joshua Abelson noted that Judaism also "gleams a far wider, more tolerant and universalist outlook" than many people think (Abelson 2001, 5). Like Sufism, Jewish mysticism "takes account of the cravings of the heart and of the great fact of the soul" (Abelson 2001, 10). In terms of Christian mysticism, *The Book of the Lover and the Beloved* by Ramon Lull, the 13th-century missionary to Muslims, draws upon Islamic sources by stating that "certain men called Sufis" set down "words of love and brief examples which give men great devotion."

See also: Ahmadiyya; Shi'ism; Sunnism; *Ummah*; Wahhabism

Further Reading

Abelson, Joshua. 2001. *Jewish Mysticism: An Introduction to the Kabbalah.* Mineola, NY: Dover Publications.

Geels, Antoon. 1996. "A Note on the Psychology of *Dhikr:* The Halveti-Jerrahi Order of Dervishes in Istanbul." *Psychology of Religion* 6, no. 4: 229–51.

Moaveni, Azadeh. 2017. "How Did Rumi Become One of Our Best-Selling Poets?" NYTimes.com, January 20, 2017. Retrieved from https://www.nytimes.com /2017/01/20/books/review/rumi-brad-gooch.html.

Naqshibandi-Haqqani Sufi Order. n.d. "About the Most Distinguished Naqshabandi Sufi Way." Naqshabandi.org. Retrieved from http://naqshbandi.org/the-tariqa /about/.

Nicholson, Reynold A. 1989. *The Mystics of Islam.* London: Penguin Books.

Oxford Dictionary of Islam. n.d. "Sufism in America." Oxford Islamic Studies Online. Retrieved from http://www.oxfordislamicstudies.com/article/opr/t125 /e2261.

Rumi, Jalal al-Din. 2004. *The Essential Rumi*. New York: HarperOne.
Rumi Forum. n.d. "About Rumi Forum." Washington, DC: Rumi Forum. Retrieved from https://rumiforum.org/about-rumi-forum/.
Safi, Omid. 2011. "Good Sufi, Bad Muslims." The Martin Marty Center for the Public Understanding of Religion: The University of Chicago–Divinity School. Last modified January 27, 2011. Retrieved from https://divinity.uchicago.edu/sightings/good-sufi-bad-muslims-omid-safi.
Safi, Omid. 2018. *Radical Love: Teachings from the Islamic Mystical Tradition*. New Haven, CT: Yale University Press.
Trix, Frances. 2009. *The Sufi Journey of Baba Rexheb*. Philadelphia: University of Pennsylvania Press.

Sunnism

The term *sunni* is derived from *sunnah*, an Arabic word referring to the normative practice of the exemplary behavior of the Prophet Muhammad. The terms *Sunnism* and *Sunni* are anglicized versions of the Arabic term *ahl al-sunnah*, or "the people of the customary way." Today, roughly 85 to 90 percent of the Muslim global population is Sunni, making Sunnism the largest "branch" of Islam in the world. The remaining percentage of the Muslim population in the world is Shi'a, or followers of Shi'ism.

The Sunni-Shi'a split dates back to the period immediately following the death of Muhammad in 632 CE. The early Muslim nation experienced divisions over succession and political authority. A significant number of Sunni Muslims claimed that the successor to Muhammad should be one of the companions closest to him, mainly those individuals from the Quraysh, or Muhammad's tribe.

An important aspect of Sunnism is the political theory pertaining to the first four caliphs of the "Muslim nation." Sunni Islam considers the *caliph* to be a guard of the *sharia* and the *ummah*, while Shi'ism saw in the "successor" a spiritual function connected with the interpretation of revelation and the inheritance of the Prophet Muhammad's teachings (Nasr 2000, 144–45). The four "rightly-guided caliphs" (*al-khulafa al-rashidun*) according to Sunni political theory are Abu Bakr Al-Siddiq, Umar Ibn Al-Khattab, Uthman Ibn Affan, and Ali Ibn Abi Talib. All were prominent companions of the Prophet Muhammad and belonged to the tribe of Quraysh. Umar, the second ruler of the *ummah* after the Prophet Muhammad's death, is a flashpoint between Sunnis and Shi'as. Sunnis consider him a role model, whereas Shi'as have mixed feelings about him: he is one of those who reportedly usurped Ali's rightful place as a successor to Muhammad, but also the ruler who ordered the successful invasion and conquest of Persia that brought the Persians into the fold of Islam (Ahmed 2007, 44). Umar is historically understood to be the dominant personality among the caliphs, establishing many of the institutions of the classical "Islamic state," whereas Utham is generally held responsible for the canonization of the Qur'an as it is known today (*Oxford Dictionary of Islam* n.d.).

The Islamic Society of North America (ISNA) is the main Sunni association of U.S. Muslims (Ul-Huda 2006, 5). According to its official website, the ISNA's mission is to "foster the development of the Muslim community, interfaith relations, civic engagement, and better understanding of Islam" (Islamic Society of North America n.d.). The annual ISNA Convention, convened during Labor Day Weekend, is "the largest gathering of [Sunni] Muslims in North America. This convention brings together more than 40,000 attendees, including individuals, families, businesses, scholars, nonprofit organizations, dignitaries, and people of other faiths" (Ul-Huda 2006, 6).

See also: Ahmadiyya; Shi'ism; Sufism; *Ummah*; Wahhabism

Further Reading

Ahmed, Akbar. 2007. *Journey into Islam: The Crisis of Globalization*. Washington, DC: Brookings Institute.

Islamic Center of America. n.d. "About." Dearborn, MI: ICOFA. Retrieved from http://www.icofa.com/about-1/.

Islamic Society of North America. n.d. "About." Plainfield, IN: ISNA. Retrieved from http://www.isna.net/mission-and-vision/.

Nasr, Seyyed Hossein. 2000. *Ideals and Realities of Islam*. Chicago: ABC International Group, Inc.

Oxford Dictionary of Islam. n.d. "Rightly Guided Caliphs." Oxford Islamic Studies Online. Retrieved from http://www.oxfordislamicstudies.com/article /opr/t125/e2018.

Pluralism Project. n.d. "Islam in America." Pluralism.org. Retrieved from http://pluralism.org/timeline/islam-in-america/.

Ul-Huda, Qamar. 2006. "The Diversity of Muslims in the United States: Special Report." Washington, DC: United States Institute of Peace. Last modified February 2006. Retrieved from https://www.usip.org/sites/default/files/sr159.pdf.

T

Taqiyya

The Arabic term *taqiyya* is literally translated to mean "shield" or "guard." Derived from the Arabic word *waqa'*, the doctrine of *taqiyya* refers to "the act of concealing one's beliefs or identity when a person's life, property, or [reputation] is in danger" (Takim 2018, 3). In modern Islamophobic discourse, however, *taqiyya* is conceived much differently, primarily as a nefarious Islamic obligation for Muslims to lie to people to serve a radical Islamic expansionist vision of the *ummah*. *Taqiyya* provides an opportunity to compare and contrast Sunnism and Shi'ism, the two major branches of the Islamic faith, in historical and contemporary terms. *Taqiyya* is primarily associated with Shi'as, who, "due to the persecution and hostilities they endured at the hands of the Sunni majority [throughout history], resorted to hiding their beliefs" (Takim 2018, 3).

The charge of *taqiyya* is often deployed by anti-Islam polemicists and politicians to marginalize Muslims as a fifth column in the United States. One of the first instances of the *"taqiyya* threat" in public discourse arose out of the "Ground Zero Mosque" controversy in 2010. The Ground Zero Mosque, officially known as Park51, was a proposed multicultural Islamic center to be built within a close proximity to the former site of the World Trade Center towers in New York City. Anti-Islam activists claimed that the building of a mosque so close to a sacred burial ground amounted to examples of "Islamic supremacy" and the historical tendency of Muslims to build mosques on cites that they have conquered. In reality, Park51 would have included interfaith dialogue services and prayer spaces for people of various faiths, a restaurant, a gym, a library, and civic meeting place, according to Imam Feisal Abdul Rauf, the leader of the Park51 movement. Frank Gaffney, an anti-Islam figure and head of the Islamophobic organization Center for Security Policy, claimed in the

Washington Times that Imam Abdul Rauf "is a skilled practitioner of the *sharia* tradition of *taqiyya*, deception for their faith."

Ben Carson, a neurosurgeon who sought the Republican nomination in the presidential election of 2016, is another case in point of U.S. citizen using the "*taqiyya* threat" as a way to depict Muslims as suspicious and untrustworthy. He claimed in an interview with The Hill website that "*taqiyya* is a component of *sharia* that allows, and even encourages you to lie to achieve your goals" (Easley 2015). In other words, as Glenn Kessler of the *Washington Post* pointed out, Carson appeared to be saying that *taqiyya* offered some kind of loophole that would allow U.S. Muslims to lie about their religious beliefs in order to pursue objectives that may be "anti-American" or "anti-Western" (Kessler 2015). Pamela Geller, the anti-Islam activist described by the Southern Poverty Law Center as a leader of a "hate group," claims that Muslims are expected to engage in *taqiyya* "in order to make non-believers think the Islamic invaders are actually peaceful neighbors. That is, until there are enough Muslims to overtake the native population." *Taqiyya* has also been used by U.S. prosecutors in the "War on Terror" to explain the uncooperative behavior of Muslim detainees. Scholars across the United States and the world disagree with Carson and Geller's understanding of *taqiyya* as an Islamic practice of deception and nefariousness. Professor John Esposito, author of *Islam: The Straight Path*, makes it clear that *taqiyya* is a practice that "permits concealment of one's belief for self-protection or survival as a persecuted minority" (Esposito 1998, 45).

The Qur'an (3:28) provides another reference point on *taqiyya*: "Let not the believers take those who deny the truth for their allies in preference to the believers—anyone who does that will isolate himself completely from God—unless it be to protect yourselves against them in this way. God admonishes you to fear Him: for, to God shall all return." This Qur'anic passage suggests that Muslims are allowed to openly embrace people of other faiths if the act ensures the safety of Muslims. In short, Muslims are permitted by the Qur'an and thus the *sharia* to deny their Islamic faith or Muslim identity if they face coerced persecution or if their lives are in danger. Indeed, as the prominent 12th-century Muslim philosopher and theologian Abu Hamid Al-Ghazali noted in *The Revival of the Religious Sciences*, the "safeguarding of a Muslim's life is a mandatory obligation that should be observed . . . lying is permissible when the shedding of a Muslim's blood is at stake."

In summary, nowhere in the Qur'an or *ahadith* does the Islamic faith grant Muslims the general permission to lie with the intention of deceiving others. The practice of *taqiyya* enables a Muslim to lie only if they face persecution or if their life is in danger. In this context, *taqiyya* is not a dangerous "anti-American" practice as argued by anti-Islam activists. It is, rather, a symbol of the Islamic faith's emphasis of the sacredness of human life and humanity over mere declaration of faith, as noted by scholar Omid Safi in the *Washington Post* (Kessler 2015).

See also: Islamophobia

Further Reading

Esposito, John. 1998. *Islam: The Straight Path*. Oxford, UK: Oxford University Press.

Kessler, Glenn. 2015. "Ben Carson's claim that 'taqiyya' encourages Muslims 'to lie to achieve your goals.'" WashingtonPost.com, September 22, 2015. Retrieved from https://www.washingtonpost.com/news/fact-checker/wp/2015/09/22/ben-carsons-claim-that-taqiyya-encourages-muslims-to-lie-to-achieve-your-goals/?utm_term=.318a14ac9b3d.

Mariuma, Yarden. 2014. "Taqiyya as Polemic, Law and Knowledge: Following an Islamic Legal Term through the Worlds of Islamic Scholars, Ethnographers, Polemicists and Military Men." *The Muslim World* 104, nos. 1–2: 89108.

Suleiman, Omar, and Nazir Khan. 2017. "Playing the Taqiyya Card: Evading Intelligent Debate by Calling All Muslims Liars." Irving, TX: Yaqeen Institute. Last modified April 27, 2017. Retrieved from https://yaqeeninstitute.org/en/omar-suleiman/playing-the-taqiyya-card-evading-intelligent-debate-by-calling-all-muslims-liars/.

Takim, Liyakat. 2018. "Policy Background: Taqiyya." Tessellateinstitute.com .Last modified January 2018. Retrieved from http://tessellateinstitute.com/wp-content/uploads/2018/01/Liyakat.-Taqiyya.2018.pdf.

Turkish American Muslims

According to estimates, there are approximately 350,000 people of Turkish descent living in the present-day United States (Turkish Coalition of America n.d.). The Turkish American population shares significant ethnic, linguistic, cultural, religious, and historical ties with over 500,000 people of "Turkic" descent, a group that includes Azerbaijanis, Kazakhs, Kirgiz,

Turkmen, Turkish Cypriots, Uzbeks, as well as Uyghur Turks from China, Turkmen of Iraq, and the Turkic communities hailing from the territories of the former Soviet Union (Turkish Coalition of American n.d.). Most of the Turkish people living in the United States are Sunni Muslims. The Islamic belief system of Sufism, the mystical form of Islam, is popular among Turkish American Muslims. The Gülen Movement, named after a prominent Turkish Muslim preacher and philosopher (Fethullah Gülen), also has an established base in the United States. The largest concentrations of Turks in the country are in the states of California, New Jersey, and New York.

Turkish Muslims, or simply "Turks" as they have been pejoratively called throughout U.S. history, started arriving on the present-day U.S. soil in the late 1500s. Writing for the *Smithsonian Magazine*, Andrew Lawler, a journalist, sheds light on an expedition led by Francis Drake, the English privateer, who attacked the important Spanish-held fort of St. Augustine in Florida. Lawler writes that Drake's warships confronted war galleys rowed by enslaved Ottoman Turks and North African Muslims, or Moors (Lawler 2018). A Spaniard taken captive by the English, as Lawler explains, told authorities that Drake also took "300 Indians from Cartagena, mostly women," as well as "200 negroes, Turks, and Moors, who do menial service."

Records from colonial Virginia also point to a possible Turkish presence in the pre–United States period. Philip A. Bruce, a 19th-century historian, wrote in *Economic History of Virginia in the Seventeenth Century* (1896) that "a number of persons of Turkish blood, who had been imported like English laborers under the terms of ordinary indentures," lived in Virginia in the 17th century. Bruce's research revealed that a man named Francis Yeardley obtained a patent to land that was to be farmed by another man named Simon, who was of Turkish descent. Furthermore, Bruce pointed out another individual, Jonathan Newell, who owned four Turkish servants. The document titled *Records of Lower Norfolk* were used by Bruce in writing his book. The *Records* provided Bruce with several other instances of "Turks" living on modern-day U.S. soil over 120 years before the United States even existed. Again, it should be noted that the term *Turks* was broadly used in the 17th century to refer to any person from the Ottoman Empire, which controlled much of Southeastern Europe, from the edge of Austria and Slovakia and as far north as Ukraine. The "Turks" mentioned in the *Records of Lower Norfolk* could have been Christians from these areas.

Legislation from the Virginian legislature also reveals an anti-Muslim and anti-Turkish sentiment in colonial America. In 1682, colonial Virginians enacted a law that read: "all servants . . . imported into this country either by sea or by land, whether Negroes, Moors [Muslims of North Africa], mulattoes or Indians who and whose percentage and native countries are not Christian at the time of their purchase . . . and all Indians . . . are hereby adjudged, deemed, and taken to be slaves to all intents and purposes of law."

Scholars Terri Ann Ognibene and Glen Browder trace the history of Turkish Americans much later, back to Yusef Ben Ali, or Joseph Benenhaley, an Ottoman refugee who had reportedly served as a scout for General Thomas Sumter in the Revolutionary War. Ognibene and Browder wrote that Benenhaley's dark-hued descendants lived insular lives in rural Sumter County, South Carolina. According to family narratives, General Sumter gave a "Caucasian of Arab descent" (Benenhaley) some land of his plantation to farm and raise a family (Browder and Ognibene 2018). Their findings, based on an extensive list of historical reports, public records, and private papers, are also confirmed through genealogical analysis and genetic testing (Ognibene and Browder 2018).

Relations between the U.S. government and the Ottoman Empire (Turkey) go back to the 19th century. The first formal act of diplomatic engagement between the United States and the Ottoman Empire occurred on February 11, 1830, when a U.S. negotiating team comprised of Captain James Biddle, David Offley, and Charles Rhind presented their credentials to the Turkish Minister of Foreign Affairs (U.S. Embassy and Consulates in Turkey n.d.). Nearly one year later, on September 13, 1831, diplomatic relations between the two states were officially established when David Porter presented his credentials to the Ottoman government in Constantinople.

Historical relations between the Ottoman Empire and the United States were addressed by President Barack Obama when he visited Ankara, the modern Turkish capital, in 2009. President Obama touched upon the contributions made by Ottoman Sultan Abdülmecid in the construction of the Washington Monument in Washington, DC. In 1854, Sultan Abdülmecid sent a marble plaque to the United States to be placed inside of the Washington Monument. A poem inscribed on the plaque reads, "So as to strengthen the friendship between the two countries." Eight years after Abdülmecid's contribution to the Washington Monument, President Abraham Lincoln agreed to the Treaty of Commerce and Navigation with the Ottoman Empire on July 22, 1862. Article II of the treaty grants all U.S. citizens the right to purchase, at all locations in the Ottoman Empire, the produce or manufacture of the Ottomans (Avalon Project n.d.). The treaty, in effect, served as the first official free-trade agreement between the two countries; however, hardly any trade was carried out between the two powers, due to the U.S. Civil War. Relations between the U.S. government and the Ottoman Empire later soured on April 20, 1917, after the United States declared war against Germany, an Ottoman ally, during World War I. Diplomatic ties between the Americans and Ottomans were formally reestablished on February 17, 1927 (U.S. Embassy and Consulates in Turkey n.d.).

The late 19th century and the first half of the 20th century witnessed the immigration of more Muslims from Ottoman territories. According to Amir Hussain, author of *Muslims and the Making of America*, many of the Muslim immigrants were itinerants who came to make money and then return to their countries of origin (Hussain 2016, 9). Some, however, were farmers and merchants who settled permanently and created mosques in states like Connecticut, Maine, New York, and North Dakota (Hussain 2016, 9). Several small towns in Maine, for example, welcomed young Muslim men from Turkey in the early 1900s. These Turkish Muslim men worked in the mill industry at York Manufacturing Co. in Saco, a neighboring town of Biddeford. Charles Butler, of the Biddeford Historical Society and author of *Images of America: Biddeford*, speculated that Turkish and Albanian Muslims created a "mosque" in the Pepperell Counting House on Main Street in Biddeford. According to historian Justin McCarthy, author of *The Turk in America: The Creation of an Enduring Prejudice*, the Turkish Muslims that immigrated to the United States in the 19th and early 20th centuries faced discrimination and false allegations mostly stemming from an antipathy in the United States toward Muslims.

Ties between the Turkish and United States governments were again strengthened in the years following World War II. During President Harry Truman's administration, the Turkish government agreed to join the North Atlantic Treaty Organization (NATO), and the United States simultaneously agreed to defend Turkey from military threats made against the country. Since then, Turkish and U.S. forces have fought alongside one another in the Afghan War, the Korean War, and the Kosovo War.

Turkish Muslims in the United States are oftentimes linked to the Fethullah Gülen movement, popularly referred to as the "Gülen movement," a transatlantic Islamic social movement that emphasizes the importance of democracy, universal education, civil society, interfaith dialogue, and peace building. The movement is named after and inspired by Fethullah Gülen, a Turkish philosopher and Islamic scholar who has lived in the United States since 1999. Gülen left Turkey at a time when he was under investigation for undermining the Turkish government—which at that point was "under control of Turkey's secular elite and backed up by the military." In 2000, he was "found guilty of scheming to overthrow the government by embedding civil servants in various governmental agencies" (Sanderson 2018).

The Gülen movement became the focus of domestic and international news during the U.S. presidential election of 2016. Michael Flynn, who briefly served as National Security Advisor under President Donald Trump, was reportedly offered $15 million to help forcibly remove Gülen from the United States and deliver him to Turkish authorities (BBC 2017). The Turkish government accused Gülen of ordering the failed 2015 coup to overthrow his chief political rival Recep Tayyip Erdogan, the president of Turkey (Sanderson 2018). Since the failed coup, President Erdogan has purged and arrested tens of thousands of people linked to the Gülen movement, which the Turkish government has branded a terrorist organization called "FETO" (Sanderson 2018).

Despite the suspicion hovering over the Gülen movement, many Turkish American Muslims are making invaluable contributions to present-day U.S. society. Mehmet Cengiz Öz, known professionally as Dr. Oz, is professor at Columbia University and television personality of *The Dr. Oz Show*. Dr. Oz grew up in a largely secular Muslim family, but he has repeatedly identified himself as a Muslim. Hikmet Ersek, who was born in Istanbul, Turkey, currently serves as president, chief executive officer (CEO), and director of the Western Union Company. According to the official website of Western Union, the company is a Fortune 500 global leader in digital and retail crossborder money transfer and payments services.

In terms of impactful Turkish organizations, the Turkish Coalition of America (TCA) is a 501(c)(3) charitable organization funded entirely by Turkish Americans who believe in a strong U.S.-Turkey relationship and who are proud of their Turkish heritage, according to the TCA website. Similarly, the Turkish Cultural Foundation (TCF), based in Washington, DC, was established in 2000 with the goal to promote and preserve Turkish culture, support education in the humanities for disadvantaged Turkish students, support research documenting the humanities related to Turkey, and help build cultural bridges of understanding between the Turkish people and the world (Turkish Cultural Foundation n.d.).

An academic paper by Ilhan Kaya examines the adoption of "American values" by Turkish Americans, specifically Muslims. Kaya found that while first-generation Turkish Americans are quite reluctant to assert their American identities, second-generation Turkish Americans openly express both their Turkish and American identities, regardless of their religious orientation (Kaya 2009, 617). The article also suggests that those second-generation Turkish immigrants who feel discriminated against believe that it is their Islamic faith rather than their ethnicity that is the cause of their lack of acceptance by the wider U.S. society (Kaya 2009, 617).

See also: African American Muslims; Arab American Muslims; Asian American Muslims; European American Muslims; Latin American Muslims; *Ummah*

Further Reading

Ahmed, Frank. 1993. *Turks in America: The Ottoman Turk's Immigrant Experience.* Columbia, MO: Columbia International Press.

Avalon Project. n.d. "Treaty of Commerce and Navigation Between the United States and the Ottoman Empire; February 25, 1862." Hartford, CT: Lillian Goldman Law Library at Yale Law School. Retrieved from http://avalon.law .yale.edu/19th_century/ot1862.asp.

Browder, Glen, and Terri Ann Obnibene. 2018. "Tracing the Mysterious 'Turks' of South Carolina Back to the Revolutionary War." Smithsonionmag.com, September 24, 2018. Retrieved from https://www.smithsonianmag.com /history/tracing-mysterious-turks-of-south-carolina-back-revolutionary -war-180970383/.

Bruce, Philip A. 1896. *Economic History of Virginia in the Seventeenth Century: An Inquiry into the Material Condition of the People, Based on Original and Contemporaneous Records.* New York: Macmillan and Co.

Hussain, Amir. 2016. *Muslims and the Making of America.* Waco, TX: Baylor University Press.

Kaya, Ilhan. 2009. "Identity across Generations: A Turkish American Case Study." *Middle East Journal* 63, no. 4 (August): 617–32.

Lawler, Andrew. 2018. "Did Francis Drake Bring Enslaved Africans to North America Decades before Jamestown." SmithsonianMag.com, August 20, 2018. Retrieved from https://www.smithsonianmag.com/history/did-francis-drake -bring-enslaved-africans-north-america-decades-jamestown-180970075/.

McCarthy, Justin. 2010. *The Turk in America: The Creation of an Enduring Prejudice*. Salt Lake City: University of Utah Press.

Ognibene, Terri Ann, and Glen Browder. 2018. *South Carolina's Turkish People: A History and Ethnology*. Columbia: University of South Carolina Press.

Sanderson, Sertan. 2018. "From ally to scapegoat: Fethullah Gulen, the man behind the myth." Deutsche Welle. Last modified April 4, 2018. Retrieved from https://www.dw.com/en/from-ally-to-scapegoat-fethullah-gulen-the-man -behind-the-myth/a-37055485.

Turkish Coalition of America. n.d. "The Turkish American Community." Washington, DC and Concord, MA: Turkish Coalition of America. Retrieved from http://tc-america.us/community/the-turkish-american-community-463.htm.

Turkish Cultural Foundation. n.d. "About Us." Washington, DC: TCF. Retrieved from http://www.turkishculturalfoundation.org/pages.php?ID=1.

U.S. Embassy and Consulates in Turkey. n.d. "History of the U.S. and Turkey." U.S. Embassy Ankara: Ankara, Turkey. Retrieved from https://tr.usembassy .gov/our-relationship/policy-history/io/.

White House, The. 2009. "Remarks by President Obama to the Turkish Parliament." ObamaWhiteHouse.archives.gov. Retrieved from https://obamawhitehouse .archives.gov/the-press-office/remarks-president-obama-turkish-parliament.

U

Ummah

Ummah is the Arabic word that literally means "nation," but it also may be understood as the "global Islamic community," or *ummah al-Islam* in Arabic. Theoretically, the global Muslim community is "one community" in the sense that each Muslim person shares an Islamic identity with approximately 2 billion other Muslims around the world. The word *ummah* in this context is linked to the concept of *ummat al-mu'minin*, or the "commonwealth of the believers," which transcends nation-state borders or transnational political unions. During the life of the Prophet Muhammad the *ummah* was unified under a single ruler, the *caliph*, but subsequent generations of Muslims ended up fracturing into political entities. This fracturing occurred because of several complex reasons, among them disagreements on the succession of leaders as well as the challenges presented by an expansive territorial *ummah* that held power as far west as Spain, into North Africa, and to west Asia.

Today, the *ummah* is more of an ideal than a political reality. Muslims worldwide are united in some ways, such as prayer and giving alms, but significantly different in other ways. The roughly 2 billion Muslims around the world, for example, are extremely diverse in terms of race, ethnicity, culture, and even sectarian preferences. In the realm of politics the *ummah* is composed of various Muslim-majority nation-states that approach and use the Islamic faith in their own unique ways. Some Muslim-majority countries like Indonesia are considered to be vibrant democracies while other Muslim-majority countries like Saudi Arabia are run by authoritarian royal families.

Contemporary ideas of the *ummah* also express a range of political and social agendas. Scholar Robert A. Saunders concluded that there is a need to recognize the *ummah*-based identity as more than just a profession

179

of the Islamic faith—"it represents a new form of post-national, political identity which is as profound as any extant nationalism" (Saunders 2008, 303). According to him, the *ummah* is fast becoming the paradigm of the nonterritorial and postnational form of allegiance once played by nation-states. Academic studies, furthermore, have found that a growing number of Muslim university students (in the case of one study, Pakistan) are disenchanted with exclusionary efforts to control state-based forms of Islamic nationalism (Nelson 2011, 565). Muslim students who reject the constraints of territorial Muslim nationalism may favor transnational movements focused on the revitalization of the *ummah* on a truly global scale (Nelson 2011, 565).

Whether the *ummah* includes—or could theoretically include—the presence of non-Muslims is a topic of speculation among Muslim jurists, theologians, and scholars. While the term is typically associated with concepts like "Muslim nation" or "global Muslim population," it has also been linked to a more liberal form of social consciousness and a universalist political idea that translates into a "community of believers." The Constitution of Medina, also known as the Medina Charter, is a case in point. Created by the Prophet Muhammad shortly after his arrival in the city of Medina, Saudi Arabia, in 622 CE, this political treatise stated that Jews, Christians, Muslims, and pagans were all part of a single political entity. The Constitution of Medina established a union of tribes and religious groups by agreeing to a set of laws including mutual defense, freedom of religion, and freedom from tyranny or rule by the majority population. This kind of political union is understood to be a civic nation in the sense that the people of Medina were united by democratic values instead of race, ethnicity, or even religion. The Prophet Muhammad's vision of this form of the *ummah* stands in contrast to the period of *jahiliyya*, or the pre-Islamic period on the Arabian Peninsula, during which Arabs were typically united by ancestry, kinship, or tribe.

In the context of the United States the Muslim population represents the entire spectrum of the *ummah* and its rich diversity. Critics, however, question whether there is sufficient space or any space at all for U.S. Muslims in the global *ummah*. The Gallup Center for Muslim Studies and the Muslim-West Initiative found that only 37 percent of U.S. Muslims say they identify strongly with the *ummah* and those who share their Islamic faith worldwide. For U.S. Muslim immigrants, the idea of the *ummah* may be more powerful because many Muslim immigrants were born and raised in regions of the world where Muslims are the overwhelming majority.

Further Reading

Arjomand, Saïd Amir. 2009. "The Constitution of Medina: A Sociological Interpretation of Muhammad's Acts of Foundation of the 'Umma.'" *International Journal of Middle East Studies* 41, no. 4: 555–75.

Hashem, Mazen. 2010. "The Ummah in the Khutba: A Religious Sermon or a Civil Discourse?" *Journal of Muslim Minority Affairs* 30, no. 1: 49–61.

Mandaville, Peter. 2011. "Transnational Muslim solidarities and everyday life." *Nations and Nationalism* 17, no. 1: 7–24.

Nelson, Matthew J. 2011. "Embracing the Ummah: Student Politics beyond State Power in Pakistan." *Modern Asian Studies* 45, no. 3: 565–96.

Saunders, Robert A. 2008. "The ummah as nation: a reappraisal in the wake of the 'Cartoon Affair.'" *Nations and Nationalism* 14, no. 2: 303–21.

Younis, Ahmed. 2012. "Is There Space for American Muslims in the Ummah?" HuffingtonPost.com, January 9, 2012. Retrieved from https://www.huffington post.com/ahmed-younis/is-there-space-for-americ_b_1179739.html.

U.S. Founding Fathers

A collection of primary documents from the 18th century shows that the U.S. Founding Fathers imagined a country rooted in freedom of religion and freedom of conscience for Muslims. These primary documents show that the U.S. Founding Fathers welcomed the presence of Muslims on U.S. soil and encouraged their integration into the fabric of U.S. social life.

Although there is no clear evidence that George Washington, the first U.S. president, was aware of the presence of Muslims on U.S. soil in the 18th century, the primary documents of his life show that he thought about the relationship of the Islamic faith to the new nation, as scholar James H. Hutson of the Library of Congress noted. Washington declared in a 1783 letter to Irish Catholic immigrants in New York City that the country was open to "the oppressed and persecuted of all Nations and Religions," a sign that he would welcome refugees and other oppressed peoples. In another 1784 letter to Tench Tighman, who asked Washington about the kind of worker he would like to see at his residence and plantation of Mount Vernon in northern Virginia, Washington stated, ". . . they may be of Asia, Africa, or Europe. They may be Mahometans [Muslims], Jews, or Christians of any sect, or atheists." The website of Mount Vernon also mentions that "elements of Islam" are found in the documentary and archaeological records of Mount Vernon's slave population (Thompson n.d.). Two slave women of West African origin—named "Fatimer" and "Little Fatimer"—were listed as two slave women on his tithe tables. Fatimer and Little Fatimer, who were mother and daughter, are likely derivatives of the name Fatima, or the Prophet Muhammad's daughter.

Thomas Jefferson, the third U.S. president and co-author of the Declaration of Independence, first engaged with the Islamic tradition when he purchased the Qur'an in 1765 while he was a law student at the College of William and Mary in Virginia (Spellberg 2014). He is said to have made the purchase for several factors including his interest in learning more about a variety of religious traditions and in part to better understand the *sharia*, or "Islamic law," especially as it related to constitutional law. This Qur'an, popularly referred to as "Jefferson's Qur'an," is held today in the Library of Congress in Washington, DC. Jefferson's Qur'an was a 1734 translation by an Orientalist academic from England named George Sale, who was sponsored by a Christian (Anglican, to be specific) missionary society. It is said to have been the definitive translation of the Qur'an during the 18th century. Sale stated in the introduction of his translation that the book is intended for Protestant audiences that were seeking to learn about the Islamic faith in the hope of arguing against the Prophet Muhammad's messages. He wrote: "It is absolutely necessary to undeceive those who, from the ignorant or unfair translations which have appeared, have entertained too favorable an opinion of the original, and also to enable us effectually to expose the imposture." Sale added that "Protestants alone are able to attack the Qur'an with success, and for them, I trust, Providence has reserved the glory of its overthrow."

Jefferson's engagement with the Qur'an and the Islamic faith led to accusations that he was a "secret Muslim," making him "the first in history of American politics to suffer the false charge of being a Muslim, an accusation considered the ultimate Protestant slur in the eighteenth century" (Spellberg 2013). During the presidential election of 1800, allies of candidate John Adams referred to Jefferson as "un-American," principally because of his deist and Unitarian religious beliefs. *The Connecticut Courant* suggested he might be a secret Muslim and complained that no one seemed to know "whether Mr. Jefferson believes in the heathen mythology or in the alcoran [*Qur'an*]; whether he is a Jew or a Christian; whether he believes in one God, or in many; or in none at all." Despite these false allegations, Jefferson insisted that the constitution of Virginia should be one in which "neither pagan nor Mohamedan [Muslim] nor Jew ought to be excluded from the civil rights of the Commonwealth because of his religion." Moreover, Jefferson's intention for the Virginia Statute of Religious Freedom was to protect the freedom of religion for "the Jew and the Gentile, the Christian and Mahometan [Muslim], the Hindoo, and infidel of every denomination," as he wrote in his autobiography.

Jefferson also is recognized as the first U.S. president to host an *iftar*, or the daily fast-breaking evening meal for Muslims during the Islamic holy month of Ramadan. President Jefferson welcomed Sidi Soliman Mellimelli, a Tunisian diplomat, to the White House during 1805. The purpose of Mellimelli's diplomatic outreach was to settle various disputes surrounding the activities of U.S. trading vessels off the coast of North Africa in the Mediterranean Sea. On the evening of December 9, Jefferson is said to have changed the time of dinner at the White House from 3:30 p.m. to "precisely at sunset" to accommodate Mellimelli's obligation to break his fast during Ramadan. The White House *iftar* was restarted in 1996 by First Lady Hillary Clinton, and the practice was continued by Presidents Bill Clinton, George W. Bush, and Barack Obama. The White House's annual *iftar* had been a staple of interfaith relations until the tradition ended in 2017 during the Trump administration.

Benjamin Franklin, the U.S. statesman of the Revolutionary War period, also imagined Muslims as part of the U.S. nation. After having grown up in 18th-century Boston, a Puritan city known for its religious intolerance and tribal orthodoxy, Franklin ran away from his birth city and moved to Philadelphia, a city where Christian populations like Lutherans, Quakers, Calvinists, and even Jews lived side by side. Franklin believed in God and in the social usefulness of religion, but he did not subscribe to any particular sectarian ideology (Isaacson 2005, 36). This led him to help raise money to build a new hall in Philadelphia that was, as he put it, "expressly for the use of any preacher of any religious persuasion who might desire to say something." Franklin added, "Even if the *Mufti* [Muslim leader] of Constantinople [modern-day Istanbul] were to send a missionary to preach Mohammedanism [the Islamic faith] to us, he would find a pulpit at his service."

James Madison, the Father of the U.S. Constitution and fourth president of the United States from 1809 to 1817, also specifically mentioned freedom of religion and freedom of conscience as they pertain to Muslims. In a 1788 letter to Thomas Jefferson, Madison wrote, "I am sure that the rights of conscience in particular, if submitted to public definition would be narrowed much more than they are ever likely to be by an assumed power" (Madison 1788). Madison had then gone on to explain why it was necessary to prohibit "religious tests" so that "Jews, Turks [Muslims], and infidels" could be free to practice their religion (or no religion) without interference from the U.S. government.

Other, less notable U.S. Founding Fathers also expressed favorable opinions of the Islamic faith and Muslims, as James H. Hutson's research at the Library of Congress shows. In 1783, the president of Yale College, Ezra Stiles, cited a study showing that "'Mohammadan" morals were "far superior to the Christian." Another New Englander around the time believed that the "moral principles that were inculcated by [Muslim] teachers had a happy tendency to render them good members of society."

See also: Civil Rights; Freedom of Religion; Integration; Pluralism

Further Reading

Considine, Craig. 2013. "George Washington Was a Friend of Muslims." Huffington Post.com, April 20, 2013. Retrieved from https://www.huffpost.com/entry /george-washington-was-a-f_b_2712606.

Considine, Craig. 2018. *Muslims in America: Examining the Facts*. Santa Barbara, CA: ABC-CLIO.

Hauslohner, Abigail. 2017. "Muslim running for U.S. Senate praised the Founding Fathers. Then the insults began." DenverPost.com. Retrieved from https:// www.denverpost.com/2017/07/20/muslim-woman-running-us-senate-insulted -arizona/.

Hutson, James H. 2002. "The Founding Fathers and Islam: Library Papers Show Early Tolerance for Muslim Faith." Washington, DC: Library of Congress. Last modified May 2002. Retrieved from https://www.loc.gov/loc/lcib/0205 /tolerance.html.

Isaacson, Walter. 2005. "Benjamin Franklin's Gift of Tolerance." In *After Terror: Promoting Dialogue Among Civilizations*. Edited by Akbar Ahmed and Brian Forst. Cambridge and Malden, UK: Polity.

Madison, James. 1788. "Letter to Thomas Jefferson, October 17, 1788 (Bill of Rights." Founding.com. Retrieved from http://founding.com/founders-library /american-political-figures/james-madison/letter-to-thomas-jefferson/.

Spellberg, Denise. 2014. *Thomas Jefferson's Qur'an: Islam and the Founders*. New York: Knopf.

Thompson, Mary V. n.d. "Islam and Mount Vernon." MountVernon.org. Retrieved from https://www.mountvernon.org/library/digitalhistory/digital-encyclopedia /article/islam-at-mount-vernon/.

W

Wahhabism

Wahhabism is the term commonly used by experts to capture the beliefs and actions of Muslims who engage in persecution of minority populations and violence as a means to a political end. Scholars specify that Wahhabism is the form of Sunnism that derives its puritanical ethos from Muhammad Ibn 'Abd Al-Wahhab, the 18th-century Muslim evangelist who lived in the Arabian Peninsula. Al-Wahhab was trained in theology and the *sharia* in Medina and Mecca, where he was drawn to the Hanbali school, the strictest school of the *sharia* in the Sunni tradition. Al-Wahhab advocated a strict literal interpretation of the Qur'an and *ahadith*, displayed a dismissiveness of intellectualism, as well as a hostility to Sufism, or "mystical Islam." According to Hamid Algar, author of "Wahhabism: A Critical Essay," Al-Wahhab engaged in a violent campaign against the communities and groups who did not share his puritanical understanding of the Islamic faith.

Ibn Tahmiyya, an Islamic scholar who lived in the 13th and 14th centuries, is said to have inspired the views and actions of Al-Wahhab. Tahmiyya had yearned to re-create the so-called "purity" of the early Muslim society, as led by the Prophet Muhammad, and to actively defend Muslim communities. According to Akbar Ahmed, a scholar of Islamic history, Ibn Tahymiyya's understanding of the Islamic faith is best summarized in modern terminology with words like "radical Islam," "political Islam," "jihadism," or "Islamo-fascism" (Ahmed 2007, 36).

Wahhabism is believed to be the central Islamic ethos of the Kingdom of Saudi Arabia. According to expert William McCants, Saudi Arabian rulers have spent billions of dollars to spread and flout Wahhabi teachings since the founding of the Kingdom in 1920. James Gelvin, whose research specialty includes the social and cultural history of the modern Middle East, claims that the Saudi Arabian government has spent approximately

$100 billion spreading Wahhabism in schools, mosques, the media, and other means since the 1960s (Kertscher 2016). The *New York Times* echoed these claims in an August 2016 article that noted how Saudi rulers have lavishly spent tens of billions of dollars on "religious outreach" (Shane 2016). On the domestic front, as McCants again noted, the Saudi Arabian government has been slow to reform the Wahhabi creed and to curb the Wahhabi influence of its clerical establishment.

Wahhabism also is considered to be the preferred ethos of Daesh, commonly referred to as the Islamic State of Iraq and Syria, or ISIS. Researcher Jeffrey R. Macris, of the U.S. Naval Academy, found that Daesh uses violence and compulsion to achieve political objectives and calls upon Muslims to return to the alleged "pure" practices of the first Muslim community (Macris 2016). Other experts, however, are not convinced that the use of the term Wahhabism as a catchall is sufficient to adequately describe the forms of Islamic militancy by Daesh and similar groups (Pew Research Center 2005).

In October 2016, Democratic politician Russ Feingold of Wisconsin accused Saudi Arabia of embracing Wahhabism and raised the question of how the United States could "allow a country [like Saudi Arabia] to be perceived as a friend—across the board, without questions—when they are doing such a terrible thing" (Kertscher 2016). Other experts like William McCants called on the Trump administration to push back against the Saudi government for its proselytization of Wahhabism. McCants claimed that Saudi rulers often flout Wahhabi teachings and have been "slow to reform the [Wahhabi] creed and to curb the influence of the clerical establishment that promotes it at home and abroad" (McCants 2017).

See also: Sunnism

Further Reading

Ahmed, Akbar. 2007. *Journey into Islam: The Crisis of Globalization.* Washington, DC: Brookings Institute.

Algar, Hamid. 2002. *Wahhabism: A Critical Essay.* Oneonta, NY: Islamic Publications International.

Kertscher, Tom. 2016. "Russ Feinghold says U.S. ally Saudi Arabia exports extreme Islam that teaches Americans are the devil." Politifact.com. Last modified October 21, 2016. Retrieved from https://www.politifact.com/wisconsin/statements/2016/oct/21/russ-feingold/russ-feingold-says-us-ally-saudi-arabia-exports-ex/.

Macris, Jeffrey R. 2016. "Investigating the ties between Muhammed ibn Abd al-Wahhab, early Wahhabism, and ISIS." *The Journal of the Middle East and Africa* 7, no. 3: 239–55.

McCants, William. 2017. "Trump should push the Saudis to scale back proselytizing—they may be more responsive than you think." Washington, DC: Brookings Institution. Last modified May 10, 2017. Retrieved from https://www.brookings.edu/blog/markaz/2017/05/10/trump-should-push-the-saudis-to-scale-back-proselytizing-they-may-be-more-responsive-than-you-think/.

Pew Research Center. 2005. "The Global Spread of Wahhabi Islam: How Great a Threat?" Washington, DC: Pew Research Center. Last modified May 3, 2005. Retrieved from http://www.pewforum.org/2005/05/03/the-global-spread-of-wahhabi-islam-how-great-a-threat/.

Shane, Scott. 2016. "Saudis and Extremism: 'Both the Arsonists and the Firefighters.'" NYTimes.com, August 25, 2016. Retrieved from https://www.nytimes.com/2016/08/26/world/middleeast/saudi-arabia-islam.html.

Women's Rights

Women's rights is a matter that is often raised in discussions on the intersection of the Islamic faith and U.S. national identity. Critics of the Islamic faith claim that Muslim women are inferior to Muslim men and that the Qur'an as well as the *ahadith* command the systematic oppression of women and the denial of their rights. In the minds of these critics, the reports of female genital mutilation, honor killings, and domestic abuse in Muslim-majority countries help to legitimize, in U.S. public discourse, the argument that women's rights do not exist in the Islamic tradition. Images of fully covered Muslim women being forced to wear the veil, forbidden from driving, and mistreated in Muslim-majority countries around the world are exacerbating the assumption that the Islamic faith oppresses women and that Muslim women need saving. The latter phrase is now a global undertaking, or a "moral crusade," in which both Muslims and non-Muslims try to rescue Muslim women from their cultures and religion (Abu-Lughod 2013). However, according to Muslims for Progressive Values (MPV), a 501(c)(3) nonprofit organization based in Los Angeles, the Islamic faith "never condones humiliation, beatings, mutilation, or outright murder, especially not as a means to exert one's own authority" (Muslims for Progressive Values n.d.). Rather, the MPV noted that the

Islamic faith teaches Muslims "to approach differences in opinion with tolerance and forbearance."

Scholar Joseph E. Lumbard stressed that Muslims recognize, or are at least commanded to recognize, that all men and women are equal before God and each gender has been measured out different qualities according to God (Lumbard 2008, 18). Muslims, he claimed, seek to establish a society that allows for the different dimensions of men and women to be fully realized (Lumbard 2008, 19). Men are commanded to provide the material needs of the household while women are responsible for the sustenance of the household. With that being said, Lumbard also pointed out that Muslim women are able to work in the public sphere and hold professional jobs.

The contemporary depictions of Muslim women in mainstream U.S. media can be tested against Islamic history. According to Karen Armstrong, author of *Islam: A Short History*, the emancipation of women was a project close to the Prophet Muhammad's heart. The Qur'an "gave women rights of inheritance and divorce centuries before Western women were accorded such status" (Armstrong 2000, 16). Muhammad, for example, ended female infanticide, a common practice in pre-Islamic Arab society, granted women the right to divorce their husbands, and provided women the right to own and purchase land.

Muslim women during the early years of Islam were involved in the development of the religion not merely as wives and daughters, but also as warriors, consultants, and scholars (Ahmed 2007, 97). In this early phase of Islamic history, women led armies (Aishah, one of the Prophet Muhammad's wives), were famous as Sufi saints (Rabia), and were rulers in their own right (Razia of India) (Ahmed 2003, 116). Their names have also been conferred on towns (Madinah Al-Zahra in Spain) and coins of the realm (the Mughal empress Noor Jahan) (Ahmed 2003, 116). In fact, the first person in history to embrace the Islamic faith is Khadijah, the Prophet's wife. Khadijah had managed successful trading caravans that crisscrossed the tribal lands of what is known today as the Middle East (Ahmed 2007, 96). She had been a widow for some time before meeting the Prophet Muhammad and decided to take a chance on him even though he was fifteen years her junior. As noted above, Aisha, another of the Prophet Muhammad's wives, had a protective, loving, and gentle relationship with her husband. She transmitted the sayings of Muhammad, called the *ahadith*, to generations after her (Ahmed 2007, 97). Aisha was also considered a legal authority, thus becoming a key figure in the transmission of the Prophet's spiritual teachings and political legacy (Ahmed 2007, 97).

While Muslim women are confined to second-class citizenship status in many parts of the so-called "Muslim world," that is not the case among U.S. Muslim women. Muslim women in the United States are one of the most highly educated female religious groups in the country, second only to Jewish American women (Younis 2009). According to the Pew Research Center (2009), roughly 62 percent of U.S. Muslims say that the quality of life for U.S. Muslim women is better than the quality of life for women in Muslim-majority countries. Women are integral parts of both the Islamic faith and Muslim communities in the United States. Countless numbers of U.S. Muslim women see themselves as strong, independent, and empowered women who are transcending the extremist narratives perpetuated by ignorance and anti-Muslim bigotry.

Further Reading

Abu-Lughod, Lila. 2013. *Do Muslim Women Need Saving?* Cambridge, MA: Harvard University Press.

Ahmed, Akbar. 2003. *Islam Under Siege: Living Dangerously in a Post-Honor World.* Cambridge, UK: Polity.

Ahmed, Akbar. 2007. *Journey into Islam: The Crisis of Globalization.* Washington, DC: Brookings Institute.

Armstrong, Karen. 2000. *Islam: A Short History.* New York: Modern Library.

Lumbard, Joseph E. 2008. *Submission: Faith & Beauty.* Berkeley, CA: Zaytuna Institute.

Muslims for Progressive Values. n.d. "Women's Rights: MPV's Stance on Women's Rights." Los Angeles: MPV. Retrieved from http://www.mpvusa.org /womens-rights/.

Pew Research Center. 2009. *Little Support for Terrorism among Muslim Americans.* Washington, DC: Pew Research Center. Last modified December 17, 2009. Retrieved from http://www.pewforum.org/2009/12/17/little-supportfor terrorism-among-muslim-americans/.

Wadud, Amina. 1999. *Qur'an and Woman: Rereading the Sacred Text from a Woman's Perspective.* Oxford, UK: Oxford University Press.

Wadud, Amina. 2006. *Inside the Gender Jihad: Women's Reform in Islam.* London: Oneworld Publications.

Younis, Mohamed. 2009. "Muslim Americans Exemplify Diversity, Potential." Washington, DC: Gallup.com. Last modified March 2, 2009. Retrieved from http://www.gallup.com/poll/116260/muslim-americans-exemplifydiversity -potential.aspx.

Z

Zakat

Zakat, the Arabic word for "purification" or "growth," is one of the Five Pillars of Islam. *Zakat* refers to the annual alms tax or tithe levied on the wealthy members of society and distributed to people in need, especially people who live in a state of poverty and severe distress. The *zakat* also may be used for purposes like freeing people from slavery or assisting individuals or organizations that have accumulated an unsustainable amount of debt.

The percentage of a Muslim's accumulated income, wealth, and assets to be given as a charitable offering is typically set at the minimum of 2½ percent in a given year. The maximum amount of money levied on wealthy and affluent Muslims in terms of the *zakat* is generally set at 20 percent. Every Muslim adult who is free and financially able to do so is required to pay the *zakat*. Muslims are also commanded to act and behave humbly in providing charity. The Qur'an (4:38) criticizes Muslims who give money to charity only to show off or boast their wealth or assets: "And [God does not like] those who spend their wealth for the sake of ostentation, who do not believe in God or the Last Day."

According to the Qur'an (9:60), which includes over 50 verses pertaining to charity, all Muslims are encouraged to give to charitable organizations or other outlets fighting a range of inequalities: "Alms are only for: the poor and the destitute, for those who collect *zakat*, for conciliating people's hearts, for freeing slaves, for those in debt, for spending for God's cause, and for travelers in need. It is a legal obligation enjoined by God. God is all-knowing and wise." As noted, the purpose of *zakat* is primarily to alleviate the suffering of the underprivileged and underserved members of a society or community, but it also serves the purpose of instilling in Muslims a sense of communal identity and responsibility to promote the common humanity. "Believers, give charitably from the good things which you have earned and what We produce for you from the earth; not worthless things which you yourselves would only reluctantly accept. Know that God is self-sufficient and praiseworthy" (Qur'an 2:267).

The Arabic term *sadaqah* is often incorporated into discussions on *zakat*. While *zakat* is often understood to be an obligatory annual alms, the *sadaqah* denotes a voluntary offering. *Sadaqah* is a necessary instrument in addition to the annual *zakat* payment. Two notable Islamic scholars in the United States, Hamza Yusuf and Zaid Shakir of Zaytuna College in Berkeley, California, encourage U.S. Muslims to commit to donating some portion of their wealth in addition to the *zakat* that they pay. More specifically, they encourage U.S. Muslims to support bona fide charitable organizations that request alms and assistance from the Muslim population in the country (Yusuf and Shakir 2008, 32).

Several charitable organizations based in the United States have emerged in recent years to tackle some of the most pressing issues facing U.S. society and the world at large. Helping Hand for Relief and Development (HHRD), a partner organization of the Islamic Circle of North America (ICNA), was selected by Charity Navigator, the United States's largest and most-utilized evaluator of charities, as the sixth highest-rated charity relying on private contributions in the United States (Islamic Circle of North America 2013). Charity Navigator also awarded four out of four stars to Islamic Relief USA, a nonprofit 501(c)(3) humanitarian agency and member of the Islamic Relief Worldwide group. Incorporated in 1993, Islamic Relief defines its mission as one that "provides relief and development in a dignified manner regardless of gender, race, or religion, and works to empower individuals in their communities" (Islamic Relief USA n.d.). According to Charity Navigator's website, Islamic Relief "operates a wide variety of projects, including education and training, water and sanitation, income generation, orphan support, health and nutrition, and emergency relief" (Charity Navigator 2018). Islamic Relief also sponsors many projects on U.S. soil, including "homeless feedings, financial assistance, healthcare in underserved areas, the annual Day of Dignity program, providing food, medical care, hygiene kits, clothes, blankets, and more to underserved communities across the United States" (Charity Navigator 2018).

The Zakat Foundation of America (ZF), founded in 2001 and based in Chicago, is unique among charitable organizations in that it exclusively supports communities abroad and reaches poor and indigent communities within the United States (Zakat Foundation of America n.d.). The range of programs offered by the Zakat Foundation of America includes emergency relief, education, development, health care, and Ramadan. Every year, the ZF also launches a campaign to provide underserved populations and communities with winter clothing during the cold months. In 2015, the "Winter Kits" program managed to distribute over 23,000 kits that provided coats, jackets, gloves, hats, scarves, and boots to underserved people around the world.

Furthermore, Muslim Aid USA, a 501(c)(3) organization, was founded by a collective of established U.S. nonprofit professionals who had envisioned a charity that would promote diversity, equity, inclusion, and transparency at all levels of operation (Muslim Aid USA n.d.). In late December 2018, Muslim Aid also embarked on a program to offer relief for underserved people suffering from colder weather conditions, particularly those people in Syria.

Further Reading

Charity Navigator. 2018. "Islamic Relief USA." Glen Rock, NJ: Charity Navigator. Last modified May 1, 2018. Retrieved from https://www.charity navigator.org/index.cfm?bay=search.summary&orgid=3908.

Islamic Circle of North America. 2013. "ICNA Partner Agency Rated among Top 10 US Charities." New York: Islamic Circle of North America. Last modified August 10, 2013. Retrieved from http://www.icna.org/icna-partner-agency -rated-among-top-10-us-charity/

Islamic Relief USA. n.d. "Mission, Vision, and Values." Alexandria, VA: Islamic Relief USA. Retrieved from http://irusa.org/mission-vision-and-values/.

Muslim Aid USA. n.d. "Who We Are." Reston, VA: Muslim Aid USA. Retrieved from https://www.muslimaidusa.org/who-we-are/.

Yusuf, Hamza, and Zaid Shakir. 2008. *Agenda to Change Our Condition.* Berkeley, CA: Zaytuna Institute.

Zakat Foundation of America. n.d. "What Makes Us Unique?" Zakat.org. Retrieved from https://www.zakat.org/en/about-us.

Annotated Bibliography

Ahmed, Akbar. 2010. *Journey into America: The Challenge of Islam.* **Washington, DC: Brookings.**
Akbar Ahmed, a leading expert on the intersection of the Islamic faith and U.S. national identity, shares his research after a one-year ethnographic study that brought his team of researchers to over 100 mosques throughout the United States. Ahmed's primary research question—"What does it mean to be an American through the lens of Muslims?"—is guided by a three-pronged theoretical framework that conceptualizes U.S. national identity in terms of its "primordial" roots, its "pluralist" vision, and its "predatorial" manifestations resulting from U.S. colonialism and imperialism. The pluralist national identity, as Ahmed notes, is rooted in primary documents that show that the U.S. Founding Fathers imagined U.S. Muslims as fully part of the U.S. nation. Ahmed found that the pluralist national identity is under threat because of the rise of anti-Muslim discrimination that is fueled largely through stereotypes of the Islamic faith and a lack of interfaith dialogue. Although *Journey into America* was published several years before the escalation of Islamophophia during the 2016 presidential election, the book offers invaluable insight into the intersection of the Islamic faith, the lived experiences of U.S. Muslims, and their historical as well as contemporary connections to different ideal types of U.S. national identity.

Arjomand, Saïd Amir. 2009. "The Constitution of Medina: A Sociological Interpretation of Muhammad's Acts of Foundation of the 'Umma.' *International Journal of Middle East Studies* **41, no. 4: 555–75.**
Saïd Amir Arjomand's peer-reviewed journal article explores the Constitution of Medina, one of the oldest documents in Islamic history, and how it informs modern thinking on the inclusion of religious minority populations

in a "Muslim nation." Arjomand breaks down the text of the Constitution in a methodical manner and aims to bridge the perceived gap between "Islamic state building" and "Western state building." His theoretical framework is informed by what he refers to as a "sociological interpretation" that is guided by three primary concepts: communal confederacy, freedom of religion, and defense of minority religious populations such as the Jews, who were living under the Prophet Muhammad's rule in Medina.

Beydoun, Khaled A. 2019. *American Islamophobia: Understanding the Roots and Rise of Fear.* **Oakland: University of California Press.**
Law professor and critical race theorist Khaled Beydoun's definitive book on Islamophobia offers one of the most comprehensive analyses of the contemporary phenomenon of anti-Muslim racism by focusing on the law, policy-making circles, and U.S. state rhetoric. Beydoun charts the history of Islamophobia in the United States, from the enslavement of African Muslims, to the antebellum South, and ultimately brings us to modern-day laws that discriminate against Muslims. The book offers a storytelling approach to show how U.S. laws detrimentally impact the lived experiences of U.S. Muslims. The stories shared by Beydoun are diverse and encompass the experiences of Muslims from a range of socio-economic, ethnic, and racial backgrounds. The end of *American Islamophobia* offers recommendations on how U.S. Muslims and their allies can build stronger coalitions across racial and religious lines in order to combat Islamophobia.

Bowen, Patrick D. *A History of Conversion to Islam in the United States: White American Muslims Before 1975.* **Leiden, The Netherlands: Brill Publishers.**
A History of Conversion to Islam in the United States is the first in-depth study on the thousands of white U.S. Muslims who converted to the Islamic faith over a span of 175 years, from the beginning of the United States in the 18th century up to 1975. Patrick Bowen, an independent scholar, investigated these conversions by studying books, periodicals, and interviews with Muslim converts that have been largely ignored by historians and scholars of Islamic studies in the U.S. context. Bowen takes the reader on a historical journey into the process of religious conversion by starting with the earliest known white converts, to Sufi reading groups in the 20th century, to women converts in the 21st century. Although the book focuses only on the history and experiences of white converts, Bowen

also wrote a second volume on African American Muslim converts and is said to be working on a third volume that documents the Latin Muslim convert perspective. His book is quintessential reading for all those who are interested in religious conversion as it pertains to U.S. Muslims.

Considine, Craig. 2016. "Religious Pluralism and Civic Rights in a 'Muslim Nation': An Analysis of Prophet Muhammad's Covenants with Christians." *Religions* **7, no. 15: 1–22.**

This peer-reviewed journal article explores the Prophet Muhammad's relations with Christians through the lens of the Covenants of Muhammad with the Christians of the world. These Covenants, which were recently documented and analyzed by scholar John Andrew Morrow, provide complete protection for Christian populations living within the borders of an "Islamic state." Using the Covenants as his units of analysis, Considine argues that the Prophet Muhammad did not merely tolerate Christians, but he engaged with them in an energetic and humane manner and offered their churches and religious leaders protection from oppression. Considine also argues that Muhammad had envisioned that Christians were "believers" and thus entitled to the same rights as the rest of the *ummah*, or "Muslim nation." While scholars continue to discuss the authenticity of the Covenants, this paper offers a sociological perspective that synthesizes modern U.S. values—like freedom of religion, separation of Church and State, and equality under the rule of law—with the life and legacy of the Prophet Muhammad. In doing so it pushes back against the validity of the "clash of civilizations" theory and promotes the "dialogue of civilizations" that shows the area in which "Islamic values" and "U.S. values" can be synthesized.

Considine, Craig. 2017. "The Racialization of Islam in the United States: Islamophobia, Hate Crimes, and 'Flying while Brown.'" *Religions* **8, no. 9: 165–84.**

The notion of the "racialization of the Islamic faith" is rooted in the idea that "Muslim identity" has been subscribed or stereotyped with certain physical features like Arab identity, brown skin, beards, or religious headgear. Considine unpacks these issues by conceptualizing the process of racialization and how it creates a "racial archetype" of Muslims in the United States. By highlighting hate crime incidents that were carried out against Sikhs and Hindus, Considine reveals how Islamophobic violence manifests itself through the dynamics of race, racialization, and racism against people who are perceived to be Muslim. The matter of racial profiling of Muslims and those people perceived to be Muslims also is examined by Considine in order to highlight how incidents infused by racial elements play out through the securitization of airports and air travel.

Considine, Craig. 2018. *Muslims in America: Examining the Facts*. Santa Barbara, CA: ABC-CLIO.
This installment of ABC-CLIO's "Contemporary Debates" series is a reference work that poses 31 questions and offers subsequent answers to some of the most pressing questions surrounding the lived experiences of U.S. Muslims. Written in an accessible prose and relying on evidence-based information, Considine's work relies on primary documents, surveys, and polls, as well as the written proclamations of U.S. Muslim organizations to provide an objective overview of the Islamic faith in the U.S. context. The book does not dedicate a lot of space to Islamic theology or Islamic history, but its abundance of hard data makes it a unique reference work for people and organizations involved in academia, interfaith work, and politics.

Curtis, Edward E., IV. 2006. *Black Muslim Religion in the Nation of Islam, 1960–1975*. Chapel Hill: University of North Carolina Press.
Edward E. Curtis IV, a historian of U.S. Muslims, pushes beyond essentialist ideas about Muslim identity by focusing specifically on localized expressions of the Islamic faith through the prisms of Islamic theology, rituals, and ethics. Using African American Muslims and the Nation of Islam as the primary frame of analysis, Curtis offers a detailed account of how African American Muslims engaged with and appropriated various Islamic traditions in the 20th century. While this valuable contribution offers insight into one of U.S. history's most well known African American Muslim separatist movements, the scope of the study is limited to a relatively short period of the 20th century. Nevertheless, *Black Muslim Religion in the Nation of Islam* is a quintessential read for those interested in critical race theory, the history of African American Muslims, and the formation as well as growth of the Nation of Islam.

Curtis, Edward E., IV., ed. 2010. *Encyclopedia of Muslim-American History*. New York: Facts on File.
Including nearly 300 entries and citing over 100 historians, scholars, and experts in the field, *Encyclopedia of Muslim-American History* is an invaluable piece of scholarship that relies on primary documents and includes an

extensive timeline of key dates and events on the lived experiences of U.S. Muslims. Curtis, a leading historian on the Islamic faith in the U.S. context, positions U.S. Muslims at the center of U.S. history and culture instead of placing them on the periphery as a marginalized religious minority population. This book is one of a handful of authoritative reference works on U.S. Muslims that provide a clear and coherent picture of the history of the Islamic faith in the United States.

Diouf, Sylviane A. 2013. *Servants of Allah: African Muslims Enslaved in the Americas*. New York: New York University Press.
Awarding-winning historian Sylviane A. Diouf offers an important and sophisticated book on the history of African American Muslims and the 400-year history of enslavement in the Western hemisphere. This well-researched piece of scholarship provides historical facts and precise insight into the lived experiences of African American Muslims. The book also reveals how these individuals were able to survive and thrive as oppressed people in the United States. Specifically, Diouf's evidence suggests that these Muslims deliberately used their Islamic education and value systems as a tool to navigate the dangerous conditions that they faced as slaves. Perhaps more importantly, *Servants of Allah* reveals that African American Muslims were not simply absorbed by Christianity and Christian slaveowners. Diouf shows how African American Muslims made their own decisions and exercised their own choices as a way to retain and re-create their culture and identity in the United States.

Feiler, Bruce. 2004. *Abraham: A Journey to the Heart of Three Faiths*. New York: Perennial.
New York Times best-selling author Bruce Feiler focuses on the life and legacy of Abraham, the first monotheistic prophet, to shed light on the commonalities across Judaism, Christianity, and Islam. Based on field-work research in war zones and religious sites in the Holy Lands of the Middle East, Feiler's book uses interviews with religious, interfaith, and community leaders to share raw as well as emotional human stories in an effort to build stronger bridges between Jews, Christians, and Muslims. *Abraham* examines the religious texts of the three great monotheistic religions and offers potential solutions to some of the more pressing conflicts in today's world. This travelogue-style book serves as an antidote to religious hatred and extremism and encourages Jews, Christians, and Muslims to reflect on their common humanity.

GhaneaBassiri, Kambiz. 2010. *A History of Islam in America.* **Cambridge, UK: Cambridge University Press.**
GhaneaBassiri's informative book offers a comprehensive portrayal of U.S. Muslims by sharing the stories of Muslims who have lived in the United States throughout history. In addition to its historical overview of U.S. Muslims, GhaneaBassiri's work covers a wide spectrum of topics like Islamic beliefs and practices in the colonial and antebellum periods, the intersection of race and Muslim identity, U.S. government immigration policies, the relationship between the Islamic faith and U.S. civil nationalism, and the impact of U.S. foreign policy on the domestic experiences of Muslims. Consisting of eight chapters, this book directly challenges the binary worldview of "Western civilization" versus "Islamic civilization" by demonstrating the relational nature of "American Islam" in modern and historic times. In doing so, GhaneaBassiri captures the various ways in which these civilizations have benefited from each other over the course of time.

Haddad, Yvonne Yazbeck. 2007. "The Post-9/11 Hijab as Icon." *Sociology of Religion* **68, no. 3: 253–67.**
Yvonne Yazbeck Haddad's peer-reviewed journal article draws on two decades of research on U.S. Muslims and in-depth semistructured interviews with U.S. Muslim youth. Haddad's article focuses on observances of *hijab* and how young Muslims of immigrant backgrounds wear an Islamic headscarf as a means to express their Muslim identity in the public sphere, an act that symbolizes their resistance to Western hegemony as well as the erasure of the Islamic faith during a time of increasing Islamophobia. Haddad concludes that young U.S. Muslim women show confidence in their observance of *hijab* because of their trust in U.S. values like freedom of religion and freedom of speech. This peer-reviewed article is accessible and avoids the kind of jargon found in most academic journals.

Haddad, Yvonne Yazbeck. 2012. *Becoming American?: The Forging of Arab and Muslim Identity in Pluralist America.* **Waco, TX: Baylor University Press.**
Becoming American? is a book that is mainly grounded in history, but it also provides significant contemporary insight into the dynamics and intersections of Arab, Muslim, and U.S. national identities. The first half of Haddad's work explores the deep history of Arab and Muslim populations living in "Western states" as early as the 19th century. Haddad pushes the reader beyond simplistic arguments that Arabs and Muslims are "new"

populations or recent immigrants to the United States. At the heart of the book is an answer to the question "What does it mean to be an American?" Haddad argues that the core of U.S. national identity rests with its tradition of religious pluralism and the energetic interaction of people of various races, nationalities, and religions.

Huntington, Samuel P. 2003. *The Clash of Civilizations and the Remaking of the World Order.* **New York: Simon & Schuster.**
The popular hypothesis of "the clash of civilizations" is largely the by-product of Samuel P. Huntington's classic book *The Clash of Civilizations and the Remaking of the World Order*. Written in the immediate aftermath of the fall of the Berlin Wall and the collapse of the Soviet Union's empire, Huntington's work claims that the next global crises will not be "capitalism versus communism," but rather "Western civilization versus Islamic civilization." Huntington's "clash of civilizations" theory gained prominence in U.S. public discourse and policy-making circles after the 9/11 attacks and the U.S. invasions of Afghanistan and Iraq. The fact that Daesh, the militant group, also expressed its belief in the legitimacy of the "clash of civilizations" binary worldview added more legitimacy to the theory in expert circles. Although Huntington's work is still influential among neoconservative and militant Muslim organizations around the world, the theory has been widely debunked as overly simplistic and dismissive of the ways that "Western civilization" and "Islamic civilization" have synthesized over the course of history.

Lambert, Frank. 2005. *The Barbary Wars: American Independence in the Atlantic World.* **New York: Hill & Wang.**
The Barbary Wars by Frank Lambert is perhaps the definitive piece of scholarship as it pertains to the Barbary Wars and the early U.S. government's relationship with the Muslim-majority countries of North Africa. Lambert's book provides an in-depth chronology of conflicts between the United States and Algiers, Morocco, and Tripoli in the late 18th and early 19th centuries. His conclusion—that commercial war was the motivating factor for the outbreak of the conflicts—is important in light of arguments that religious differences between the Christian and Islamic faiths were the reasons why the United States went to war with the Barbary States. While the book does not offer deep insight into the actual naval battles fought between the opposing sides, Lambert's thesis remains pertinent today as a means to counter the argument that religious differences have been the

reason why "Western civilization" and "Islamic civilization" have been at odds with each other since the creation of the United States in the 18th century.

Lean, Nathan. 2012. *The Islamophobia Industry: How the Right Manufactures Fear of Muslims*. London: Pluto Press.
The Islamophobia Industry is the definitive book on the coordinated network of anti-Muslim activists, bloggers, philanthropic organizations, politicians, and religious leaders that work to spread fear and hatred of U.S. Muslims. Lean's book is an invaluable resource on how the right-wing religious and political arenas manufacture anti-Muslim sentiments among U.S. citizens and how the manufacturing has deep roots in U.S. history. One of the chapters—"We Come Bearing Crosses: The Christian Right's Battle For Eternity"—provides insight on the dominant views of evangelicals and their perspectives on the Islamic faith, an especially important topic considering that evangelical Christians are the religious population with the highest levels of anti-Muslim sentiment in the United States. Perhaps most importantly, Lean makes a persuasive argument that there is a direct connection between the activities of the Islamophobia industry and the rise of anti-Muslim hate crimes as well as anti-Muslim legislation in the United States today.

Malcolm X. 1987. *The Autobiography of Malcolm X: As Told to Alex Haley*. New York: Ballantine Books.
The Autobiography of Malcolm X: As Told to Alex Haley is the conclusive book on Malcolm X, the African American Muslim civil rights and anti-racism activist. The book is written in an ongoing, first-person style as a series of chapters based on the stages of Malcolm X's life. Some critics say that the style is a confessional narrative, which provides readers with a window into his deepest experiences. The structure of the book is linear in that Malcolm X takes the reader on a journey from his childhood, to his years as a gangster, to his imprisonment, to his conversion to the Islamic faith, and to his ultimate break with the Nation of Islam in favor of mainstream Sunnism after his pilgrimage to Mecca. Themes covered in the book include black nationalism, civil rights activism, pan-Africanism, racial inequality and racial equality, and U.S. national identity. *The Autobiography of Malcolm X* is essential reading for anyone who is seeking to better understand U.S. history, the Nation of Islam, as well as the historical experiences of African American Muslims.

Morales, Harold D. 2018. *Latino and Muslim in America: Race, Religion, and the Making of a New Minority.* **Oxford, UK: Oxford University Press.**
Latino and Muslim in America is one of the first books to focus specifically on U.S. Muslims of Latin descent. Morales structures the book in a historical manner by following the lives of several Latin Muslim leaders from the 1970s to the present and documenting three waves of immigration of Latinos to the United States. One of the core theories that is offered by Morales—intersectionality—provides readers with an in-depth analysis of how U.S. Latin Muslims navigate their way around complex identities and stereotypical representations of their cultures, ethnicities, and religion. He also gives significant attention to stories of "reversion" or conversion to the Islamic faith and the role that the 9/11 attacks played in the lived experiences of Latin Muslims.

Morrow, John Andrew. 2013. *The Covenants of the Prophet Muhammad with the Christians of the World.* **Brooklyn, NY: Angelico Press-Sophia Perennis.**
John Andrew Morrow's groundbreaking book is the first piece of scholarship to comprehensively assess the authenticity, symbolism, and potential impact of the Prophet Muhammad's treaties, or Covenants, with the Christians of his time. The book begins with a reference on how the mostly neglected Covenants are an important source of inspiration that can improve relations between Christians and Muslims. Morrow follows the introduction by providing a detailed biography of the Prophet Muhammad. Morrow focuses on six Covenants, each of which has its own chapter, in order to refute the argument that Christians and Muslims are eternal enemies and that "Islamic values" are incompatible with modern-day narratives surrounding civil rights as well as human rights. One of Morrow's arguments—that the Covenants should be treated as the third pillar of Islamic theology outside of the Qur'an and *ahadith*—is persuasive, but it has yet to enter into "mainstream" thinking among U.S. Muslims. Scholars and critics, nevertheless, have described *The Covenants of the Prophet Muhammad with the Christians of the World* as even-handed and scholarly, but also overly sympathetic in terms of the debate on the authenticity of the Covenants.

Patel, Eboo. 2007. *Acts of Faith: The Story of an American Muslim, the Struggle for the Soul of a Generation.* **Boston: Beacon Press.**
Acts of Faith is Eboo Patel's personal account of growing up as a second-generation Muslim in the United States. The two overarching themes of

the book—religious extremism and religious pluralism—are colorfully unpacked in a memoir-like style. The first half of the book provides insight on Patel's personal journey as a young, disaffected man in search of meaning, purpose, and spirituality. Patel shares stories from his life and offers reflective reactions on how young U.S. Muslims may be able to successfully synthesize the various elements of their identity—culture, ethnicity, family, and faith. The second half of the book explores how young people may be susceptible to radicalization by hate preachers as well as terrorist organizations. The end of Patel's accessible book offers practical solutions on how leaders can create programs to foster social justice and stronger interfaith bonds.

Rashid, Qasim. 2013. *The Wrong Kind of Muslim: An Untold Story of Persecution & Perseverance.* **Amazon Digital Services LLC.**
While it is not a traditional piece of academic scholarship, this book by human rights lawyer and activist Qasim Rashid provides an illuminating memoir of his life experiences as an Ahmadi Muslim, or what he refers to as "the wrong kind of Muslim." Rashid shares his lived experience as being part of a persecuted religious minority population that is targeted both inside and outside of the wider Muslim populations in which Ahmadis live. *The Wrong Kind of Muslim* gives a history of several key issues like the Ahmadiyya movement, the Pakistani government's relationship with religious minority populations, as well as the U.S. Ahmadiyya community. This vivid narrative, which gives glimpses into graphic violence, but also stories of transcending hate and bigotry with compassion and peace, also concludes by reminding the reader of the importance of education, compassion, and inclusion. For Rashid, these are the solutions for extremism regardless of its sources.

Runnymede Trust. 1997. "Islamophobia: A Challenge for Us All." TheRunnymedeTrust.org. Retrieved from http://www.runnymede trust.org/uploads/publications/pdfs/islamophobia.pdf.
This flagship report published in 1997 by the Runnymede Trust, a liberal U.K.-based think tank focusing on community building and policy engagement, is one of the first attempts by scholars and experts to define anti-Muslim sentiments and discrimination, or what we may refer to as Islamophobia. The Runnymede Trust outlined eight primary components that capture the essence of Islamophobia, among them closed-minded views of Islam and Muslims and viewing both of these entities as

monoliths. While the report is a must-read for researchers who focus on the growing phenomenon of Islamophobia, scholars and experts have criticized it for its lack of discussion on the role that race and racialization play in anti-Muslim racist hate crimes.

Salaita, Steven. 2006. *Anti-Arab Racism in the USA: Where It Comes From and What It Means for Politics Today*. London: Pluto Press.
Steven Salaita offers a passionate and scholarly analysis of the roots and rise of anti-Arab racism in the United States. Focusing on the impact of colonialism and imperialism and moving gradually toward the 9/11 attacks, the book explores the impact and evolution of white supremacy, stereotypical depictions of Arabs as "savages" and "barbarians," and the racism that emerged out of political scandals like the Abu Ghraib torture center in Iraq. One of the primary findings of Salaita's book is that anti-Arab racism does not stem merely from conservative circles, but that it also is rising out of liberal discourse among left-leaning Democrats. Despite being published in 2006, *Anti-Arab Racism in the USA* still provides invaluable insight due in large part to the rise of anti-Arab and anti-Muslim racism in the United States.

Shaheen, Jack. 2004. *Reel Bad Arabs: How Hollywood Vilifies a People*. Petaluma, CA: Olive Branch.
Award-winning film critic Jack Shaheen's groundbreaking book explores the historical depiction of Muslims and Arabs in the cinematic industry, especially that of Hollywood. *Reel Bad Arabs* explores the degrading representations of Arabs and Muslims by critically examining the stereotypical images of them as barbaric, backward, machoistic, violent, and terrorism-prone. As a method of analysis, Shaheen viewed over 1,000 films produced between 1896 to 2000 and found that 936 titles portray Arabs and Muslims in a derogatory manner. Approximately 5 percent of the films studied by Shaheen had depicted Arabs and Muslims as "normal" or "human" characters. Shaheen's research also was turned into a popular documentary that is called *Reel Bad Arabs* like the book itself.

Spellberg, Denise. 2014. *Thomas Jefferson's Qur'an: Islam and the Founders*. New York: Knopf.
Denise Spellberg, a leading scholar on the U.S. Founding Fathers' views on Muslims and the Islamic faith, focuses on the themes of freedom of religion and religious tolerance through the life and legacy of Thomas Jefferson, the

co-author of the Declaration of Independence and third president of the United States. This book provides valuable evidence that the U.S. Founding Fathers intended for the Islamic faith to be part of the U.S. religious landscape. Spellberg's main argument is that the U.S. Founding Fathers "imagined" Muslims as future citizens of the United States even though there were already Muslims living in the country. This is a must-read for anyone studying Thomas Jefferson's political philosophy and religious beliefs.

Uddin, Asma T. 2019. *When Islam Is Not a Religion: Inside America's Fight for Religious Freedom*. **New York: Pegasus Books.**
Written by religious liberty lawyer Asma Uddin, *When Islam Is Not a Religion* sheds light on the movement to criminalize the Islamic faith and marginalize U.S. Muslims from the guaranteed civil rights protections as outlined in the U.S. Constitution. Uddin draws on her personal experiences as a lawyer and U.S. Muslim, but also deploys legal and philosophical underpinnings in this key primer on freedom of religion and freedom of conscience in the modern-day United States. Uddin's passionate defense of the U.S. Constitution and the rights of U.S. Muslims is timely in light of the recent increase in anti-Muslim sentiment and racism toward U.S. Muslims.

Williams, Rhys H., and Gira Vashi. 2007. **"***Hijab* **and American Muslim Women: Creating the Space for Autonomous Selves."** *Sociology of Religion* **68, no. 3: 269–87.**
This peer-reviewed article by two leading scholars on the sociology of U.S. Muslims uses *hijab* as a unit of analysis to examine how the Islamic faith is practiced and adapted into a "new culture" like that of the United States. Williams and Vashi carried out semistructured interviews with second-generation U.S. Muslim women between the ages of 18 and 22 years old and found that these young women observe *hijab* for various personal, familial, cultural, and religious reasons. Williams and Vashi conclude that *hijab* is a symbol of how young Muslim women carefully navigate expectations of them both as U.S. residents or citizens and as children of immigrants.

Index

Abdul Rauf, Feisal (*imam*), 169

Abrahamic tradition (interfaith dialogue concept), **1–5**; academic initiatives and, 3; description of, 1–3; George Washington and, 63; interfaith dialogue and, 26; Muhammad and, 15; Qur'an and, 127, 140

Abu Ghraib (prison in Iraq), 205

Activism (social process): anti-Islam, xx, 48–49, 66–67, 89, 90, 102, 113, 118, 140; civil rights, 30; human rights, 75; LGBTQ, 100; "radical," 43; U.S. Muslim, 22, 31, 97; young Muslim, xxi

Adams, John (U.S. president), 182

Adams, John Quincy (U.S. president), xxx, 160

Afghanistan (country): border of, 59; immigration policy towards, 24; LGBTQ rights in, 101; migrants from, xxxi, 27; U.S. foreign policy towards, 27, 57; U.S. invasion of, xxxiii, 58, 201; W.D. Fard Muhammad and, 9

African American Muslims (ethno-religious group), **5–13**; Ahmadiyya and, 8; athletes and, xxxiii; demographics of, 9–10; freedom of speech and, 66; history of, xxii, 5–8; *jihad* camps and, 89; mosques and, 113; North African, xxix, 108, 172; slavery and, 158, 198; Timbuktu and, xxx, 160; war in, 174

Ahadith (hadith), **13–14**; apostasy and, 19; description of, 13–14; freedom of speech, 69; *jihad* and, 88; Khadijah in, 133; LGBTQ and, 101–102; *sharia* and, 151; slavery and, 160; *taqiyya* and, 171; use of, xx; Wahhabism and, 187–188

Ahl al-Kitab ("People of the Book"), xx, 63, 127, 140

Ahmadiyya (Islamic movement), **14–18**; African Americans and, 8, 40; description of, 14–15; emergence of, 8; Islamic sects and, xxii; Latin Americans and, 96;

missionaries and, xxxi, 8, 17, 25; Pakistan and, 15–16, 204; *sharia* and, 150

Al-Qaeda (violent group): Afghanistan and, 58; 9/11 and, 108; "radical Islam" and, 56; rise of Daesh and, 59; U.S. Muslim condemnation of, 44

Albanian American Muslims (ethno-religious group), xxiv, 51, 165–166, 174

Ali, Muhammad (civil rights activist and athlete), 29, 40

Ali, Shamsi (*imam*), 26–27

American-Arab Anti-Discrimination Committee (organization), 107

American Civil Liberties Union (ACLU) (organization), 43–44, 64, 72

Apostasy (process of "leaving" religion), **18–20**, 41–42

Arab-American Association (organization), 20–23, 30, 163

Arab American Muslims (ethno-religious group), **20–23** activism and, 163; anti-Arab racism and, 205; experiences of, 200; history of, xxxi, 113; Hollywood films and, 21; mosques and, 113; organizations of, 30, 163; overview of, 20–22; political engagement of, 22; population of, xxii; veterans and, 21

Asian American Muslims (ethno-religious group), xxii–xxiii, **23–28**

Bannon, Steve (political figure), 35

Barbary States (North African country), xxx, 39, 55–56, 201

Battle of Gettysburg (Civil War), 27

Bhojani, Salman (politician), 3

Bilal (companion of Muhammad), 8, 161

Bin Laden, Osama (former Al-Qaeda leader), 58, 90, 108

Black Lives Matter (social movement), xxi, 30; 163

Blasphemy (act of criticizing religion), 66–69, 135

Bolton, John (politician), 59

Bosnian American Muslims (ethno-religious group), xxiv, 52

Bush, George H.W. (U.S. president), 58

Bush, George W. (U.S. president), xxxiii, 59, 134, 183

Central Intelligence Agency (CIA) (U.S. intelligence agency), 57, 107, 122

Civil rights (social movement), **29–34**; activists for, 31; "anti-terrorism" actions and, 43; freedom of religion and, 72, 183; hate crimes and, 146; *jizya* and, 92; media coverage of Muslims and, 106; mosque attacks and, 90; overview of, 29–32; protection of, xxiv; racial profiling and, 32; U.S. Muslim involvement in

movement of, xxii, xxv,
29–30, 114–115, 140
Civil Rights Act (1964)
(legislation), xxxiii, 76
"Clash of civilizations" (academic
theory), **34–38**; apostasy and,
18; *hijab* and, 75;
Islamophobia and, 80;
overview of, xix, 34–37;
Samuel Huntington and, 201;
sharia and, xxv, 32
Chinese Exclusion Act (U.S.
foreign policy), 24
Christians (religious group):
anti-Islam views among, 34;
Benjamin Franklin's views
on, 134; Catholics and, 153,
181; Daesh and, 92; freedom
of religion and, 62; the *jizya*
and, xx, 91–92; LGBTQ and,
102; Muhammad's
relationship with, xx, 92–93,
112, 133, 146–147; pluralism
and, 127; polygamy and,
130; Puritans and, 128;
Qur'an and, 140, 147;
rejection of Islamophobia by,
64; *sharia* and, 153;
similarities between Muslims
and, 85; Sufism and, 166;
Thomas Jefferson and, 182;
ummah and, 180; U.S.
Founding Fathers and, 184
Clinton, Bill (U.S. president), 183
Clinton, Hillary (politician), 22,
183
CNN (news outlet), 35, 36, 72
Columbus, Christopher (explorer),
xxiii, xxix, 5

Constitution of Medina, the
(Islamic document), xx, 4,
63–64, 180, 195
Converts (switching religions),
38–43; 49, 196
Cooper, Anderson (CNN anchor),
35
Council on American-Islamic
Relations (CAIR)
(organization): civil rights
work of, 31; description of,
114–115; hate crimes
statistics and, 71, *jihad* camps
and, 90; Islamophobia
industry and, 81–82; mosque
statistics and, 113; Muslim
Brotherhood and, 118; Qur'an
and, 140–142; *sharia* and,
149; voting statistics and, 78
Countering Violent Extremism
(CVE) (U.S. government
program), **43–45**
Cruz, Ted (politician), 117

Daesh (or ISIS) (violent group):
Barbary States and, 56; *jizya*
and, 92; LGBTQ and, 101;
media coverage and, xxiv;
"Muslim Travel Ban" and,
122; "radical Muslims" and,
43–44; rise of, 59; *sharia*
and, 160; slavery and, 160;
U.S. foreign policy and, 59–
60; Wahhabism and, 186
Da'wah (act of spreading Islamic
teachings), 41, 163
Declaration of Independence, the
(U.S. political document),
xxvii, 182, 206

Deferred Action for Childhood
Arrival (DACA)
(legislation), xxi, 31, 164
Democrats (political party),
47–50, 78, 164, 186
Dhimmi, **47–50**
Dialogue of civilizations
(academic theory), xvi, xxvii,
27, 35–36, 197
Drake, Sir Francis (explorer),
xxix, 172
Drew, Timothy (Noble Drew Ali)
(U.S. Muslim), 7, 40

Eisenhower, Dwight D. (U.S.
president): Abdullah Igram
and, 21; mosque visit by,
xxxi; views on "Judeo-
Christian" nation of, 2
Ellison, Keith (politician), xxxiii,
10–11, 140–141
European American Muslims
(ethno-religious group):
history of, xxiii–xxiv, xxix;
overview of, **51–54**; Sufism
and, 165–166
Evangelical (branch of
Christianity), 45, 99

Federal Bureau of Investigation
(FBI) (U.S. government
organization), 71–72, 89
Five-Percent Nation (branch of
Nation of Islam), 9
Five Pillars of Islam (guiding
principles of Islam), xxvii,
88, 110, 156, 191
Flynn, Michael (politician), 35,
175

Foreign policies, **55–61**
Fox News (news outlet), 105–107
Franklin, Benjamin (U.S.
statesman), 135, 183
Freedom of religion (value),
61–66; Council on American
Islamic Relations and, 114;
hijab and, 75; Islam and,
206; James Madison and,
184; overview of 61–65;
Qur'an and, xxi, 19; *sharia*
and, 152; Thomas Jefferson
and, 183–184; Roger
Williams and, 128
Freedom of speech (value), **66–69**

Graham, Franklin (Christian
evangelist), 45
Gülen Movement (Islamic
movement), 172, 174–175

Hate crimes (violence), **71–74**;
Council on American-Islamic
Relations statistics on, 3;
definition of, 71; racialization
and, 144
Hezbollah (political group), xxxii,
58
Hijab (process of modesty),
74–76; discrimination and,
xxiv, 81; experiences of
women and, 206; U.S.
Supreme Court ruling and,
xxxiii; overview of, 74–76
Hollywood films (entertainment),
21–22, 107, 205

Ibn Said, Omar (slave), xxx, 6–7,
22

Ibrahim, Abdul-Rahman (slave), xxx, 160

Iftar (act during Ramadan), xxx, 112, 140, 183

Igram, Abdullah (U.S. soldier), 21

Immigration Act of 1917 (legislation), xxxi, 24, 123

Immigration and Nationality Act of 1965 (legislation), xxii, xxiii, xxvi, xxxii, 10,

Indonesia (country), 24, 26, 68, 117, 179

Integration (social process), 77–79

Iran (country): Hollywood films and, 107; LGBTQ in, 101; "Muslim travel ban" and, 120, 122; president of, 36; Shias in, 156; U.S. foreign policy towards, 24, 27, 57–58, 60

Iraq (country): Daesh in, xxiv, 43, 92, 122, 160, 186; Hollywood films and, 22, 107; invasion of, xxxiii; LGBTQ in, 101; "Muslim travel ban" and, 120; 9/11 attacks and, 201; Shias in, 156; U.S. foreign policy towards, 24, 57–59

Islamberg, New York (town of "*jihad* camp"), 89

Islamic Circle of North America (ICNA) (organization), 115, 192

Islamic Relief USA (organization), 147, 192

Islamic Society of North America (ISNA) (organization), 113, 114–115, 118, 168

Islamophobia (process of discrimination), **80–83**; definitions of, 204; industry of, 119, 202; overview of, 80–82; racialization and, 197

Israel (country), 35, 56, 60, 119

Jefferson, Thomas (U.S. president): biography of, 205–206; James Madison and, 183; *iftar* and, xxx, 183; Muslims and, xxvii; Qur'an of, xxxiii, 11, 140–141, 182–183

Jesus (founder of Christianity): depiction in the Qur'an of, xxi, 85–87, 147; Islamic teachings and, 40; phrase used by, 7

Jesus and Mary, **85–87**

Jews (religious group): Constitution of Medina and, xx, 63–64, 180; freedom of religion and, 62; freedom of speech and, 66; George Washington and, 181; hate crimes and, 71; integration of, 77; "Islamic Spain" and, 95; James Madison and, 184; *jizya* and, xx, 91; Palestinians and, 56, 90; polygamy and, 130; pluralism and, 127; Qur'an and, 47–48, 140; Roger Williams and, 129; *sharia* and, 153; slavery and, 161; Sufism and, 166; Thomas Jefferson and, 182; *ummah* and, 180; voting patterns of, 78

Jihad (Islamic value), **88–91**;
Ahmadiyya and, 15;
Afghanistan and, 57;
civilizational, 118–119, 142;
definition of, xxv; Muslim
Brotherhood and, 117;
"Muslim Travel Ban" and,
122; overview of, 88–90;
"radical," 113; slavery and,
161
Jizya (process of taxing), xx,
91–93
Johnson, Lyndon B. (U.S.
president), xxxii
Judeo-Christian (interfaith
tradition), 2, 5, 35, 102

Kafir (Islamic concept), 15–16,
56, 62–63, 92
Kahn, Mohammed (U.S. soldier),
xxxi, 27
Khaldun, Ibn (scholar), 163
King, Martin Luther, Jr. (U.S. civil
rights activist), 30

Latin American Muslims (ethno-
religious group), **95–99**;
converts and, 38, 40–41, 196;
experiences of, 203; legacy
of, xxiii; overview of, 95–98
Lebanon (country), xxxi, xxxii, 9,
20, 58, 112, 157
LGBTQ (group), xxi, **99–103**,
163, 164
Lincoln, Abraham (U.S.
president), xxxi, 173

Madison, James (U.S. president),
39, 183–184

Malcolm X (black nationalist and
civil rights leader):
assassination of, xxxii;
autobiography of, 202;
background of, 29–30;
conversion of, 40–41; the
Five-Percent Nation and, 9;
Latin American Muslims
and, 97; Nation of Islam
(NOI) and, 29
Mamout, Yarrow (slave), 7
Mary (Jesus's mother): depiction
in *Qur'an* of, xxi, 86–87, 147
Marrakesh Declaration, the
(statement and document), 4
Massignon, Louis (scholar), 1
Media coverage and the
entertainment industry
(depiction of Muslims),
105–110
Mellimelli, Sidi Soliman
(diplomat), xxx, 183
Mohammed, Wallace D. (W.D.)
(*imam*), xxxii, 11
Moorish Science Temple (group),
7–8, 40, 96
Mormons (religious group), 65
Mosques (place of worship):
attacks on, xxiv, 72; historical,
51, 52, 174; LGBTQ friendly,
100–101; opposition to, 64;
overview of, 110–114; social
services and, xxvi–xxvii;
surveillance of, 32, 106;
Wahhabism in, 186
Mosques and Organizations,
110–116
"Mother Mosque of America"
(mosque), xxxi

MPower Change (grassroots organization), 31, 164

Muhammad (prophet of Islam): "anti-," xx; blasphemy and, 69; cartoon depictions of, 134; Byzantine Empire and, 92–93; the Constitution of Medina and, 63; Covenants with the Christians of the World and, xx, 4, 93, 197, 203; *dhimmi* and, 47–48; drawing contests of, 67; Farewell Sermon of xx; freedom of religion and, 19; freedom of speech and, 66; *hijab* and, 74; "Islamic Spain," 95; Jesus and, 85; *jihad* and, xxv, 88; overview of, 132–136; pluralism and, 127; Qur'an and, 139; Ramadan and, 111; refugees and, 146; *shahada* and, 38; *sharia* and, 150; Shias and, 155–156; slavery and, 160; Sunnism and, 167; teachings of xix–xx; *ummah* and, 179; U.S. Constitution and, 63; U.S. Founding Fathers and, 182; Wahhabism and, 185; women's rights and, 188. *See also* The Prophet Muhammad

Muhammad, Bilali (slave), 159

Muhammad, Elijah (Nation of Islam), 9, 11, 40

Muhammad, Ibtihaj (athlete), xxxiii, 11

Muhammad, Wallace Fard (W.F.) (Nation of Islam), xxxi, 8–9, 27, 40

Muslim Aid USA (organization), 193

"Muslim Brotherhood" (political group), 92, **116–120**

Muslim Public Affairs Council (MPAC) (organization), 100, 108, 115

Muslims for Progressive Values (MPV) (organization), 100, 101, 187

Muslim Travel Ban and Immigration Policies, **120–125**

"Muslim Travel Ban" (legislation): overview of xxxiii, 120–124; refugees and, 145; "religious test" and, 65; U.S. Supreme Court and, xxxiv, 62

Nation of Islam (NOI) (ethno-religious group): background and history of, 8, 198; civil rights and, 29; converts to, 40, 96–97; founder of, xxxi; Malcolm X and, xxxii;

National Security Entry-Exit Registration System (legislation), 124

9/11: Afghanistan and, xxxiii, 57–58; Ahmadiyya and, 17; anniversary of, 72; attacks on, xxxii; civil rights and, 32; clash of civilizations and, 35; George W. Bush and, xxxiii; 57–58, "Ground Zero Mosque," 169; first hate crime after, 144; media coverage and movies about

Muslims after, 105–108;
Muhammad Ali and, 29;
National Security Entry-Exit
Registration System
(NSEERS) and, 124

Obama, Barack (U.S. president):
"Cairo Speech" of, xxxiii;
Countering Violent
Extremism (CVE) and, 43;
Daesh and, 59; freedom of
speech and, 67–68; *jizya* and,
92; Linda Sarsour and, 31;
media depiction of Muslims
according to, 108–109;
Pakistan and, 59; presidential
medal of freedom given by,
11; Ramadan and, 183;
Republican rally and, 89;
Turkey and, 173
Omar, Ilhan (U.S. politician),
xxxiv, 22, 106
Ottoman Empire (Turkey): Barack
Obama and, 173;
civilizational contributions
of, 36; Muslim immigrants
from, 21; slaves from, 172;
U.S. government relations
with, xxx, xxxi, 173

Pakistan (country): freedom of
religion on, 62; freedom of
speech in, 68, 135; history of,
25; nationalism and, 180,
treatment of Ahmadiyya in,
15–16, 204; treatment of
women in, 75; U.S. foreign
policy and, 27, 57, 59; U.S.
Muslims from, 3, 24

Palestine (country), 56, 90, 108,
114, 119
Patel, Eboo (scholar), 128
Peale, Charles Wilson (painter), 7
Pew Research Center
(organization): Asian
Americans and, 23–24;
converts and 41–42;
integration and, 77;
Islamophobia and, 81;
LGBTQ and, 99;
radicalization and, 44;
refugees, 145–146; voting
patterns and, 78; women's
rights and, 189
Pluralism (social process), **127–
129**, 203
Polygamy (marriage), **129–132**
The Prophet Muhammad, **132–
137**. *See also* Muhammad
(prophet of Islam)

Qur'an (Islamic holy book), **139–
142**; anti-Islam activists and,
66; blasphemy in, 68;
Christians and, 147; the
dhimmi and, 48; freedom of
religion and, xxi, 19, 62–63;
hijab in, 74–75; Jesus in the,
xxi; *jihad* and, 85–86, 88;
jizya and, 92; LGBTQ and,
100–102; Mary in the, xxi,
86–87; overview of, 139–
141; pluralism and, 127;
refugees and, 146; slavery
and, 161; U.S. Muslim
history of, 6; U.S. Supreme
Court and, 136; *taqiyya* and,
170; Thomas Jefferson and

the, 11, 182; women's rights
and, 188; *zakat* and, 191

Racialization (social process),
143–145; Caucasian Muslims
and, 53; hate crimes and,
197; Muslim stereotypes
and, xxii, 20–21; overview
of, 143–144; racial
profiling, 32
Ramadan (Islamic holy month),
111–112, 140, 183
Rashid, Qasim (U.S. politician),
16, 17, 75
Reagan, Ronald (U.S. president),
57–58
Refugees (group), **145–148**
Religious pluralism (social
process): Ahmadiyya and,
17; description of, xxvii;
"Islamic Spain" and, xxiii;
Muhammad and, 133, 197;
overview of, 127–129; U.S.
Muslims and, xxi; U.S.
national identity and, 64, 201
Republicans (political party): the
"clash of civilizations" and,
35; condemnation of
Islamophobia by, 64;
debates of, 43; *jihad* and,
88; the "Muslim Travel Ban,"
120; refugees and, 145;
sharia and, 153; *taqiyya*
and, 170
Roosevelt, Franklin D. (U.S.
president), 136
Rubio, Marco (U.S. politician),
43
Rumi (philosopher and poet), 166

Sadiq, Mufti Muhammad
(missionary), xxxi, 8, 16–17,
25, 40
Said, Edward (scholar), 80
Sapelo Island, Georgia (slavery),
6, 159
Sarsour, Linda (U.S. activist), xxi,
30–31, 163–164
Saudi Arabia (country), freedom
of religion in, 62; immigrants
from, 25; Muhammad in,
132, 139–140; LGBTQ in,
100; mosque and, 112;
ummah and, 179; U.S.
foreign policy with, 60; U.S.
Muslim criticism of, 22;
Wahhabism and, 185
Scalia, Antonio (U.S. Supreme
Court justice), 76
Shahada (Islamic declaration of
faith), 38–39, 110
Shakir, Zaid (*imam*), 163, 192
Sharia ("Islamic law"), **149–155**;
activists and, 31–32, 49;
apostasy and, 18; "creeping,"
xxv; *dhimmi* and, 47–48;
family and, 150; Fox News,
106; *khutba* and; 111;
legislation against, xxv, 32;
"March Against," 152;
polygamy and, 129–130;
public discourse on, xix–xx,
31; Shias and, 157, Sunnism
and, 167; Wahhabism and, 185
Shias (Islamic sect), xxii, 155–
158, 168, 169–170
Shi'ism, **155–158**
Slavery (social process), xxx, 6–7,
158–162

Social justice activism (social process), **162–164**

Sotomayor, Sonia (U.S. Supreme Court justice), xxxvi, 62, 122

Sufism (branch of Islam), 150, **165–167**, 172, 188, 196

Suleiman, Omar (*imam* and activist), 31, 100

Sunnis (Islamic sect), 167–168; population of, xxii; 167; population of Asian American, 24; Shias compared to, 156; *taqiyya* and, 169; Turkish American, 172; Wahhabism and, 185

Sunnism, **167–168**

Syria (country): Christianity in, 34; Daesh and, xxiv, 43, 59, 92, 101, 122, 160, 186; history of immigrants from, xxxi, 20, 21, 113; "Muslim Brotherhood" in, 119; "Muslim travel ban" and, 120, 122; refugees from, xxvi, xxxiv, 145; U.S. foreign policy and, 59

Tatars (ethno-religious group), 25, 52

Taqiyya (Islamic concept), xxvi, **169–171**

Terrorism (violence), Ahmadiyya views on, 15; Islamophobia and, 80; media coverage of, 105–106; Muhammad and, 134; Muslim Brotherhood and, 117–119; racialization of, 143–144; "radical Muslims" and, 43; Ugyhurs

as, 26; U.S. Muslims denouncing, 29

Tlaib, Rashida (U.S. politician), xxxvi; 22

Treaty of Peace and Friendship (legislation), xxx, 55

Tri-Faith Initiative (organization), 3

Truman, Harry (U.S. president), 174

Trump, Donald (U.S. president): advisors of, 35; Countering Violent Extremism (CVE) and, 44; Daesh and, 59–60; *jihad* and, 89; the "Muslim travel ban" and, xxvi, xxxiii, xxxvi, 22, 120–122, 145; refugees and, 146; Republicans disagreeing with, 65; *sharia* and, 153

Tunisia (country), xxx, 183

Turkey (country), immigrants from, 25; media depiction of families from 108; "Muslim Brotherhood" and, 117; Roger Williams and, 129; Sir Francis Drake and, xxix; Sufis and, 165; Turkish American Muslims, 171–176; U.S. diplomacy and, xxx; 40

Turkish American Muslims, **171–177**

Ummah ("Muslim nation"), **179–181**; freedom of religion and, 19; polygamy and, 130; population of the, xxii; radicalization and the, 43; Shias and, 156; Sufis in, 165,

Sunnism and, 167; *taqiyya*, 169; Universal Islamic Society, 7; U.S. Muslim population and, xxi–xxii

U.S. Civil War (history), xxxi, 174

U.S. Commission on International Religious Freedom (USCIR) (organization), 68

U.S. Constitution (political document): *ahadith* and, xx; civil rights and, 32, 62, 68, 206; First Amendment of, 32, 61, 66, 122; freedom of religion and, 49, 183; Muhammad and, 63–64; Qur'an and, xxxiii; *sharia* and, xix, xxv, 32, 150, 152; slavery and, xxx, 160

U.S. Department of Justice (branch of government), 72, 92

U.S. Department of State (branch of government), 146

U.S. foreign policy (legislation), 55–60

U.S. Founding Fathers (U.S. Revolution), **181–184**; Muhammad and, 134; overview of Islam and, 181–184; pluralism and, 195; Turkish Americans and, 173; vision of, xxvii; xxix; 63, 195;

U.S. Muslims (religious group): athletes and, 11, 29; discrimination of, xxiv; freedom of speech and, 66–69; history of, xxii; Islamophobia and, 81; organizations of, xxiv; U.S. national identity and, xxv;

U.S. Revolutionary War (history), 173, 183

U.S. Supreme Court (laws): job discrimination and, 76; Muhammad frieze in the, 136; the "Muslim travel ban" and, xxvi, xxxvi, 122; slavery of Muslims and, xxx, 160

Uyghur (ethno-religious group), 25–26, 172

Vietnam War (history), 11, 29, 58

Wahhabism (branch of Islam), 101, **185–187**

Wahhaj, Siraj (*imam*), xxxii, 11, 131

War of 1812 (history), 39, 159

Washington, George (U.S. president), xxix, 27, 63, 181

Webb, Alexander Russell (convert to Islam), 39

Williams, Roger (Christian leader), 128

Women's Mosque of America (women's rights), 114

Women's Rights (Islamic values), **187–189**

World War I (history), 25, 174

World War II (history), 21, 57, 17

Yemen (country), 22, 25, 101, 120, 122

Yusuf, Hamza (scholar), 163, 192

Zakat (charity), xxvii, 116, 162, **191–193**

Zaytuna College (education), 163, 192

About the Author

DR. CRAIG CONSIDINE is a U.S. Catholic of Irish and Italian descent. He is currently a faculty member of the Department of Sociology at Rice University in Houston, Texas. Considine is the author of *Muslims in America: Examining the Facts* (ABC-CLIO, 2018) and *Islam, Race, and Pluralism in the Pakistani Diaspora* (2017). He holds a PhD from Trinity College Dublin (Republic of Ireland), an MSc from the University of London–Royal Holloway, and a BA from American University in Washington, DC. Considine is a native of Needham, Massachusetts.